"In the current political climate, it has become increasingly common to suggest that we are witnessing 'the end of the European project'. Eurosceptic attitudes are widespread, not only in the UK but also in continental Europe, including in those countries that have traditionally been regarded as 'Europhile' or 'pro-European'. In this tension-laden and crisis-ridden context, more and more people seem to take the view that European matters – notably, European politics – are, at best, boring or, at worst, largely irrelevant to our lives. William Outhwaite is to be applauded for having done a superb job in deconstructing this prevalent misconception. His book is a powerful reminder of the fact that, in order to face up to the key civilizational challenges of our time, we need more, rather than less, pan-European – and, indeed, global – co-operation."

Dr Simon Susen, *Reader in Sociology, City University London*

"The European Union is at a critical stage of its evolution. It is more necessary than ever to understand the nature of the enterprise, to situate it in relation both to European developments generally and to the world at large. William Outhwaite, an established and astute commentator on contemporary Europe, in this succinct and highly readable book, provides all the necessary historical and theoretical tools for the job."

Krishan Kumar, *Professor of Sociology, University of Virginia*

"Refreshingly, this is a book about Europe in its proper sense, which means Europe in more than one sense. The discussion of the European Union as a transnational form of governance that intersects and doubles-up with nation-state governance obviously looms large in William Outhwaite's narrative of *Contemporary Europe*. Tellingly, the author's alternative title for his book was *Europe and the European Region in the Age of the European Union*. The EU therefore qualifies what Europe is nowadays, but neither defines nor exhausts it. The coherent pursuit of this line of interpretation (not an obvious one in the current panorama of European studies) makes this socio-political-historical account of the European region and of its peoples both interesting and distinctive.

In engaging and thoughtful style, Outhwaite offers an interdisciplinary panorama of what Europe has become, particularly as the effect of the end of the Cold War and the process of European integration. The book therefore examines the Europe of the EU and the Europe outside it, well aware that these two areas have been continuously changing in both their borders and self-understandings. But geopolitics is not the only way in which different Europes are defined in this book. Outhwaite illustrates in rapid prose and colourful figures how the continent has been dramatically reshaped economically, institutionally, politically, territorially and demographically, in the course of the last few decades.

A *tour de force* that remains critical of the (ir)resistible progress of European integration, and of the place of Europe in the world, but nevertheless confident that there is something valuable in the present European experience. *Contemporary Europe* is both a lively introduction to European studies, and a shrewd reflection on their multi-faced object of investigation."
    Dr Dario Castiglione, *Associate Professor of Politics, Exeter University*

"Outhwaite's *Contemporary Europe* is a critical diagnosis of one of the most advanced political projects after World War II. The book is one of the two or three great books on Europe. It takes reality as seriously as the dream of European Unification. Insisting in particular that the dream is one of democratic growth, the present reality looks gloomy but not hopeless. There are already unique institutional advances of transnational democracy. Today they are under sharp restriction and hegemonic control, but restrictions and controls can be overcome, and the present crisis, therefore, is a great but probably the last chance of Europe."
    Hauke Brunkhorst, *Professor of Sociology and Head of the Institute of Sociology at the University of Flensburg, Germany*

Contemporary Europe

Europe is one of the most dynamic and interesting areas of the world, pioneering in the European Union a new form of governance for half a billion people, represented in the world's first directly elected transnational parliament. This book situates the European Union in a broader European, global, historical and geographical context, providing a readable presentation of the most important facts and drawing on the theoretical approaches which have transformed the study of contemporary Europe over the past two decades.

The European Union is still on the road to what has been called 'an unknown destination', and this book presents its economic, political, legal and social trajectory from the middle of the last century to the present. *Contemporary Europe* covers some of these issues in an interdisciplinary framework, aiming to situate the development of the European Union in a broader context of pan-European and global processes. Europe has been cut down to size, but it does not have to become a global backwater, and the study of contemporary Europe's institutional reality does not have to be boring. The book counters this misperception, conveying the essential facts and theories of contemporary European reality in a clear and approachable analysis. It will serve as a readable introduction both to the academic field of European studies and to contemporary Europe itself.

William Outhwaite, FAcSS, Emeritus Professor of Sociology at Newcastle University, is the author of *European Society* (Polity 2008), *Critical Theory and Contemporary Europe* (Continuum 2012), *Europe Since 1989* (Routledge 2016), and a large number of journal articles and book chapters on contemporary Europe. He taught European studies and the sociology of contemporary Europe at the University of Sussex (in the School of European Studies) and Newcastle University (in the School of Geography, Politics and Sociology). He is an associate editor of the *European Journal of Social Theory* and *European Societies*, the journal of the European Sociological Association, and is a member of editorial boards of a number of other journals.

I dedicate the book to the memory of Chris Rumford (1958–2016), from whom I also learned much about contemporary Europe.

Contemporary Europe

William Outhwaite

LONDON AND NEW YORK

First published 2017
by Routledge
2 Park Square, Milton Park, Abingdon, Oxon OX14 4RN

and by Routledge
711 Third Avenue, New York, NY 10017

Routledge is an imprint of the Taylor & Francis Group, an informa business

© 2017 William Outhwaite

The right of William Outhwaite to be identified as author of this work has been asserted in accordance with sections 77 and 78 of the Copyright, Designs and Patents Act 1988.

All rights reserved. No part of this book may be reprinted or reproduced or utilised in any form or by any electronic, mechanical or other means, now known or hereafter invented, including photocopying and recording, or in any information storage or retrieval system, without permission in writing from the publishers.

Trademark notice: Product or corporate names may be trademarks or registered trademarks, and are used only for identification and explanation without intent to infringe.

British Library Cataloguing-in-Publication Data
A catalogue record for this book is available from the British Library

Library of Congress Cataloging-in-Publication Data
Names: Outhwaite, William, author.
Title: Contemporary Europe/by William Outhwaite.
Description: New York, NY: Routledge, 2016.
Identifiers: LCCN 2016008785| ISBN 9781138125674 (hardback) | ISBN 9781138125681 (pbk.) | ISBN 9781315647340 (ebook)
Subjects: LCSH: European Union countries–Politics and government. | European Union countries–Social conditions. | Europe–Politics and government–1945-Classification: LCC D1060.O96 2016 | DDC 940.56–dc23
LC record available at https://lccn.loc.gov/2016008785

ISBN: 978-1-138-12567-4 (hbk)
ISBN: 978-1-138-12568-1 (pbk)
ISBN: 978-1-315-64734-0 (ebk)

Typeset in Scala
by Sunrise Setting Ltd, Brixham, UK

Contents

List of figures viii
Preface ix
Acknowledgements x
Abbreviations xi
Key words xiii

1 European unity: dream and reality 1
2 Globalisation and the European economy 19
3 Territory and governance 41
4 Institutional Europe 57
5 European democracy 76
6 People's Europe 98
7 Europeans against 'Europe' 117
8 The future of Europe in the world 134

Postscript 153
Appendix 158
Index 161

Figures

1.1	Europe polar stereographic Caucasus Urals boundary	10
1.2	Earthlights 2002	11
1.3	Density of population in EU 2014	12
1.4	Gross domestic product (GDP) per inhabitant, in purchasing power standard (PPS), by NUTS 2 regions, 2011	13
2.1	Institutions across sub-spheres of the political economy	26
3.1	Regional eligibility for structural funds, NUTS 2 regions, 2014–20 (per cent of EU-27 average)	43
3.2	North West European Metropolitan Area (NWMA)	47
4.1	The Three Pillars	67
6.1	UK Passport front cover	103
6.2	Results of the EU?	111

Preface

People sometimes still suggest that European matters, particularly European politics, are boring. This belief has somehow survived the events of the past few years, in which the European Union has become a major force in the world and European affairs have become as dramatic as anyone could wish. This book aims to counter such a misperception, conveying the essential facts and theories of contemporary European reality in a clear and approachable analysis.

This book covers some of these issues in an interdisciplinary framework, aiming to situate the development of the European Union in a broader context of pan-European and global processes. It should serve as a readable introduction both to the academic field of European studies and to contemporary Europe itself.

Acknowledgements

I am extremely grateful to David Spence for his comments on this book; any remaining errors are my own.

Abbreviations

AfD	Alternative für Deutschland
CAP	Common Agricultural Policy (PAC in French)
CDU	Christlich-Demokratische Union (Christian Democratic Union)
CETA	Comprehensive Economic and Trade Agreement (EU-Canada)
CMEA	(Comecon) Council for Mutual Economic Assistance
COREPER	Committee of Permanent Representatives (from the French *Comité des représentants permanents*)
DVU	Deutsche Volksunion (German People's Union)
ECJ	European Court of Justice; now Court of Justice of the European Union (CJEU)
ECR	European Conservatives and Reformists
ECSC	European Coal and Steel Community
ECU	European Currency Unit, forerunner of the euro
EEAS	European External Action Service
EEC	European Economic Community
EFA	European Free Alliance (civic nationalist parties)
EFTA	European Free Trade Area
EP	European Parliament
ERASMUS	European Region Action Scheme for the Mobility of University Students

ERT	European Round Table
EU	European Union
GAL/TAN	Green-Alternative-Libertarian versus Traditional-Authoritarian-Nationalist
GDP	gross domestic product
GNP	gross national product (includes foreign trade etc.)
JHA	Justice and Home Affairs (now Police and Judicial Co-operation in Criminal Matters (PJCC))
KKE	Communist Party of Greece
M5S	Five Star Movement
MEP	Member of the European Parliament
NAFTA	North American Free Trade Association
NATO	North Atlantic Treaty Organization (OTAN in French)
NGO	non-governmental organisation
NKVD	People's Commissariat for Internal Affairs; Soviet police and secret police
NPD	Nationaldemokratische Partei Deutschlands
N-VA	New Flemish Alliance (Belgium)
NWMA	North West European Metropolitan Area
ODS	Civic Democratic Party (Czech)
OECD	Organisation for European Cooperation and Development (OCDE in French)
OEEC	Organisation for European Economic Co-operation
PDS	Partei des Demokratischen Sozialismus (Germany)
PEGIDA	Patriotic Europeans Against the Islamisation of the Occident (Germany)
PHARE	Pologne, Hongrie: Activité pour la Restructuration Économique
PiS	Law and Justice Party (Poland)
PPP	purchasing power parity
PVV	Party for Freedom (Netherlands)
SHAPE	Supreme Headquarters Allied Powers Europe
SPD	Sozialdemokratische Partei Deutschlands
TACIS	Technical Assistance to the Commonwealth of Independent States
TEN	Trans-European Network
TFEU	Treaty on the Functioning of the European Union (Lisbon Treaty)
TiSA	Trade in Services Agreement
TTIP	Transatlantic Trade and Investment Partnership
TTP	Trans-Pacific Agreement
UKIP	United Kingdom Independence Party
USSR	Union of Soviet Socialist Republics

Key words

Europe, European Union, European identity, democracy, globalisation, migration, euroscepticism, European foreign policy.

chapter 1

European unity

Dream and reality

Fernand Braudel's classic book of 1949, *The Mediterranean and the Mediterranean World in the Age of Philip II*, opens with a long discussion of the physical geography of the Mediterranean region and gradually introduces the human dimension. With the same idea in mind I might have called this book *Europe and the European Region in the Age of the European Union*. Here *region* replaces *world*, to avoid the suggestion that the contemporary world is shaped by Europe, even to the extent it was in the late nineteenth and early twentieth centuries, when European colonies covered much of the world map. The name of a monarch (1527–98), King of Spain, Portugal and (briefly) England, is replaced by the name of a political entity whose nature remains quite unclear.

Europe as a geographical entity, the western peninsula or subcontinent of the Eurasian land mass, would have been as it is without the European Union (EU). Even Europe as a political entity, made up of the national states which have become the default model of political organisation in the world (and divided from the middle of the twentieth century till close to its end into two distinct halves, East and West), would probably have looked much the same without European integration. What was called *communism* or *state socialism*, and the hegemony of the Union of Soviet Socialist Republics (USSR), would probably have run out of steam some time in the late twentieth or early twenty-first century in the absence of any moves towards integration in Western Europe. But separate processes can intersect, as when you arrive late for a train and find to your relief that the train, for quite other reasons, is itself running late. The political shape of contemporary Europe has been drawn by these two processes: the end of the Cold War and the ongoing process of European integration.

There are basically two ways of thinking about the unity of Europe. One is as a 'federalist' political project begun after World War II of an 'ever-closer union' aiming at something like a United States of Europe; this is now substantially abandoned or indefinitely deferred. The other approach is to focus instead on the growing integration between European states, economies and societies, punctuated and qualitatively transformed by the fall of the Iron Curtain in 1989. The EU is a crucially important aspect of this second process but only part of the story; its development over the past sixty years needs to be put in context.

Take an imaginary trip across the European Union to illustrate these two dimensions. Depending on where you're starting from and how you travel, you may or may not need your passport or national identity card or to change some money. If you don't, it's because you're already in the 'Schengen' area of passport-free travel and the eurozone – both, of course, creations of what is now the European Union, though not coextensive with it. (If you're in Switzerland, you need the money but not the identity document; if you're in the UK, you need both.) If you're flying, you may need to show your identity documents for security reasons anyway – something imposed by most national states following the 9/11 terrorist attack of 2001. If your plane ticket is cheap, it's because of budget air travel which has transformed mobility within Europe and elsewhere – nothing specific to the EU here, though the coordination of air traffic is partly under EU control and the EU has also supported road and rail links. If you want to work during your trip, you won't need a work permit, thanks to European provisions for freedom of movement – unless you're from a recently joining member state with a transitional arrangement for a short period. The laws to which you're subject are partly local, especially the criminal law, but also partly European – or even international in the case of some human rights law (just in case you were planning on genocide). The political geography of Europe makes it possible for some Europeans to walk easily from one country to another – something which is difficult in the United States unless you live near the Canadian or Mexican border. As an EU citizen resident in another member state, you can usually vote in European and local elections – something which was unusual in the past except for special cases, for example in Ireland or for Commonwealth citizens resident in the UK.

What comes into your mind when you think of Europe? For me, it's a mental map of the (sub)continent, shading off to the east. For some people, it will be the EU as a political entity, as when there is talk of a trade deal between the United States and 'Europe', meaning the EU. Here's another thought experiment. Which of these countries do you think of as being part of Europe? The UK, the Channel Islands, Iceland, Martinique, Turkey, Ukraine, Morocco, Russia? Well, people in the UK often talk about going 'to Europe' for their holidays, but it's joined to the rest of Europe by a rail link under the Channel and is (still) a member of the EU and a number of other European organisations. The Channel Islands off the French coast are dependencies of the British Crown but are not part of the UK, nor of the EU, though they have access to it through the Treaty on European Union of 1992, and Channel Island citizens are also citizens of the Union. Iceland is a good deal further into the Atlantic, but most people would think of it as European and it is a member of the European Economic Area, along with Liechtenstein and Norway, giving it access to the EU's single market. In 2009, Iceland applied to join the EU in response to the financial crisis which broke in 2007 to the present, but public opinion was negative and the country is currently not pursuing its application. Martinique in the Caribbean is an 'overseas department' of France, along with Guadaloupe, French Guiana and Réunion off the coast of Africa, and therefore part of the EU. Turkey applied for full membership of what is now the EU in 1987, but most of its territory would normally be thought of as lying in Asia rather than Europe, and this, along with its large and Muslim population (approaching 80 million, the same as Germany), has made its membership application problematic, especially in the eyes of centre-right Christian democratic politicians elsewhere in Europe. Ukraine is of course geographically and culturally European, indeed on some measures containing its geographical centre, but the prospect of its accession to the EU is now more remote than it seemed a few years ago. Morocco, by contrast, is not in geographical Europe, though I have included it here because it made an unsuccessful application in 1987 to join what is now the EU; the application was rejected on the grounds that it is not a European country. Russia, like Turkey, has much more of its territory in Asia than Europe, but its culture is European. With a population of 144 million and falling, it is much less than twice that of Turkey or Germany, but it is probably too big to think of as a possible member even of a vastly enlarged European Union.

These examples show how the boundaries of political and geographical Europe can vary. Does it make sense to think of Europe as a single entity? Yes, I think, for both geographical and political/cultural reasons. It now has a transnational polity which has expanded from its initial core of six member states to twenty-eight, with half a billion people, and acts as the main reference point, along with Russia, for the rest of the continent. Why do I use the possibly unfamiliar term *polity* rather than *state*? As we shall see, the EU is not a state like the United States, and unlikely to become one in the foreseeable future, but nor is it just an intergovernmental institution linking its member states. It is still, as Jacques Delors, then president of the European Commission, described it in 1985, an 'unidentified political object'.

In this chapter I describe the unification of Europe in the second half of the twentieth century along these two tracks. First, the informal process. In 1950, most of Europe was still recovering from the war which had ended five years earlier. Food rationing, for example, continued in the UK till 1954 and in West Germany right through the 1950s. There had been vast migrations in the immediate post-war period: between 1944 and 1948 over thirty million people moved (or more often were moved by force) west from central and eastern Europe, around half of them Germans. Europe had been effectively partitioned between a communist East and a capitalist West, mostly democratic but including two post-fascist dictatorships, Spain and Portugal, and a shaky democracy in Greece following the Civil War. In a mini-version of this partition, Germany now consisted of two states, and Berlin and (most of) Vienna were divided between a Soviet sector and Western sectors under British, French and US control.

As for the formal processes of unification, the two *halves* of Europe had begun to integrate, with the formation of the Western military alliance North Atlantic Treaty Organization (NATO) in 1949, followed in 1955 by the Warsaw Treaty Organisation, or Warsaw Pact. Comecon, the Council for Mutual Economic Assistance (CMEA), was formed in 1949 by the USSR and Bulgaria, Czechoslovakia, Hungary, Poland and Romania, with Albania and East Germany joining shortly afterwards. In Western Europe, the Marshall Plan of 1948 for European economic recovery, funded by the US, included a requirement for economic cooperation between the recipient states, coordinated by the Organisation for European Economic Co-operation (OEEC), which later became the Organisation for Economic Co-operation and Development (OECD). A more ambitious and, given that the war had ended only five years earlier, rather surprising move to integration was also underway, with the proposal in 1950 to form what in 1951 became the European Coal and Steel Community (ECSC), prefiguring in its membership and institutions the European Economic Community (EEC) of 1957. In 1967 they combined for practical purposes, along with the European Atomic Energy Community, in what was called the European Communities or, more often, Community. There were still just the original six member states: Belgium, the Netherlands and Luxembourg (Benelux for short), France, West Germany, and Italy. The Benelux countries had already formed a customs agreement in 1944, but the main impetus behind the formation of the ECSC came, as in so much of European politics in the following decades, from France and Germany.

For the EU the rest is history – a story of gradual extension by successive 'enlargements', with this 'widening' accompanied by a 'deepening' of integration: the strengthening of some of the linking tissue between the member states and the transnational institutions to which they increasingly had to relate. How did it come about? The idea of a united Europe had been around for a long time. For example, two of the founders of social science, Henri de Saint-Simon and Emile Durkheim, had talked about it in 1814 and 1893 respectively, as had one of the classic theorists of nationalism, the historian Ernest Renan, in 1882. The Second World War, not surprisingly, gave a sharper focus to federalist proposals, and Winston Churchill, in a speech in 1947, supported the idea of European unification, though without the UK's active participation.

There was always a dual motivation: to preserve peace and to derive what economists call *economies of scale* from bringing together the rather small states of Europe. Both motives were present in the formation of the ECSC: the recent memory that heavy industry had been linked to arms production and the fact that coal and steel were declining industries in Europe, which called for rationalisation. There were plans for two other 'communities', a Political Community and a Defence Community, but neither came to much, leaving the EEC as the powerhouse of integration. With hindsight, looking at the continuing difficulties of coordinating political approaches and defence and foreign policies in the EU, this is perhaps not surprising.

Both Marxist and non-Marxist commentators tend to stress the primacy of economic motives in the process, but it is important to not overlook the element of chance and the political entrepreneurship of Jean Monnet and others in the early years of what became the Union. For the next few decades, the pace of integration was fastest when economies were thriving and the Soviet threat seemed greatest. Though the details of the timing of enlargements were influenced by chance (in the case of the UK, the departure of De Gaulle and the pro-European policy of Edward Heath), they were often made possible by major political upheavals, notably the collapse of the post-fascist dictatorships in Spain and Portugal, of the Greek colonels' dictatorship, and of those in communist Europe.

The extensive growth of the Union through successive enlargements was governed by the simple principle that membership should be open to any democratic European country which also met certain fairly basic economic conditions.[1] An important element of the underlying 'dynamic' has been brilliantly analysed by the German sociologist Georg Vobruba (2005). If you're on the external border of the Union at any given time, it's in your interest, other things being equal, to support the membership applications of your immediate neighbours, to avoid irritating border problems, undesirable economic competition, and so on. This process may, however, cause the Union to overreach itself and expand too quickly. Intensive growth, by contrast, was the result of unclear and conflicting motives, with some member states motivated by the idea of 'ever-closer union' and others favouring more limited forms of cooperation. Vobruba has more recently identified another dynamic here: that of inadequate institutionalisation, where launching an initiative without the institutional complex required to sustain it leads to the need to develop and retro-fit additional institutions. The sad saga of the euro is the best illustration of this. Set up without proper coordination of tax policy, the eurozone has been searching since the 2008 crisis for one expedient after another to hold itself together.

On the ground, Europe was already relatively well integrated, with quite good transport networks compared to those of regions which had been colonised and where routes tended to run just from the interior to the main ports. Roads were primitive in Europe by North American standards, but rail transport was vastly superior. Trains rolled even across the Iron Curtain, though with stops for passport and customs controls. What came to be called *globalisation* in the 1990s began much earlier, and, in Europe, tends to mean *Europeanisation*, with links developing both between the six member states of the ECSC/EEC and those outside, many linked in the European Free Trade Association, formed in 1960.

How much had the world changed at the middle of the twentieth century? Two world wars had put into question the model of the independent national state. There was a serious risk of a new type of war which could at least destroy all the major population centres in Europe, and, at worst, extinguish all human life on the planet, through radiation and/or the scenario which came to be called a *nuclear winter* in which soot in the atmosphere from nuclear firestorms might drastically reduce global temperatures. The First World War had eliminated the empires which had been for centuries a major element of European political organisation, the Austro-Hungarian and Ottoman (Turkish) empires, leaving only the Russian Empire in the transfigured form of the USSR. Though the European colonial empires (British, French, Belgian, Dutch and Portuguese) still survived, the default model in Europe became the independent national state whose emergence is often, though problematically, associated with the peace of Westphalia in 1648 which had brought to an end the Thirty Years War. After World War II, some people began to think of the two world wars, with a troubled interwar period, as another thirty years war whose end called for a new form of political organisation, at least in Europe, with the deliberately modest title (replicated after 1991 in what had been the USSR) of 'community'.

Whether the new European Communities were intended to supplant the member states or, as Alan Milward (1992: 3) put it, to 'rescue' them, was something which has been left vague throughout their development:

> The evolution of the European Community since 1945 has been an integral part of the reassertion of the nation-state as an organisational

concept. ... Without the process of integration the west European nation-state might well not have retained the allegiance and support of its citizens in the way that it has. The European Community has been its buttress, an indispensable part of the nation-state's post-war construction. Without it, the nation-state could not have offered to its citizens the same measure of security and prosperity which it has provided and which has justified its survival.

These Community nation-states had no founding constitution, just sets of international treaties, mostly named after the places where they were signed: Paris, Rome (this was enough to alarm some Northern Irish protestants!), Brussels, Schengen (in Luxembourg), Maastricht, Amsterdam, Nice, Lisbon. No 'government', just a 'high authority' (ECSC) or 'commission' (EEC/EU), and an intergovernmental 'council' of national ministers. No parliament initially, just an 'assembly'. No 'laws', just 'regulations' and 'directives'. No national anthem, just the music (by Beethoven) without the words (by Schiller).

Take a look at a euro coin if you have one to hand. The one I just picked out of my coin bag happens to be from Greece, and has, like others, European symbols on one side and a national one (owls in this case) on the other. The Greek side also just has the word Euro in Greek; a French one has the symbol (Marianne) and the initials R. F. for République Française. The banknotes feature architecture of a variety of European and international styles, but no specific buildings.

This cautious approach to national representation can also be seen in the institutions. The clumsily named Court of Justice of the European Union has a judge from each member state, and there are also twenty-eight Commissioners. The representation of smaller member states in the Parliament is enhanced, so that it takes many fewer Luxembourg voters to elect an MEP than Germans. (This apparently harmless gesture got up the nose of the German Constitutional Court, which cited it as a reason for the incompleteness of EU democracy.) Minority national languages, too, are provided for, though often by complicated relays of interpreters, translating, say, Lithuanian via English into Finnish or Greek. For a long time, decisions in the Council, where they did not have to be unanimous, required a 'qualified majority'; France under De Gaulle was able to block all Community business for six months in the mid-1960s by leaving an 'empty chair' (the phrase was used earlier by Stalin). For all this positive discrimination, the larger states still tend to dominate discussions, with France losing its leading role to Germany in the present century. Of the other larger states, the UK and Spain have always been somewhat marginal, and Italy often in political crises of one kind or another. All member states are notionally equal, but some are more equal than others. It is difficult to imagine that a small state threatening to withdraw would have received such a patient hearing as the UK did in 2015–16.

'Follow the actors' is a great principle for social research (Latour 2005), but in the case of Europe it's not clear which actors we should concentrate on: national political leaders, European activists, entrepreneurs and financiers, or migrant workers (Kaiser and Meyer 2013)? Experts are divided between those who stress an intergovernmental approach and those who concentrate more on the supranational European level. This difference in research approach also goes alongside the more important division, among both outside observers and practitioners, between those who believe the EU *should* be an intergovernmental cooperative organisation and those who see it as an example of 'governance beyond the national state' and a foretaste of a more cosmopolitan future in other parts of the world as well. The German philosopher and social theorist Jürgen Habermas, for example, has written of a 'post-national constellation' (Habermas 1998) and of European integration as 'Europe's second chance' (Habermas 1994).[2] Europe, having pioneered the model of the independent national state and of nationalism, is now pioneering another form of democratic cosmopolitan governance which some people have seen as a kind of democratic empire, where people of different nationalities and citizenships interact closely in political, economic and cultural settings (Ziełonka 2006; Foster 2015).

This, then, is a dramatic story: the emergence of a new political entity towards the end of what Westerners call the second millennium. Two social scientists who have analysed these developments particularly well are Adrian Favell (2008) and Kathleen McNamara (2015). Favell has looked in particular at young mobile professionals ('Eurostars') in the 'Eurocities' of London, Paris, Brussels and Amsterdam in the context of what the EU calls *Free Movement* (Recchi 2015; see also Amilhat-Szary and Giraut 2015). McNamara stresses the political and cultural dimensions of the EU and its self-presentation. Here, however, it is important to note the rather muted way in which the EU has portrayed itself. It is often said that generals tend to fight the last war rather than the current one, and what has become the EU has tended to portray its great achievement as preventing another World War II. Seventy years on, this narrative has worn a little thin, even (or particularly) after the EU was awarded the Nobel Peace Prize in 2012. The unification of (most of) Europe in 1989 is a less remote date, but the EU's efforts to mobilise it as a propaganda theme have run into controversy. The emphasis on the fall of the Berlin Wall is questioned both locally, in Leipzig, the main site of the early protest marches, and in Poland, where Solidarity had been contesting communist rule through the 1980s (Auer 2010, 2012). Although the idea of rejoining the (Western) European mainstream was a major theme of anti-communist opposition movements in the 1980s, the EU had only a marginal role in

1989 and the early 1990s.³ It absorbed the former German Democratic Republic when it became part of the Federal Republic (Spence 1991), but it was distinctly hesitant about further eastern enlargements; the first of these did not happen until 2004, followed by the accession of Bulgaria and Romania in 2007 and Croatia in 2013, and they remain a work in progress, with Albania and most of the former Yugoslav republics, along with Turkey, remaining candidates or potential candidates.⁴ The EU was of course crucial in the economic and, later, political integration of the former communist countries into the rest of Europe, but it was essentially responding to a *fait accompli* rather than driving the process. There are parallels in the way the existence of the EU has helped to open up the prospects for regional nationalist movements such as those in Spain and the UK. (As I discuss more fully in Chapter 3, an independent Scotland, Catalonia or Basque Country taking their place within the EU is a much easier prospect than independence in the absence of such a transnational entity, despite the fact that the EU has so far officially discouraged separatist movements.)

Enough of generalities. Let me end this introductory chapter with a portrait of Europe, drawing on statistical sources covering the (sub)continent as a whole which have only recently been developed. Some observers of the UK have suggested that we should think of it as containing five nations rather than the four usually referred to: England, Scotland, Wales and Northern Ireland (Bryant 2005). As well as these, they argue, we should count the UK itself.⁵ In this chapter, and in the book as a whole, I shall move between the European (and global) levels and national and subnational ones, looking at interrelations between them. The British sociologist Michael Mann (1998) asked 'Is there a society called Euro?' as a question expecting, and getting, the answer 'no'. Whatever answer you give, the question remains, I think, worth asking.

How many Europes are there? There's the Europe of the EU, growing gradually over time. The Council of Europe has forty-seven members, including all European states except Belarus and Kazakhstan, currently excluded because of their human rights records, and the theocratic Vatican State. There's the Europe of the OECD, which also includes Norway, Switzerland, Liechtenstein, Iceland, Turkey and three former Yugoslav republics. The United Nations Statistical Department adds Georgia, Armenia, Azerbaijan as well as Turkey. The European Bank for Reconstruction and Development differentiates three broad European regions: Central Europe and the Baltic, Eastern Europe and the Caucasus, and southeastern Europe, as well as Russia and Turkey. The boundaries assigned to geographical Europe tend to run along the Caucasus Mountains, the Ural River, and the Urals mountain range⁶ – thus including part of Russia and western Kazakhstan.

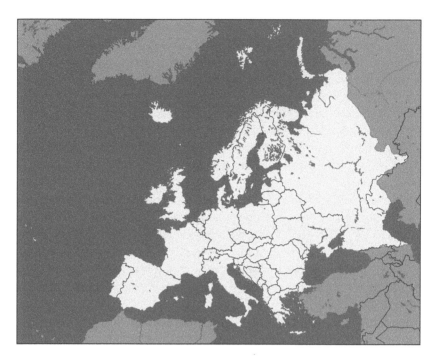

Figure 1.1 Europe polar stereographic Caucasus Urals boundary.

© *Ssolbergj, Wikicommons.*

The satellite map of Europe by night (Figure 1.2) gives a good sense of the distribution of its population, shown more precisely in the population density map of the EU (Figure 1.3). Note the diagonal strip in Figure 1.2 running from northwest England to northern Italy, with pockets also around major cities such as Paris, Madrid, Barcelona, Stockholm and Budapest, and in Bavaria and southern Poland and adjacent parts of the Czech and Slovak Republics. In only four states (Ireland, France, Sweden and the UK) have fertility levels been close to that required to replace the native population, and immigration, except in Germany, has tended to benefit the more fertile states, with very high levels of emigration in the Baltic States and more recently in southern Europe.

A fairly typical Eurostat map of gross national product (GNP) per head (Figure 1.4) shows regional inequalities across Europe, with most of the west around the average (75–125 per cent), but significantly less in most of post-communist Europe, plus a few pockets of poverty in Portugal, Spain and southern Italy.[7]

The richest, dark blue regions, apart from those around capital cities, tend to be clustered in the European 'core', the 'blue banana' running roughly along the Rhine and down into northern Italy. A simplified version shows a stark contrast between the northwest and the south and east of the EU.[8]

Figure 1.2 Earthlights 2002.
© NASA.

The banana is one of the most striking images of Europe. Developed to illustrate urbanism and economic activity, it also corresponds to the core Europe of the ninth-century Carolingian empire. A more elaborate version would have it curve over the Channel into southern and central England, and down along the Mediterranean into northeast Spain.[9] Other historical borders include the northern extent of the Roman Empire, running through southern Scotland and Germany, and, more importantly for the present, the border of the Austro-Hungarian Empire, which still marks substantial cultural differences between regions of Poland, Romania and former Yugoslavia. Islam in Europe is the result not just of recent migration, but also of the original reach of the Ottoman Empire, for example in Bosnia. In European Christendom, the north of Europe (and of Germany) is mostly protestant, the south catholic, and the east of Europe orthodox.

These divisions make Europe, particularly western and central Europe, particularly diverse across often short distances, and yet there are strong commonalities running across these political boundaries. Language is a good example. National languages have been shaped and monitored

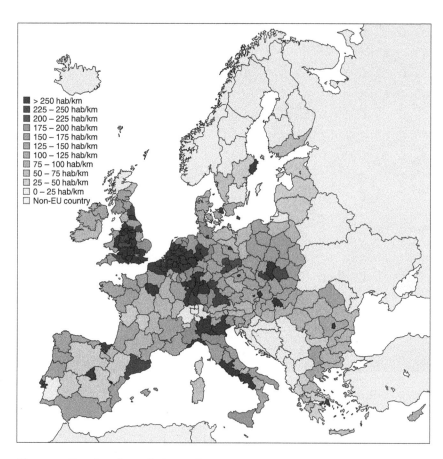

Figure 1.3 Density of population in EU 2014.

© CGN2010.

by national states, which in the past often tried to eradicate regional languages such as Breton in France or Welsh in Britain. Local dialects, however, are more likely to overlap boundaries so that firms setting up new operations across state borders find that, although the managers crossing the border to work in the new plant had to be taught the new language, the workers could communicate in dialects which had some of the features of both, say, German and Dutch. More significantly, the Scandinavian languages are mutually intelligible, with only minor differences in vocabulary which may occasionally require explanation between speakers of the different languages. There is nothing specifically European about this phenomenon of the 'dialect continuum', but with the increased frequency of transnational communication in Europe it is probably becoming increasingly common for two speakers of different languages each to use their own, knowing that it will be understood by the other. Alternatively, the

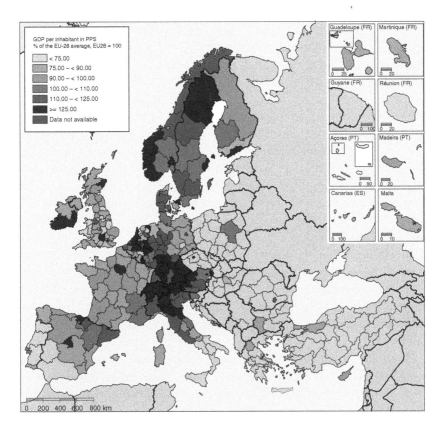

Figure 1.4 Gross domestic product (GDP) per inhabitant, in purchasing power standard (PPS), by NUTS 2 regions, 2011.

break-up of a state like Yugoslavia, where 'Serbo-Croat' was a common language, has led to the separation and often fabrication of languages corresponding to the former republics which are now separate states. The EU, as we saw earlier, has made a principle of facilitating the use of any official member state language, to the extent that a substantial part of its administrative costs are for translation and interpretation. Meanwhile, however, English has become more and more the common language of the EU, with French, the second language, increasingly marginalised except in the Court, where the judges continue to deliberate in French.

Its linguistic diversity is an obvious reason why mobility across Europe remains low by North American standards. Annual migration between EU member states amounts to around 0.75 per cent of the resident population. This contrasts with geographical mobility in the United States, where approximately 2.4 per cent of the population moves between states. Apart from the rather exceptional circumstances of Luxembourg and Ireland (with its land boundary to the north), no member state has figures for lifetime intra-EU mobility in double figures (European Commission 2008: 33). Even the most mobile professionals studied by Adrian Favell (2008) experienced a number of legal and other administrative inconveniences, especially if they had children.

Another question which has attracted a lot of attention is whether EU citizens feel European, in the way that US citizens feel 'American', as well as Texan, Californian, etc. Eurobarometer surveys tracked this systematically over a number of years but found only a very small minority saying they felt European *rather than* their nationality. The majority were evenly divided between those feeling *only* national and those feeling national and European (European Commission 2012: 22). The same survey (European Commission 2012: 9) found fewer than half declaring themselves 'attached' to the EU, and only a quarter in the UK.

Interestingly, the change which people felt would most strengthen a sense of European citizenship was a 'harmonised' social welfare system (health care, education, pensions, etc.), something which the EU has always steered clear of getting involved in (European Commission 2012: 26). When asked what features of the EU contributed most to a feeling of European identity, the euro was first, followed by 'democratic values'. This is particularly striking, given that only around half the member states were already using the euro, and that some of the deficiencies in the governance of the eurozone had already become evident (European Commission 2012: 27).

Another common (and related) topic has been the question whether there is something like a European public sphere. The fact that there is no European newspaper (despite a couple of attempts in past years) may be regrettable, but is perhaps not so significant; regional papers are also more important in the United States, though the *New York Times* and the *Wall Street Journal* have something like the national prominence of the *Financial Times* in Europe. Unlike the situation in the United States, however, the European TV channel *Euronews* is unevenly available across the continent except online. European news tends to be filtered through national channels and 'frames', with relatively little syndication of newspaper columns of the kind familiar in North America. Social movements tend to be national or international rather than European in their focus, except for those thoroughly embedded in the 'Brussels bubble', through which the Union rather complacently presents its engagement with 'civil society'.[10]

Finally, it is worth considering how far the EU acts like a state in the area of foreign and security policy. The short answer is 'not much', despite the establishment of a Common Foreign and Security Policy in the Maastricht Treaty of 1992 as one of the three 'pillars' of the Union, along with the European Community (EC) and the area of Justice and Home Affairs. In the Lisbon Treaty of 2009, the division into legally distinct pillars was abandoned and the foreign policy element was strengthened by the creation of a 'High

Representative', a kind of EU Foreign Minister, and a diplomatic service which operates alongside and in some countries stands in for those of member states. The EU currently has more substantial foreign missions, both civil and in some cases military, in Ukraine, Kosovo, Bosnia and Herzegovina, and Georgia, and outside Europe in Libya, Mali, Niger, the Democratic Republic of the Congo, Afghanistan, Palestine, the Central African Republic and the Horn of Africa. It remains the case, however, as the former US Secretary of State Henry Kissinger used to say, that if you want to talk to Europe you don't know who to call: the 'High Representative' is only one likely addressee, along with the President of the European Commission, the President of the European Council, or (more probably) the leaders of one or more of the major member states.

All these topics are discussed in more detail in the following chapters.

Summary points

A 'united Europe' can mean two different things. One, an incomplete and perhaps unrealistic project of political union in a federal state. Two, the ending in 1989 of the division of Europe between two power blocs and social systems and the increasing integration of European states.

The integration process was driven partly by the project of 'ever closer union' and partly by piecemeal practical steps to create a single market with free movement of goods, capital and people.

Europe remains substantially divided between a mainly richer north and west, centred on the original member states of what is now the EU, and a poorer south and east.

Further questions

Where is Europe?
What is European? Think of some ways in which the adjective has been used.
Which are more important in contemporary Europe: the differences between northern and southern Europe or between east and west?

Further reading

For an overview, a good place to start would be Anna Triandafyllidou and Ruby Gropas', *What is Europe?* (London: Palgrave 2015). The edited book by Richard Sakwa and Anne Stevens, *Contemporary Europe* (Basingstoke: Palgrave Macmillan, 3rd ed. 2012) has chapters on the topics covered in later chapters, as does Chris Rumford (ed.), *The SAGE Handbook of European Studies* (London: SAGE 2009). Among the excellent histories of contemporary Europe, I particularly recommend Béla Tomka's, *Social History of Twentieth-Century Europe* (Abingdon: Routledge 2013); also Eric Hobsbawm's, *Age of Extremes: The Short Twentieth Century 1914–1991* (London: Michael Joseph 1994) and Tony Judt's, *Postwar: A History of Europe Since 1945* (New York: Penguin 2005). Many websites also have timelines which are a useful reference point. Gerard Delanty examined the history of the idea of Europe in, *Inventing Europe: Idea, Identity, Reality* (Basingstoke: Palgrave Macmillan 1995). See also Delanty's *Formations of European Modernity: A Historical and Political Sociology of Europe* (London: Palgrave Macmillan 2013) and my *Europe Since 1989* (London: Routledge 2016). More specifically on the EU, see Luuk van Middelaar's, *The Passage to Europe. How a Continent Became a Union* (New Haven and London: Yale University Press 2013) and Gerard Delanty and Chris Rumford's *Rethinking Europe: Social Theory and the Implications of Europeanization* (London and New York: Routledge 2005).

For a territorial focus on Europe, see Jönsson, Tögil and Törnqvist's *Organizing European Space* (London: SAGE 2000) and Ole B. Jensen and Tim Richardson's, *Making European Space: Mobility, Power and Territorial Identity* (London: Routledge 2004).

Books with a primarily sociological orientation include three outstanding handbook-length works: Steffen Mau and Roland Verwiebe's, *European Societies* (Bristol: Policy Press 2010) and Stefan Immerfall and Göran Therborn's *Handbook of European Societies* (New York: Springer 2011). Other primarily sociological works include my *European Society* (Cambridge: Polity 2008), Maurice Roche's *Exploring the Sociology of Europe* (London: SAGE 2010) or Adrian Favell and Virginie Guiraudon's (eds), *Sociology of the European Union* (Basingstoke: Palgrave Macmillan 2011). Kathleen McNamara's, *The Politics of Everyday Europe* (Oxford: Oxford University Press 2015) interestingly relates these themes to the politics of the EU, as does Cris Shore's *Building Europe: The Cultural Politics of European Integration* (London: Routledge 2000). Chris Rumford's, *The European Union: a Political Sociology* (Oxford: Blackwell 2002) and Nathaniel Copsey's, *Rethinking the European Union* (London: Palgrave 2015) provide superb critical analyses of the EU.

There are also a host of books on more specific political, economic, legal and other aspects of the EU, as well as overviews such as John McCormick's, *Understanding the European Union* (Basingstoke: Palgrave, 6th ed. 2014). More specialised books include Simon Hix and Bjørn Høyland's *The Political System of the European Union* (Basingstoke: Palgrave 2011), Helen Wallace, Mark A. Pollack and Alasdair R. Young's, *Policy-Making in the European Union* (Oxford: Oxford University Press, 7th ed. 2015), and Michelle

Cini and Nieves Pérez-Solórzano Borragán's (eds), *European Union Politics* (Oxford: Oxford University Press, 5th ed. 2016).

Later chapters of this book include more specific suggestions for further reading.

Notes

1. On the 'Copenhagen criteria' for accession, formulated in 1993, see http://eur-lex.europa.eu/summary/glossary/accession_criteria_copenhague.html
2. Habermas's more recent books (Habermas 2012, 2015) have been more pessimistic.
3. On the evolution of European foreign policy, see Bickerton (2012), Chapter 5.
4. http://ec.europa.eu/enlargement/countries/check-current-status/index_en.htm. For a useful overview of post-communism, see Szelenyi (2015) and his other work referred to there; also Outhwaite (2016).
5. London has become so different from the rest of England that it might be counted as a sixth nation.
6. The Urals are actually more like modest hills.
7. http://ec.europa.eu/eurostat/documents/4031688/6917606/KS-04-14-908-EN-N.pdf/ccc77eb9-8ec4-4e5a-ad79-2d721ae5c582 (accessed 12.2.16). On inequalities *within* member states as well as between them, see, for example, the recent summary study by Jutta Allmendinger (European Commission 2015).
8. http://ec.europa.eu/eurostat/tgm/mapToolClosed.do?tab=map&init=1&plugin=1&language=en&pcode=tec00114&toolbox=types
9. See Chapter 3 below for more detail on this image.
10. See http://ec.europa.eu/transparency/civil_society/; www.eesc.europa.eu/

References

Amilhat-Szary, Anne-Laure and Frédéric Giraut (2015) *Borderities and the Politics of Contemporary Mobile Borders*. Basingstoke: Palgrave Macmillan.

Auer, Stefan (2010) 'Contesting the origins of European liberty. The EU narrative of Franco-German reconciliation and the eclipse of 1989', *Eurozine*. www.eurozine.com/articles/2010-09-10-auer-en.html

Auer, Stefan (2012) *Whose Liberty Is It Anyway? Europe at the Crossroads*. London, New York and Calcutta: Seagull Press.

Bickerton, Christopher (2012) *European Integration: From Nation States to Member States*. Oxford: Oxford University Press.

Braudel, Fernand (1972) [1949] *The Mediterranean and the Mediterranean World in the Age of Philip II*. Tr. Siân Reynolds. London: Fontana/Collins.

Bryant, Christopher G. A. (2005) *The Nations of Britain*. Oxford and New York: Oxford University Press.

European Commission, DG Employment, Social Affairs and Equal Opportunities Final Report (2008) *Geographic Mobility in the European Union:*

Optimising its Social and Economic Benefits. Luxembourg: European Commission.
European Commission (2012) *Standard Eurobarometer 77*. Luxembourg: European Commission.
European Commission (2015) *An Ever Closer Union Among the Peoples of Europe? Rising Inequalities in the EU and their Social, Economic and Political Impacts. Outcomes of EU–Funded Research*. Luxembourg: Jutta Allmendingen.
Favell, Adrian (2008) *Eurostars and Eurocities. Free Movement and Mobility in an Integrating Europe*. Oxford: Blackwell.
Foster, Russell (2015) *Mapping European Empire*. Abingdon: Routledge.
Habermas, Jürgen (1994) *The Past as Future*. Lincoln: University of Nebraska Press, pp. 73–94.
Habermas, Jürgen (1998) *Die postnationale Konstellation*. Frankfurt: Suhrkamp.
Habermas, Jürgen (2001) *The Postnational Constellation*. Cambridge: Polity.
Habermas, Jürgen (2012) *The Crisis of the European Union*. Cambridge: Polity.
Habermas, Jürgen (2015) *The Lure of Technocracy*. Cambridge: Polity.
Kaiser, Wolfram and Jan-Henrik Meyer (eds) (2013) *Societal Actors in European Integration: Polity-building and Policy-making 1958–1992*. Basingstoke: Palgrave Macmillan.
Latour, Bruno (2005) *Reassembling the Social. An Introduction to Actor-Network Theory*. Oxford: Oxford University Press.
Mann, Michael (1998) 'Is There a Society Called Euro?' In Roland Axtmann (ed.), *Globalization and Europe*. London: Pinter, pp. 184–207.
McNamara, Kathleen (2015) *The Politics of Everyday Europe*. Oxford: Oxford University Press.
Milward, Alan [1992] (2000) *The European Rescue of the Nation-State* (2nd ed.). Abingdon: Routledge.
Outhwaite, William (2016) *Europe Since 1989*. London: Routledge.
Recchi, Ettore (2015) *Mobile Europe: The Theory and Practice of Free Movement in the EU*. London: Palgrave Macmillan.
Spence, David (1991) 'Enlargement Without Accession. The EC's Response to German Unification', Royal Institute of International Affairs, Discussion Paper 36.
Szelenyi, Ivan (2015) 'Capitalisms After Communism', *New Left Review* 96, Nov–Dec: 39–51.
Vobruba, Georg (2005) *Die Dynamik Europas*. Wiesbaden: Verlag für Sozialwissenschaften.
Ziełonka, Jan (2006) *Europe as Empire. The Nature of the Enlarged European Union*. Oxford: Oxford University Press.

chapter 2

Globalisation and the European economy

Globalisation, a term in common use since around 1990, has been less prominent a topic in European studies than one might expect. Europeanists have tended to look inward to the growth of the EU, and international relations scholars, who often enthusiastically adopted globalisation theory,[1] tended to see the EU as just a particularly intensive form of international organisation.

As a process, globalisation – the extension of economic, cultural and political relations to a global scale – long precedes the use of the term. Some people have talked of globalisation in relation to the Stone Age, and long-distance international trade and other economic relations were certainly a feature of the world in the early twentieth century, and long before (Wallace 2000: 372). The period of the two world wars and the years between them, marked by economic dislocation, is rather exceptional in this respect, and after 1945, global economic relations reverted to earlier patterns. As noted in the previous chapter, the United States was particularly concerned that the West European economic recovery should include coordination between what seemed from a US perspective to be rather small states. The ECSC was a dramatic example of European-level coordination, and the United Nations, with its New York headquarters, represented a more truly global focus. The Cold War encouraged military coordination within the two opposed blocs.

When people came to speak of globalisation, the world had become networked to a much greater extent, and the collapse of communism in Europe, including the USSR, meant that a large part of the world which had previously been relatively detached from these processes became more fully involved, with 'Western' conceptions of economic and political rights implemented more or less rapidly across the former communist bloc (Outhwaite 2016). China and southeast Asia, too, entered world markets. And the fact that people were *thinking* in terms of globalisation made a big practical difference: European integration seemed to fit a multilateral world of big trading blocs in Europe, America and Asia. George Orwell's dystopian vision of a tripartite division of the world into Oceania (North America and the UK), Eurasia and Eastasia seemed to be coming true in a more benign form, without the wars which were a feature of Orwell's *Nineteen Eighty-Four* (1948).

Within Europe, economic globalisation often tended in practice to mean Europeanisation, with large corporations like Dutch-based Phillips and Anglo-Dutch Shell and Unilever operating across Europe and the rest of the world. The integration of economic processes and consumer markets, including those for cultural production, corresponds to global processes outside Europe, but there was also a specifically European dynamic, with textile and car production, for example, tending to shift from northern to southern Europe, and then, in the 1990s, to eastern Europe (Hudson 2002). The EU can be seen as reinforcing these trends, in its long-standing pursuit of a unified market, and also by regulating access to European markets of products from outside the Union.

Helen Wallace (1996: 17) wrote that

> European integration can ... be seen as a distinct west European effort to contain the consequences of globalization. Rather than be forced to choose between the national polity for developing policies and the relative anarchy of the globe, west Europeans invented a form of regional governance with polity-like features [to extend the state and harden the boundary between themselves and the rest of the world].[2]

Pascal Lamy, working for Commission President Jacques Delors from 1984 to 1994 and Trade Commissioner from 1999 to 2004, popularised the term *mondialisation maîtrisée* or *managed globalisation*. There had however been a clear shift of policy from the first Delors Presidency of 1985–88, which worked closely with industrialists but tended towards protectionism for the European economy, to a much more liberal approach as European capital became more globalised in its orientation, continuing to exercise influence through the European Round Table (ERT) of industrialists and other similar groupings.[3] An ERT document of 1993 stated:

> Industry wants a strong Europe in a growing world economy, which cannot be achieved by building a fortress closed against our neighbours.

> The large companies of the European Round Table operate on a global scale and can clearly identify the causes of declining competitiveness. . . . Industry . . . expects more open access to world markets, in return for giving our competitors better access to the Single Market in Europe.
>
> (ERT 1993: 10, 14)

Whereas deregulation measures in the EU can sometimes be agreed by the Commission and/or the Court even against the wishes of the member states, regulatory measures require the agreement of a qualified majority of member states in the Council. This means that 'industries have lost protection at the national level and have been unable to re-establish it at the EU level' (Hansen 1998: 67). The idea of the EU as a 'competition state' (Cerny 1997) remains, but in a very different form.[4] US anxieties about the formation of a 'fortress Europe' proved groundless, and the EU negotiated a major trade agreement, the Transatlantic Trade and Investment Partnership (TTIP), with the United States based on the Trans-Pacific agreement (TTP). The TTIP encountered significant public opposition in Europe, particularly for its provision for investor-state dispute settlements which enable corporations, including cigarette manufacturers, to sue states for imposing health and safety and other regulations which impede their activity. The EU has currently proposed an alternative court structure for the settlement of such trade disputes, but anxieties remain over, for example, the poor state of labour protection in the United States and divergent regulatory standards.[5] Along with the TTIP are a similar deal with Canada, the Comprehensive Economic and Trade Agreement (CETA), and an agreement with the World Trade Organisation on trade in services (Trade in Services Agreement [TiSA]).

As for economic diversity *within* the EU, a jokey article in *The Guardian* (Atkinson and Elliott 1999: 26) predicted a future for the United States of Europe in 2010 in which 'Germany makes all the cars, France the booze, Italy the fridges and washing machines, Finland the mobile phones and the UK the drugs'. Citing a business economist, the authors pointed to the comparative advantage of 'engineering in Germany . . . alcoholic beverages in France and Portugal, household goods in Italy, engineering vehicles in Spain, chemicals in the Netherlands, electricity in Austria, paper and packaging in Finland and Sweden, electronics in Ireland, tobacco in Greece, food in Denmark and pharmaceuticals in the UK'. Taking up the theme in a more serious analysis, Smith *et al.* (1999: 5) pointed to the persisting diversity of capitalism even in Western Europe, and set to increase with the accession of most of East-Central Europe, and 'the unevenness and instability of European territorial development'. In fact, as Chris Bickerton (2012: 118–120) points out, there has been much less specialisation than economic theories of comparative advantage would expect. France and Germany, for example, both produce cars and sell in each other's markets.

Germany however stands out for its high proportion of machinery exports, and the UK for services, mostly consumed domestically, apart from some financial services. Construction is prominent in Spain, Cyprus and Italy; transport and storage in the Baltic states; information technology (IT) in Ireland and Luxembourg; and administrative services in Belgium.[6]

Seen from Europe, then, integration is both a positive response to globalisation and a basis for possible resistance to it, as well as a basis for the maintenance, for example, of what has been called the *European social model*, which includes a developed system of labour law that often goes well beyond, and supersedes that in member states such as the UK, and of substantial welfare state provision. Like many models, this looks more impressive on paper than in reality. Legal provision against discrimination was a necessary part of the early treaties, concerned as they were with the prevention of discrimination against other European nationals and the fairness of competition between member states and, for example, their airlines. A classic court judgement in a case in 1976, in which a Belgian flight attendant contested her compulsory retirement at the age of forty, when male colleagues were allowed to continue in work, cited this as well as the principle of non-discrimination embodied in the relevant treaty article: 'The aim of article 119 is to avoid a situation in which states which have actually implemented the principle of equal pay suffer a competitive disadvantage.'[7]

The EEC however avoided intervening in the complex social policy arrangements of member states, and this policy has continued to the present, with a focus instead on 'benchmarks' of minimal standards of provision. Court judgements have been mainly concerned with ensuring that European citizens have access to benefits despite residing in other member states, as in the case of Tas-Hagen and Tas of 2006. Despite the diversity of social models across Europe which results both from long-standing historical patterns and (especially in the East) from more recent policy choices, it remains the case that most Europeans, even in the English-speaking periphery, are accustomed to patterns of social provision which remain contentious or even utopian in the United States and much of Asia and Africa.

The area where the EEC did develop something like a social policy from an early stage was in the Common Agricultural Policy (CAP), which for a long time accounted for three quarters of the total budget and is still around 40 per cent. The CAP relied on a combination of farm price support and a tariff on imports from outside the Community, thus preserving the incomes of otherwise unviable farmers (though also providing massive subsidies to large agribusiness). Like the coal and steel community, it also supported restructuring of agriculture, and cushioned, for example, a massive decline in French agricultural employment in the 1950s and 1960s (Mendras 1967). It was not only quantitatively the biggest common policy for many years, it was also the one which, long before the introduction of the common currency and more cosmetic changes to passports, driving licences and so forth, brought European-level policies close to home across Europe.

Long-standing controversies over the global impact of the CAP on lower-cost producers elsewhere in the world point to the broader issue of policy choices for the EU between an emphasis on internal and external trade relationships. For impoverished agricultural and other producers in what used to be called the 'third world', Europe appears as a selfish protectionist club of excessively rich states, now urging measures to mitigate climate change which further reduce the prospects of other states catching up. On the other hand, as discussed in more detail in Chapter 8, Europe's share in world output is diminishing, and its role in the world is perhaps correspondingly reduced. Supporters of a common foreign policy see this as a reason to develop this aspect of the EU's activity, along with economies of scale, in diplomatic representation overseas.

The rest of this chapter examines the political economy of contemporary Europe in more detail. To begin with the long term, Europe was of course the main site of industrialisation in the nineteenth century, beginning in Britain and adjacent parts of northwest Europe (Belgium, northern France) and gradually and unevenly extending east and south in the course of the century. A classic work of historical sociology, Barrington Moore's *Social Origins of Dictatorship and Democracy*, is still worth reading as an account of this process. To sum it up very briefly, the later you industrialise, the faster you are likely to do it and the greater the role the state is likely to be in the process. This in turn reinforces authoritarian tendencies in the state, as it did in Germany, Russia and Japan. The 'end of the peasants' described by Henri Mendras took place centuries earlier in England, with the surplus capital and labour, released by the shift from small arable farming to sheep rearing, available for early industrialisation. In Germany, the class alliance between big landowners and industrialists sustained the Empire until the revolution of 1918. At the cultural level, duelling persisted in Germany into the early twentieth century (Elias 1996). In Russia, another imperial state on the old model, with a land empire stretching across much of Asia, serfs were freed at around the same time as slaves in the United States (1861), but even for much of the Soviet period, collective farmers were not allowed the internal passports which would enable them to move legally around the country.

Industrialism in Europe was further shaped by communism from the late 1940s to the end of the 1980s. Czechoslovakia and East Germany were advanced industrial states, but the rest of the bloc was not, and it was industrialised on the soviet model with priority given to heavy industry – a policy followed to some extent even in Czechoslovakia and Germany.

Agriculture was collectivised, except in Poland where collectivisation was abandoned in the face of opposition. Economies of scale were however balanced out by inefficiencies in production and distribution. (In 1983, the future Soviet leader Mikhail Gorbachev was astonished to see how few workers were needed to run a gigantic Canadian farm.)

The Soviet Union, it was said, boasted the twentieth century's leading *nineteenth* century economy, and the same was true to some extent of the rest of Communist Europe. Especially in Germany, there were stories of Western industrialists crossing the border in search of plants which might be worth taking over, but finding that only the real estate was of interest. After 1990, the East German economy was wrecked by a politically understandable but economically disastrous decision to treat the East German mark as equivalent to the West German Deutsche mark, and even in Russia there was a flood of imports which wiped out many local producers. The new German government ran what was effectively a fire-sale of East German assets, and elsewhere in the bloc the privatisation policy was similarly hasty and often chaotic. A quarter of a century later, average living standards in almost all of post-communist Europe are still lower than anywhere except Greece, Portugal and southern Spain – all of them suffering badly from austerity policies.

An economic policy for Europe faces the dilemma of whether to look first at the South or the East. Historically, of course, it was the South which first became the focus, with regional policy initially directed to southern Italy and southwest France, followed by the accession of Greece in 1981 and Spain and Portugal in 1986. Three of the founding members, Italy, Belgium and West Germany, themselves had significant north–south divides, with Italy's the most extreme. In Germany, the South has now become more prosperous relative to the earlier industrialising North, much of it now in relative decline, while in Belgium it was the French-speaking South which had industrialised early and was overtaken by the Flemish North.

In the run-up to the main post-communist enlargement of 2004, southern Europeans feared that they would lose out as what have been called since 1986 *cohesion policies* to reduce inequalities between member states shifted their attention towards the East. The EU as a whole feared the consequences of an eastern enlargement to which it was inevitably committed, and therefore adopted a strategy which has been called 'putting down and putting off' (Kovács 2001). As it turned out, the 2004 accession states, which had suffered a very severe 'transition shock' in the 1990s, slotted fairly comfortably, both politically and economically, into the enlarged Union. Though badly hit, like the rest of Europe, by the 2008 crisis, they weathered it better than the South, where austerity policies have been even more damaging. Ireland may no longer be an honorary 'southern' state, but Italy, France and Belgium are not in a very secure position.

Can we really speak of the European economy, or are the different economic regimes across the continent too diverse to be described in this way? The large body of literature known under the heading 'varieties of capitalism' suggests, if we take the biological analogy seriously, that they are at least not different species (Streeck 2012). There are indeed substantial overlaps and affinities between, say, British and US capitalism at one extreme, and more statist forms in parts of southern and southeastern Europe and those in Latin America. The simplest contrast is that between 'liberal' and 'coordinated' market economies. Hall and Soskice (2001) assigned the major advanced English-speaking countries to the former category, and Germany, Austria, Scandinavia and Japan to the latter. Their figure (see Figure 2.1) suggests a clear-cut division, but they also allow for a 'hybrid' category in Mediterranean Europe.

More importantly, Europe displays a striking polarisation in intra-EU trade between export-oriented economies (Germany, Netherlands, Belgium) and importers (Greece, Spain, UK), indicating a more fundamental division between their degree of competitiveness. While in the UK the continuing balance of payments deficit has not so far led to a loss of confidence in the currency,[8] within the eurozone trade deficits were part of the problem in Ireland, Italy, Greece, Portugal and Spain (Bickerton 2012: 118). This polarisation means that the Europe of the EU has something like a triple division, between the Northwest, with some very strong economies, such as Germany, and weaker ones, such as France and the UK; the South, from Portugal to Greece; and the East, with again some differentiation between stronger (Slovenia, Czech Republic, Slovakia, the Baltic States) and weaker (Romania, Bulgaria) performers.

The Europeanness of the European economies resides not so much in these resemblances and differences as in the fact that they are linked, loosely in the single European market and more tightly in the eurozone, which is set to include all member states except the UK, though with Denmark (whose krone is, however, pegged to the euro and likely to remain so) and Sweden currently postponing entry, which has become a less popular prospect over the past few years in the wake of the eurozone crisis.

Although the immediate cause of the crisis was the very particular public debt problem in Greece, whose economy represents only 2 per cent of the eurozone and 1.3 per cent of the EU, the crisis revealed a much more fundamental problem of imbalances in the European (and eurozone) economy. Seen in global terms, not just Greece but most of western Europe, along with the United States, Canada and Japan, make up the countries with the highest proportion of debt to GNP. As rich and stable countries, they can afford it, just as your bank may raise your overdraft limit if you get a permanent job. In Greece, however, where the level of debt was finally revealed at the height of the global recession following the 2007–08 global financial

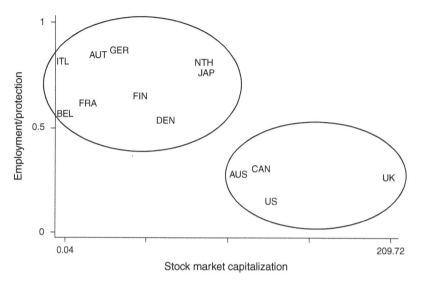

Figure 2.1 Institutions across sub-spheres of the political economy.

Source: International Federation of Stock Exchanges, Annual Report. See www.lse.ac.uk/government/whosWho/Academic%20profiles/dwsoskice@lseacuk/Hall-Soskice-Intro-VoC-2001.pdf, p. 19.

crisis, this provoked fears of a default in Greece itself which might then spread to other eurozone countries. This in turn led to panic about a break-up of the eurozone, beginning with Greece's exit from it. Chancellor Merkel, the only effective head of a major European state (with Sarkozy a lame-duck president, Berlusconi facing court proceedings and also on the way out, and the British outside the eurozone and of course marginal in other ways), proclaimed that 'if the euro falls, Europe falls'.[9]

It is important to distinguish these panic phenomena from the underlying problems of the eurozone, which would have existed in the absence of the banking crisis and the foolish lending by banks in France, Germany and (outside the eurozone and the EU) Iceland; the mendacity of successive Greek governments; and the unsustainable property booms, particularly in Spain, Ireland and elsewhere. The underlying problem is that of a monetary union which lacks a common tax policy and other elements of political coordination. These have now been bolted onto the existing formal structures of political and monetary policy at the European level, but in a messy and uncoordinated way.

To understand the impact on Europe of the world economic crisis which broke out in the United States in 2006, it is worth looking briefly at Asia. There, the impact was somewhat delayed, until the collapse of Lehman

Brothers raised doubts about the stability of capitalist institutions worldwide and demand for Asian goods fell drastically in Europe and North America (Goldstein and Xie 2009; Kawai, Lamberte and Park 2012). European countries, like Russia and the other former communist countries in the Community of Independent States, were much more exposed to the crisis. The EU amplified its impact on Europe, especially in the form of the eurozone: it encouraged states and individuals to accumulate dangerous levels of debt. As Wade Jacoby (2014: 54) writes of the new member states, 'The perceived safety of EU Member States allowed private actors to increase their borrowing well above the already high flows elsewhere in post-communist Europe.' These countries, apart from Slovenia, were not yet in the eurozone.[10] The issue of eurozone membership raised by the position of Greece sharpened up the dilemma between closer integration to sustain the currency and, alternatively, a much more restricted set of entry criteria, perhaps to be imposed retrospectively on problem states. (At both ends of this argument – Germany and Greece – there were calls for the respective state to opt out of the euro.)

> An optimal currency area is a region where economic efficiency is maximised if the region shares a single currency. It may be larger than a state, like the eurozone, or smaller (e.g. Scotland in the UK). What makes it optimal are similarities across the region (gross domestic product (GDP) per head, timing of business cycles, etc.) and high mobility of labour and capital. The United States is therefore closer to an optimal currency area than the eurozone because, despite substantial differences in prosperity between regions, Americans are much more mobile than Europeans and capital flows more easily across state lines.

Within the eurozone itself, which lacked the high mobility of capital and labour and the internal transfers normally considered necessary for an 'optimal currency union', Europe relied on short-term convergence programmes and failed to address the imbalances between member states.[11] In the post-crisis Union, as Fritz Scharpf wrote,

> Like the provinces or cantons in a federal state, they lose control over the instruments of macroeconomic management, and they are likely to suffer from uniform national policies that do not fit their regional economy. At the same time, however, the EU budget is minuscule in comparison to the budget of federal states, there are no European taxes and there is no European social policy to alleviate interregional imbalances. Instead, member states are expected to cope with all

economic problems by relying entirely on their own policy resources ... [and] ... are subject to the intrusive supervision and potential punishment imposed by supranational authorities.

(2011: 31–32)

Scharpf (2011: 37) concluded that 'In the worst case ... the attempts to save the Euro through the policies presently enacted may either fail on their own terms, or they may not only undermine democracy in EU member states but endanger European integration itself.' (There were voices suggesting that the EU had overburdened itself with its southern and some of its eastern accessions.)

This, then, is a second way in which Europe, in the form of the eurozone, amplified a global crisis. However, states outside the eurozone, such as the UK and Hungary, also adopted damaging austerity programmes. As Steffen Lehndorf (2015: 23) puts it, 'You don't need the Troika[12] to wreak havoc'. In post-communist Europe, the impact was most acute in a second wave, in 2011, particularly in the Baltic states (of which only Estonia was at that time joining the eurozone), where unemployment doubled before falling back to more normal levels around the middle of the European range (EBRD 2012; Leschke, Theodoropoulou and Watt 2015: 297). The post-communist states most closely engaged with the eurozone and the outside world in general, such as Hungary, were the most affected (EBRD 2012; Myant and Drahokoupil 2012; Jacoby 2014). One impact has been to put in question existing governmental trajectories, whether these are at the more strongly neoliberal end of the spectrum, as in Estonia, or more corporatist, as in Slovenia (Bohle and Greskovitz 2012: 256–258; Lindstrom 2015: 53–73).

Did Europe also provide some protection? Iceland certainly thought it would, applying to join the EU in the summer of 2009 and negotiating from 2010 until 2013, when it stopped pursuing its application. (What would have happened if it had been *in* the eurozone when the crisis hit is anyone's guess.) In the short term, however, any benefit the eurozone members derived from the European Central Bank's guarantee of the currency and from direct support through bond purchases, accelerated disbursements of structural funds and other measures was probably less than they could have achieved by devaluing the local currencies they had abandoned. More broadly, however, and despite appalling levels of social dislocation and emigration, it is probably true that 'the new member state (NMS) economies are better off than they were before EU membership and better off than they would have been without membership' (Jacoby 2014: 67). In this context, it is interesting to see that the crisis has not prevented, though it may have delayed, new accessions to the eurozone, and even the political forces most opposed to current EU policies, such as Greece's Syriza and Spain's Podemos, are not calling for exit from the eurozone. At the other end of the political spectrum, the strongly neoliberal economist Anders Åslund (2010) combines a blistering critique of the European Central Bank with strong support for the expansion of the eurozone (see also Wyplosz 2014).

Wolfgang Streeck (2014) has provided the most compelling analysis of the crisis, and one which has inspired many subsequent analyses, such as those discussed below.[13] It is striking that the first two of the three main chapters of his book barely mention Europe, with the implication that the changes he describes would have taken place even if the international and transnational regime in Europe had been very different. In his account, the EU is what he calls a *neoliberal transnational consolidation state*, presiding over those of the member states. In Europe and elsewhere, capitalism bought time, 'deferring ... social conflicts, at first by means of inflation, then through increased government borrowing, next through expansion of private loan markets[14] and finally (today) through central bank purchases of public debt and bank liabilities' (Streeck 2014: xiv). Modern governments have two constituencies: the voters and the markets. International capital now influences politics not just indirectly, by choosing to invest or not to invest in national economies, but directly, 'by financing or not financing the state itself' (Streeck 2014: 84). Debt policy becomes 'international financial diplomacy' (Streeck 2014: 90). Or, one might add, in the European case, (also) the domestic policy of the transnational European polity. In Streeck's analysis, then, we are not so much in late capitalism as in late democracy or post-democracy. The circumvention and undermining of democratic institutions in member states and at the European level is not just a reaction or overreaction to the current crisis but something intrinsic to the 'international consolidation state' which the EU has become.

This is one dimension of the EU's amplification of the crisis. The second dimension relates specifically to the eurozone and hence, in the longer term, to the Union as a whole (leaving aside for the moment the prospect that the UK and Sweden might remain outside the eurozone, without, like Denmark, pegging their currency to the euro).[15]

Streeck argued:

> In the years after 2008, distributional conflict under democratic capitalism has turned into a complicated tug-of-war between global financial markets and sovereign national states. Where in the past workers struggled with employers, citizens with governments, and private debtors with private creditors, it is now financial institutions wresting with the same states that they had only recently successfully blackmailed into saving them from themselves.
>
> (2011: 11–12)

Fritz Scharpf (2011: 37) similarly concluded that 'In the worst case . . . the attempts to save the Euro through the policies presently enacted may either fail on their own terms, or they may not only undermine democracy in EU member states but endanger European integration itself.'

Assuming that the immediate eurozone crisis has ended, as Mario Draghi claimed on March 5th, 2015, where does all this leave the EU? The most dramatic diagnosis is that the eurozone crisis is merely the tip of an iceberg which has holed and is about to sink the entire flawed project of European integration. A weaker form of this diagnosis suggests that, while a modest degree of integration, such as the single market, was and remains worthwhile, monetary union should not have been on the agenda, or at least not so early or on such an indiscriminate basis. The last of these variants suggests the policy of disaggregating the euro into a northern, hard, and/or southern, soft, version, or cutting adrift either the southern 'problem children' or, alternatively, Germany and possibly other more robust member states. Meanwhile the 2010–15 UK government echoed Winston Churchill's view of European integration, that it would be a good idea *for them*, by endorsing further integration within the eurozone while allowing for a semi-detached and more independent position outside it.

As for the impact of the crisis on the institutional and political future of the Union, it is clear that it opened up a latent but now serious political division between the North (especially Germany) and the South, with anti-austerity parties or movements strongest in Greece and Spain, though less so in Italy and Portugal.[16] In institutional terms, the crisis has consolidated a tendency already present in the strengthening of the European Council (which brings together heads of state and govenment), in the Maastricht Treaty of 1992 and the Lisbon Treaty of 2009, towards what Jürgen Habermas (2012), following Philipp Dann and Stefan Oeter, has called 'executive federalism' and Hauke Brunkhorst (2014) 'collective Bonapartism'. In a context of crisis management, Angela Merkel, with a mixture of careful and more perfunctory consultation with other heads of government or state, drove through a set of measures, often in conjunction with the European Central Bank (sidelining the Commission and the Parliament) and the International Monetary Fund. However damaging many of these policies may have been, things had to be done, and done quickly, and Merkel filled a leadership vacuum, given the weakness of the French president, Sarkozy and his successor, Hollande, a lame duck from the outset, the marginality, for various reasons, of Italy and the pathetic irrelevance of the UK.[17]

Anthony Giddens (2014: 6) has brilliantly distinguished between what he calls EU1, the formal institutions of the Union, and EU2, the ad hoc groupings of heads of state or government in the leading member states 'where a lot of the real power lies, exercised on a selective and informal basis'. In his argument,

> Europe must choose a new future, and this time the citizens must be directly involved. The eurozone countries have to set the pace, but the states outside the euro will be affected just as much by the innovations that are made. ... The Union must develop an EU3 – a system conferring more dynamic leadership and political legitimacy as well as greater macro-economic stability than exists at present ... economic federalism, now inevitable if the euro is to be saved, has to be accompanied by political federalism in some guise or other.
>
> (Giddens 2014: 9, 29)

This is a third response to the crisis, one which recognises the imperative of further integration, but in a different and more democratic form. Giddens' book is full of policies for a new Europe, but merely hopeful about the possibility of mobilising a political consensus around them. Vivien Schmidt (2015) similarly outlines a number of proposals for the governance of the eurozone but is sceptical, despite the surge of anti-austerity political controversy since 2014, about the capacity of the EU to reform itself (see also Schmidt 2014).

I shall not linger further on the analysis and prognosis of the current crises. The underlying issues, as noted earlier, are the ways in which the EU can manage its internal diversity and its position in global economic relations.

First, diversity. A crude but important indicator is GDP per capita, or purchasing power parity (PPP).[18] Leaving out Luxembourg and tiny San Marino, and also non-EU Norway and Switzerland, this ranged in 2014 from $49,000 USD in Ireland and only a little less in the Netherlands, Austria, Germany, Denmark and Sweden, to less than $20,000 in Romania and Bulgaria. Italy and Spain were in the mid-30s, Portugal and Greece in the mid-20s. Apart from Slovenia and Croatia, the former Yugoslav republics which are candidates for EU membership are close to the bottom, in the mid-teens (Serbia and Macedonia) or around $10,000 (Montenegro, Bosnia and Herzegovina).[19]

More significant even than these differences between member states, which are gradually reducing, are those between *regions*, where these are understood both transnationally, at a European scale, and within national states. Starting with the European level, a map of light pollution neatly shows the location of economic activity across Europe and its concentration in a (slightly flattened) banana shape running from southeast England through northern France and Germany to northern Italy (Baldwin and Wyplosz 2012: 270).[20] Average incomes in sub-national regions range from a quarter of the EU average in rural Romania to three and a half times in London, and disparities within member states are tending to increase, particularly in the UK and Poland (Baldwin and Wyplosz 2012: 273–274;

see also the EU's Cohesion Reports[21]; also the EU's GINI project [see Salverda et al. 2014; Nolan et al. 2014]).

A more subtle indicator of diversity is the 'real effective exchange rates', based on labour costs and productivity and disguised by the fact of eurozone membership. As Scharpf (2011: 17–18, 49) showed, there is now a wide and persisting spread between Germany and the 'problem' states unkindly referred to as *PIGS*: Portugal, Italy, Greece and Spain. The 'southern problem' was however grotesquely overblown in the eurozone crisis, and as Vivien Schmidt (2015: 37) points out, 'framing the crisis as one of public debt in the periphery fueled resistance to any form of deeper economic integration'. Schmidt notes that most analyses

> tend to assume by definition that the EU cannot share risk the way equally heterogeneous entities like the United States do through fiscal federalism. ... But although the EU will certainly never become a federal state like the US, there are many ways to deepen economic integration so as to make it more robust.
>
> (2015: 38)

Sara Hobolt (2015) provides an interesting analysis of whom EU citizens *blame* for the economic crisis. Initially, even in Britain, it was understandably the US banks which got most of the blame (70 per cent). By 2012, after the world crisis had led into the Euro crisis, the EU's share of the blame rose from 20 per cent to around 40 per cent, catching up with the level score of the British government.[22] Across the EU as a whole, the Union itself gets relatively little of the blame for 'current economic problems', even among *opponents* of the EU in France and Germany, who score just over 40 per cent in each country.[23] Support for the euro has halved in the states with opt-outs (UK, Denmark, Sweden), from just over 40 per cent to just over 20 per cent, but has remained more or less constant in the eurozone itself. In other EU member states, which are committed to adopting the euro in the short or medium term, there was a slight drop in support from around 50 per cent to around 40 per cent between 2007 and 2013.[24] The most recent survey of prospective eurozone members (including Sweden) shows opinion evenly split, with a decline from 2009 in those who would like it to be introduced as soon as possible and a rise in those who would like it to be introduced as late as possible (Eurobarometer 2015: 65–68).

As Hobolt (2015: 63) concludes, the EU and the euro may not be seen as part of the problem, but (except in the euro opt-out states) also seen as part of the solution, with a majority, even in the currently victimised 'debtor' states, viewing the EU as more effective than national governments at handling the crisis.

By now the governance problems of the eurozone have been, if not resolved, at least patched up in a way that may or may not be good enough for the time being. What remains is the bigger issue of Europe's economic place in the world. It is interesting to see how much of the emphasis in the Cohesion Report, referred to earlier, despite its primarily internal focus, is on the comparison between the EU and the United States and other major world economic powers (see, for example, pages 8–9, 19–20, 33, 70, 93 of the Report).

With half a billion people in the EU, plus another 145 million in Russia, 40 million in Ukraine and 10 million in Belarus (to take just the main countries), the EU's share of world population (7 per cent) and output is shrinking, but it is still a major world region, third after China and India in population, currently running equal with the United States in share of global output and likely to be a close third after the United States and China in a year or two.[25]

Very broadly, Europe is distinguished from North America and Asia in having a more substantial welfare state, often presented in rather exaggerated terms as the *European social model*. I discuss this in more detail in Chapters 6 and 8, but it is worth considering here the economic dimensions. Though the EU imports and exports rather more than the United States or China, much EU trade is internal, like that of the United States. In both, external trade amounts to only a third of GNP. Intra-EU trade is close to twice the volume of that with the rest of the world, including close neighbours like Switzerland and Norway.[26]

The EU is however not exempt from global competitive pressures, and its long-term future is likely to lie in areas of design, high-value manufacturing and services. A 2013 survey of international managers by Ernst and Young placed Germany sixth as a favoured site for investment, followed by Poland, the UK and France.[27]

Europe is also a favoured destination for tourism, with much potential still under-exploited in post-communist Europe, and for longer-term migration. Here, Europe's demographic position as an ageing and relatively infertile subcontinent is a crucial part of the picture (Therborn 2004; 2011). The UN's Population Division expects the population of geographical Europe to fall by 2100 from 738 million in 2015 to 646 million, against a world population growing from just over 7 billion to over 11 billion (with estimates ranging from 9.5 to over 13), and Africa moving from 1.2 billion to almost catch up with Asia at over 4 billion.[28] The report notes:

> Fertility in all European countries is now below the level required for full replacement of the population in the long run (around 2.1 children per woman, on average), and in the majority of cases, fertility has been below the replacement level for several decades. Fertility for

Globalisation and the European economy

Europe as a whole is projected to increase from 1.6 children per woman in 2010–2015 to 1.8 in 2045–2050, but such an increase will not prevent a likely contraction of the total population size.

Across post-communist Europe, from rich Eastern Germany to poor Moldova, the decline is particularly sharp. There are exceptions, such as Catholic Poland (and, in western Europe, Ireland), but these are a tiny proportion of the total, and the experience of southern Europe is that catholicism does not reliably preserve fertility.

Of the eight independent countries[29] with the oldest population in 2015, seven (after Japan) are in Europe. Of the seven least fertile in 2010–15, five are in Europe. The safest expectation is that, with substantial immigration by populations whose age structure and culture make them more fertile, Europe will become more like North America in its ethnic diversity. The EU is of course a region with free movement between its member states; movement is limited mostly by employment opportunities and also by language diversity, and we probably have to take into account the possibility that some member states will try to restrict border-free travel, at least for non-citizens such as the asylum-seekers who provoked a moral panic in 2015. (The UK and Ireland are currently outside the Schengen Area, with a permanent opt-out,[30] though this anomaly may be removed if the UK leaves the Union after the 2016 referendum or at some later date.)

It used to be said of West Germany that it was an economic giant and a political dwarf. This is no longer true of Germany, but it is certainly true of the EU. Its political role in the world is distinctly muted. Despite all the talk of 'normative power Europe', it is the EU's economic role which predominates in the world, and it therefore tends to be perceived as self-interested, exploitative and even imperialistic (Bialasiewicz 2011: 7). The formation of European foreign policy, broadly conceived, depends on questions of how the EU manages its territory and organises its internal political processes. These are discussed in the following chapters.

Summary points

Although the term *globalisation* did not come into use until the 1990s, world trade was re-established after World War II and the United States encouraged the economic integration of western Europe.

Globalisation in Europe often means in practice *Europeanisation*, with the same goods marketed across the EU and increasing numbers of transnational European corporations.

The EU now has a similar economic presence to the United States, with a much larger population.

Contemporary Europe displays a number of different 'varieties of capitalism', as well as a residual communist-style economic order in Belarus. The wave of economic crises after 2008 have exposed weaknesses in the way the eurozone is managed and even more substantial disparities and tensions within the Union.

Further questions

What is meant by *Europeanisation*? How does globalisation relate to it?
Is there a European economy, or just a whole lot of national economies?
What are the most important types of economy found in contemporary Europe?

Further reading

Aldcroft, Derek H. and Steven Morewood (2013) *The European Economy Since 1914* (5th ed.). London and New York: Routledge.

Eichengreen, Barry (2007) *The European Economy Since 1945: Coordinated Capitalism and Beyond*. Princeton, New Jersey and Woodstock: Princeton University Press.

Fligstein, Neil (2011) 'Markets and Firms' in Adrian Favell and Virginie Guiraudon (eds), *Sociology of the European Union*. Basingstoke: Palgrave Macmillan, pp. 100–124.

Ray, Larry (2007) *Globalization and Everyday Life*. Abingdon: Routledge.

Notes

1 For a readable exception to the latter consensus, see Rosenberg (2000). On the impact of globalisation on the EU, see also Kriesi *et al.* (2012).
2 See also the special number of the *European Journal of Public Policy* (2010).
3 The ERT was set up in 1983, but preceded by, for example, the Groupe des Présidents des Grandes Entreprises Européennes in 1967. It is one of a number of 'Round Tables' in the US, Japan and Africa.
4 Alex Warleigh (2002: 114) argues that 'the single market and currency were forged not out of idealism but to enable the EU to rival the USA and Japan'. He cites Sandholtz and Zysman (1989), who 'hypothesize that change in the international economic structure was necessary for the revival of the European project' (Sandholtz and Zysman 1989: 34). In his study of Cohesion policy, Chris Rumford (2000: 3) writes: 'It is interesting to see how the EU has steadily redefined concepts such as harmonization and cohesion away from their redistributive or social market meaning, increasingly aligning them with notions of competitiveness and stressing their compatibility with neoliberal growth.'

Bickerton (2012, Chapter 4) stresses the differences between early form of integration and those which got going in the 1980s.
5 On TTIP, see for example a recent (August 2015) brief by Volkswagen, prior to the revelation that it had itself subverted testing regimes, www.viavision.org.uk/ftp/1887.pdf
6 See Eurostat (2009).
7 See appendix for this case (*Defrenne v. SABENA*) and other major legal cases in the history of the EU.
8 There are however regular warnings, as noted by Allen (2015) and a growing number of bankers in early 2016.
9 See Meiers (2015) and www.bundestag.de/dokumente/textarchiv/2010/29826227_kw20_de_stabilisierungsmechanismus/201760
10 Slovenia joined in 2007, Slovakia in 2009, Estonia in 2011, Latvia in 2014 and Lithuania in 2015. Kosovo and Montenegro use the euro, without (yet) being members of the EU.
11 See the appendixes to Fritz Scharpf's paper, comparing Germany with the GIPS countries (here Greece, Ireland, Portugal and Spain).
12 The committee made up from the European Central Bank, the European Commission and the International Monetary Fund. The word is derived from a Russian three-horse sledge, but was also used, more ominously, of the summary courts of the Soviet NKVD.
13 See also the excellent review of the German original by Colin Crouch (2013).
14 A process aptly described by Colin Crouch (2009) as 'privatised Keynesianism'.
15 Streeck (2015) continues to argue powerfully for its abandonment.
16 Historically, of course, these countries had a good deal in common with the later post-communist accessions; Louka Katseli (2001: 85–86) gave a very similar analysis of their trajectories. More recently, they have been competitors for structural funds and their relative prosperity, even after the crisis broke, has made post-communist member states like Slovakia unwilling to support aid packages.
17 The critique of 'Merkiavelli' by the late Ulrich Beck (2013) seems to this extent unfair.
18 This measure of PPP gives a better picture of relative wealth in countries where prices are very different, though many commodities, especially in the EU, exchange at similar prices. The euro was of course intended in part to increase price transparency across member states.
19 http://statisticstimes.com/economy/european-countries-by-gdp-per-capita.php
20 The banana image comes from the media response to a study by Roger Brunet (Datar/Reclus 1989), referring to a 'dorsal' spine or 'megalopolis', along with its peripheries and in particular the 'finisterres' along the Atlantic coast; see Brunet (2002). For a follow-up to the 1989 study see Rozenblat and Cicille (2003).
21 http://ec.europa.eu/regional_policy/en/information/publications/reports/2014/6th-report-on-economic-social-and-territorial-cohesion
22 Hobolt (2015: 50), citing the *British Election Study* CMS 2008–2012.

23 Hobolt (2015: 53), citing the *PEW Global Attitudes Project*, Spring 2011. See also Hobolt and Tilley (2014).
24 Hobolt (2015: 58), based on *Eurobarometer*.
25 www.global-vision.net/blogging-brussels--beyond/eu-28-is-no-longer-the-worlds-largest-economy
26 http://trade.ec.europa.eu/doclib/docs/2013/december/tradoc_151969.pdf
27 www.welt.de/wirtschaft/article116837465/In-Europa-kommt-keiner-an-Deutschland-heran.html
28 http://esa.un.org/unpd/wpp/Publications/Files/Key_Findings_WPP_2015.pdf
29 The UN also lists Martinique and Hong Kong.
30 Bulgaria, Romania, Croatia and Cyprus are currently in a transitional period but legally bound to join Schengen in due course.

References

Allen, Katie (2015) 'Trade imbalance hampers UK growth', *The Guardian* (28.12.15), p. 43.

Åslund, Anders (2010) *The Last Shall Be the First: The East European Financial Crisis, 2008–10*. Washington DC: Peterson Institute.

Atkinson, Mark and Larry Elliott (1999) 'Where the jobs will be in the US of €', *The Guardian* (13.2.99), p. 26.

Baldwin, Richard and Charles Wyplosz (2012) *The Economics of European Integration* (4th ed.). London: McGraw-Hill Higher Education.

Beck, Ulrich (2013) *German Europe*. Cambridge: Polity.

Bialasiewicz, Luiza (ed.) (2011) *Europe in the World: EU Geopolitics and the Making of European Space*. Farnham: Ashgate.

Bickerton, Christopher (2012) *European Integration: From Nation States to Member States*. Oxford: Oxford University Press.

Bohle, Dorothee and Béla Greskovitz (2012) *Capitalist Development on Europe's Periphery*. Ithaca and London: Cornell University Press.

Brunet, Roger (2002) 'Questions sur la banane bleue' www.mgm.fr/ARECLUS/page_auteurs/Brunet14.html

Brunkhorst, Hauke (2014) *Das doppelte Gesicht Europas*. Berlin: Suhrkamp.

Cerny, Philip G. (1997) 'Paradoxes of the Competition State: The Dynamics of Political Globalization', *Government and Opposition*, 32(2): 251–274.

Crouch, Colin (2009) 'Privatised Keynesianism: An Unacknowledged Policy Regime'. *The British Journal of Politics & International Relations*, 11(3): 382–399.

Crouch, Colin (2013) 'The Debtor State', *European Journal of Sociology*, 54(3): 477–484.

Datar/Reclus (1989) 'Images de l'Europe', in *Les villes européennes*. Paris: La Documentation Française, pp. 11–13.

Elias, Norbert (1996) *The Germans*. Cambridge: Polity.

ERT (1993) *Beating the Crisis – A Charter for Europe's Industrial Future.* Brussels: ERT. http://ert.eu/document/beating-crisis-charter-europes-industrial-future

Eurobarometer (2015) http://ec.europa.eu/public_opinion/flash/fl_418_en.pdf

European Bank for Reconstruction and Development (2012) *Transition Report: Integration Across Borders.* www.ebrd.com/downloads/research/transition/tr12.pdf

Eurostat (2009) 'Specialisations Within EU Manufacturing', Number 62. http://ec.europa.eu/eurostat/documents/3433488/5283793/KS-SF-09-062-EN.PDF/aa7ac08f-b0cc-4a34-bf39-4b1216c62c54?version=1.0

Giddens, Anthony (2014) *Turbulent and Mighty Continent. What Future for Europe?* Cambridge: Polity.

Goldstein, Morris and Daniel Xie (2009) 'The Impact of the Financial Crisis on Emerging Asia'. "Asia and the Global Financial Crisis", Santa Barbara, October 18–20.

Habermas, Jürgen (2012) *The Crisis of the European Union.* Cambridge: Polity.

Hansen, Brian T. (1998) 'What Happened to Fortress Europe? External Trade Policy Liberalization in the European Union', *International Organization*, 52(1): 55–85.

Hall, Peter and David Soskice (eds) (2001) *Varieties of Capitalism.* Oxford: Oxford University Press, pp. 1–68.

Hobolt, Sara (2015) 'Public Attitudes towards the Euro Crisis', in Olaf Cramme and Sara B. Hobolt (eds), *Democratic Politics in a European Union under Stress.* Oxford: Oxford University Press, pp. 48–65.

Hudson, R. (2002) 'Changing Industrial Production Systems and Regional Development in the New Europe'. *Transactions of the Institute of British Geographers*, 27(3): 262–281.

Jacoby, Wade (2014) 'The EU Factor in Fat Times and in Lean: Did the EU Amplify the Boom and Soften the Bust?' *Journal of Common Market Studies*, 52(1): 52–70.

Katseli, Louka (2001) 'The Internationalization of Southern European Economies', in Heather D. Gibson (ed.), *Economic Transformation, Democratization and Integration into the European Union.* Basingstoke: Palgrave, pp. 75–118.

Kawai, Masahiro, Mario B. Lamberte and Yung Chul Park (eds) (2012) *The Global Financial Crisis and Asia: Implications and Challenges.* Oxford: Oxford University Press.

Kovács, Melinda (2001) 'Putting Down and Putting Off: The EU's Discursive Strategies in the 1998 and 1999 Follow-up Reports', in József Böröcz and Melinda Kovács (eds), *Europe's New Clothes. Unveiling EU Enlargement.* Telford: Central European Review, pp. 196–234.

Kriesi Hanspeter, Edgar Grande, Martin Dolezal, *et al.* (2012) *Political Conflict in Western Europe*. Cambridge: Cambridge University Press.

Lehndorf, Steffen (2015) 'Europe's Divisive Integration – An Overview', in Lehndrof (ed.), *Divisive Integration: The Triumph of Failed Ideas in the EU-Revisited*. Brussels: ETUI (European Trade Union Institute), pp. 7–37.

Leschke, Janine, Sotira Theodoropoulou and Andrew Watt (2015) 'Towards Europe 2020? Austerity and New Economic Governance in the EU', in Steffen Lehndorf (ed.), *Divisive Integration: The Triumph of Failed Ideas in the EU – Revisited*. Brussels: ETUI (European Trade Union Institute).

Lindstrom, Nicole (2015) *The Politics of Europeanization and Post-Socialist Transformations*. Basingstoke: Palgrave Macmillan.

Meiers, Franz-Josef (2015) *Germany's Role in the Euro Crisis: Berlin's Quest for a More Perfect Monetary Union*. Cham, Switzerland: Springer.

Mendras, Henri (1967) *La Fin des Paysans*. Paris: SEDEIS; 2nd ed. Arles: Actes Sud, 1992. Translated as *The Vanishing Peasant: Innovation and Change in French Agriculture*. Cambridge, MA: MIT Press, 1970.

Myant, Martin and Jan Drahokoupil (2012) 'International Integration, Varieties of Capitalism and Resilience to Crisis in Transition Economies', *Europe-Asia Studies*, 64(1): 1–33.

Nolan, Brian, Wiemer Salverda, Daniele Checchi *et al.* (2014) *Changing Inequalities and Societal Impacts in Rich Countries: Thirty Countries' Experiences*. Oxford: Oxford University Press.

Outhwaite, William (2016) *Europe Since 1989: Transitions and Transformations*. Abingdon: Routledge.

Rosenberg, Justin (2000) *The Follies of Globalisation Theory: Polemical Essays*. London: Verso.

Rozenblat, Céline and Patricia Cicille (2003) *Les Villes Européennes: Analyse Comparative*. Paris: La Documentation Française.

Rumford, Chris (2000) *European Cohesion? Contradictions in EU Integration*. Basingstoke: Macmillan.

Salverda, Wiemer, Brian Nolan, Daniele Chicchi, *et al.* (2014) *Changing Inequalities in Rich Countries: Analytical and Comparative Perspectives*. Oxford: Oxford University Press.

Sandholtz, Wayne and John Zysman (1989) '1992: Recasting the European Bargain', *World Politics*, 42(1): 95–128.

Scharpf, Fritz (2011) 'Monetary Union, Fiscal Crisis and the Preemption of Democracy', London School of Economics: LEQS Annual Lecture Paper 2011.

Schmidt, Vivien (2014) 'Why are Neo-Liberal Ideas so Resilient in Europe's Political Economy' (with Mark Thatcher), *Critical Policy Studies*, 8(3): 340–347. http://dx.doi.org/10.1080/19460171.2014.926826

Schmidt, Vivien (2015) 'Changing the Policies, Politics, and Processes of the Eurozone in Crisis: Will This Time Be Different?', in David Natali and

Bart Vanhercke (eds), *Social Policy in the European Union: State of Play 2015*. Brussels: ETUI, pp. 33–64.

Smith, Adrian, Al Rainnie, Mick Dunford *et al.* (1999) 'Where the Jobs Will Be in the United States of Europe': Networks of Value, Commodities and Regions in Europe After 1989', Working Paper 1–99. www.sussex.ac.uk/webteam/gateway/file.php?name=workpaper1.pdf&site=2

Streeck, Wolfgang (2011) 'The Crises of Democratic Capitalism', *New Left Review*, 71, Sep-Oct. www.newleftreview.org/?page=article&view=2914

Streeck, Wolfgang (2012) 'Varieties of What? Should We Still Be Using the Concept of Capitalism?', in Julian Go (ed.) *Political Power and Social Theory*, 23: 311–321.

Streeck, Wolfgang (2014) *Buying Time: The Delayed Crisis of Democratic Capitalism*. London: Verso.

Streeck, Wolfgang (2015) 'Why the Euro Divides Europe', *New Left Review*, 95, Sep-Oct: 5–26. http://newleftreview.org/II/95/wolfgang-streeck-why-the-euro-divides-europe

Therborn, Göran (2004) *Between Sex and Power: Family in the World 1900–2000*. Abingdon: Routledge.

Therborn, Göran (2011) *The World. A Beginner's Guide*. Cambridge: Polity.

Wallace, Helen (1996) 'Politics and Policy in the EU: The Challenge of Governance', in Helen Wallace and William Wallace (eds), *Policy-Making in the European Union*. Oxford: Oxford University Press, pp. 16–17.

Wallace, William (2000) *Regional Integration: The West European Experience*. Washington DC: Brookings Institution Press.

Warleigh, Alex (2002) 'Towards Network Democracy? The Potential of Flexible Integration', in Mary Farrell, Stefano Fella and Michael Newman (eds), *European Integration in the Twenty-First Century: Unity in Diversity?* London: SAGE, pp. 101–118.

Wyplosz, Charles (2014) 'The Eurozone Crisis: A Near-Perfect Case of Mismanagement', http://graduateinstitute.ch/files/live/sites/iheid/files/sites/international_economics/shared/international_economics/prof_websites/wyplosz/Papers/The%20Eurozone%20Crisis%202.pdf

chapter 3

Territory and governance

For over forty years, at the time the EU was being established, there were two Europes. There was a Western Europe centred on the six member states of the ECSC and then of the EEC. A number of other states were associated with this Europe through some combination of trading links with the Communities and/or membership of the alternative European Free Trade Area (EFTA), established in 1960 by seven states: Austria, Denmark, Norway, Portugal, Sweden, Switzerland and the UK. These were often called the 'outer seven', by contrast with the 'inner six', and three of them (Denmark, Norway and the UK, along with Ireland) also made an unsuccessful application to join the EEC. The UK's application was finally vetoed in 1963 by the French President, General De Gaulle, who argued, with some justification, that the UK was subservient to the United States and would not be a satisfactory member. Portugal's membership of EFTA is surprising, since it was still under the post-fascist dictatorship of Salazar, which had survived, along with Franco's regime in Spain, the defeat of European fascism in 1945.

With the exception of Spain and Portugal, Western Europe could reasonably present itself as democratic, in opposition to the communist dictatorships in Eastern Europe. The other main Western European organisation was NATO, linking most of the 'Western' European states (including Greece and Turkey) with the United States and Canada in an alliance for military defence and cooperation, based in Brussels and with its European military command (SHAPE) nearby in Mons. The reference to Greece and Turkey points to the fact that 'Western' Europe was a political, not a geographical, label.

Mirroring the EEC/EFTA and NATO in the communist bloc were the CMEA (or Comecon) and the Warsaw Treaty Organization or Warsaw Pact. Europe was divided between East and West, with Germany as a microcosm of this division and Berlin a further microcosm within Germany.

After the 1989 anti-communist revolutions, the east–west division in Europe has been relativised, though it still remains as a structuring feature of European society and of the way it is imagined by its inhabitants. Even within Germany (including Berlin), where reunification was accomplished in less than a year, what was known as the [Berlin] 'wall in the head' persisted for a whole generation, with West Berliners, for example, for a long time more likely to marry a foreigner than a German from the eastern part of the now undivided city (Bausinger 2000: 134). Elsewhere in Europe, the old divisions were slow to fade, with most eastern regions still poorer than most in the west.

A related map displaying eligibility for EU structural funds over the period 2014–20 is shown (see Figure 3.1). Looking at this map, however, one can see elements of a north–south division as well, with poorer areas not only in the old communist east but also in the south (Portugal, Spain, Italy, Greece), and particularly the south of some of the southern countries, notably Spain and Italy.

These are also the regions where the effects of the current economic crisis continue to be particularly strong. Elsewhere, countries like Ireland and the Baltic States have recovered relatively quickly, though often with unemployment reduced by high levels of emigration. Some of the more specifically economic aspects of these differences were discussed in the previous chapter. But what is special about the EU is the kind of territorial thinking represented by the notion of cohesion and by the prominence of maps and other forms of data in much of this analysis. This is partly a matter of a worldwide trend towards what is sometimes called 'evidence-based policy', but it is important to see that this takes on a particularly striking quality when it is a question of formulating policy for what are now nearly thirty highly diverse states.

Going back to the beginnings of the integration process, the political goal of bringing together two states, France and (West) Germany, which had been at war only a few years ago, with one occupying the other and deporting and murdering a substantial part of its population, was combined with the economically rational motivation to solve the problems of overproduction in an increasingly obsolete iron and steel industry in northeast France and northwest Germany (and southern Belgium). This underlying logic of doing political work by economic means was also a territorial logic which was well established by the time Michel Foucault (1975)

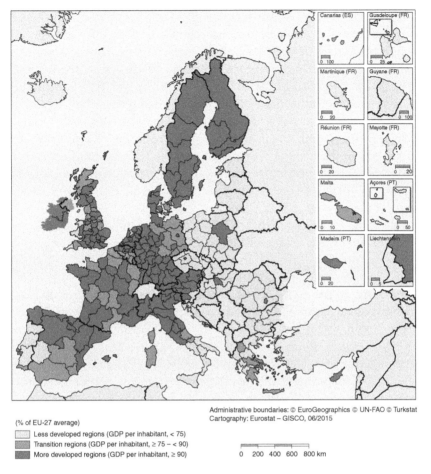

Figure 3.1 Regional eligibility for structural funds, NUTS 2 regions, 2014–20 (per cent of EU-27 average).

© Eurostat.

Source: http://ec.europa.eu/regional_policy/sources/docoffic/official/reports/cohesion6/6cr_en.pdf

developed his historical analysis of *governmentality* and *surveillance* which are the terms in which we now tend to conceive it.

The economic recovery of Europe was not just a goal in itself, but (as the United States recognised in designing the Marshall Plan in the late 1940s) an essential element in halting the advance of Soviet communism. Analysts of Europe noted that the pace of integration was substantially dependent on two factors: how well the economies were doing and how serious the Soviet threat seemed at a given moment. Apart from the first enlargement of 1973 (Denmark, Ireland and the UK), all the following ones

Territory and governance 43

were accompanied by concerns for democracy preservation: 1981 (Greece after the end of the dictatorship of the 'colonels'); 1986 (Spain and Portugal after their return to democracy); 1995 (consolidating the post-war status of Austria, and the full independence of Finland after the end of Soviet influence, and also including Sweden, whose neutrality and independence had never been in doubt); and the three mainly post-communist enlargements of 2004, 2007 and 2013. This leaves unfinished business in the western Balkans (Albania and the remaining states of former Yugoslavia), and Turkey, where the hope of preserving something like Western democratic values may have been lost for ever because of the reticence and procrastination of Christian Democrats and some other politicians in the existing member states.

Following the precedent of the ECSC, the main policy of the emergent EEC and one which bridged economic, social and territorial policy was the CAP. Introduced in 1962, this constituted two thirds of the Communities' budget for a long time, peaking at three quarters in 1985, and is still around 40 per cent.[1] It was also, until the introduction of the euro, the most obvious expression of European integration, at least for Europeans not regularly crossing the borders between EU member states. Farmers, traditionally remote from the political games in national capitals, became among the closest Brussels-watchers. In the absence of a European social policy, the CAP filled the gap to some extent for agricultural workers, cushioning the major shifts out of agriculture in many areas of Europe.[2] It also acted as a surrogate for regional policy, which was for a long time a low proportion of EU expenditure, though it now represents nearly a third.[3]

As with other EU initiatives, one can argue that much of this process of agricultural modernisation and concentration would have happened anyway, as it did in North America. National states might have picked up the tab for the social costs of what Henri Mendras called 'the end of the peasants'.[4] But the fact that this was a European policy, and one which stood out in its size and range in the early history of the Union, makes it exceptionally important. It was also deeply problematic, with much of the support going to larger farms which were competitive anyway and resulting in surplus production which was dumped on the world market to the detriment of poorer producing countries. Wyn Grant (2009: 274) argues that 'the greatest damage that is done by CAP is to Europe's image in the wider world (and many of the European countries outside the EU are, if anything, more protectionist)'. These countries are also as generous (or profligate) in subsidising agriculture. Taking as a measure the proportion of gross farm receipts, the EU's subsidy of 19 per cent in 2012 is dead on the OECD average, and well below Switzerland (57 per cent) and Norway (63 per cent) (Copsey 2015: 109).

The CAP however fell into the trap of reinforcing of what the sociologist Robert Merton called 'the Matthew effect': those who already have something get more.[5] This tends to mean larger farms, such as those in the UK, northern France, Germany and Austria.[6] As Nathaniel Copsey (2015: 108) points out, 'meaningful direct benefits from the CAP in money terms appear to accrue to fewer than 500,000 people', or less than 0.1 per cent of the EU population. To give another, minor, example of the CAP's inflexible application of its rules: hilly regions in the UK came off badly for support payments because the hills weren't high enough above sea level to qualify.

What about regional policy itself? Part of the rationale of what became the EU was the idea later expressed in the ideas of subsidiarity and multi-level governance: that powers previously concentrated at the level of the national state (and often localised in the national capital) should spread upwards to the European level and downwards to regions within states, so that decisions would ideally be taken at the most appropriate level. For example, local decisions about the collection of household waste; European decisions about nuclear waste management. These ideas were not however prominent in policy until the 1980s. Although the Rome Treaty included a clause that 'the Community shall aim at reducing the disparities between the levels of development of the various regions', regional policy in the early days of the EEC was really just a very limited policy for backward regions, particularly southwest France and the south of Italy. The European Regional Development Fund, set up in 1975 after the accession of Denmark, Ireland and the UK, provided some limited support for projects conceived by the member states themselves, but it was only in 1988 that Structural Funds were introduced, and the Committee of the Regions, which incorporates regional representatives into the preparation of legislation, was not established until 1994, when Cohesion Funds were added.[7] Cohesion Policy today amounts to 50 billion euro, a third of the EU budget, though still with a confusing mixture of separate funds and 'objectives' (Rumford 2000).[8]

Copsey (2015: 110) puts together agricultural and infrastructure spending, calculating that its 'direct beneficiaries' amount to around 20 million people, or 4 per cent of the EU's population, but most agricultural support goes to a small number of large farmers or absentee landowners – among them the British Queen and other members of the Royal Family.

Stepping back from the details, it is interesting to reflect on this as an example of what Michel Foucault called *governmentality*, closely linked to ideas of territory. Even if his analysis is not always reliable (Elden 2013: 8–9, Elden and Crampton 2007), the basic idea of the link between power and territory, ruling (*regere* in Latin) and region, is an important one. It is most powerfully discussed in relation to Europe by Jensen and Richardson

(2004), who develop a notion of European planning as the pursuit of a 'monotopia' in which Europe is conceived as a whole and all internal obstacles are removed. Given the 'four freedoms' (the free movement of goods, capital, services and people), they focus in particular on the EU's encouragement of transport networks and infrastructure and on transnational or polycentric development plans, especially in border regions.

An image or 'vision' from the North West European Metropolitan Area planning group (NWMA 2000), cited by Deas and Lord (2006: 1860), illustrates the conceptual framework of this approach as it bears on a core region of the EU (Figure 3.2). The central zone represents southeast England, northern France, Belgium and the Netherlands, and western Germany, including the 'global cities' of London and Paris and 'polycentric' urban areas,[9] linked by 'Eurocorridors' of transport and development.[10] The English Channel and the overcrowded rail and road links between London and Birmingham appear as 'communication bottlenecks'.[11] North and south of the core are an 'Island Zone' including the rest of England (except the far southwest), southern Scotland, and the northeast and east of Ireland; an 'Open Zone' with the rest of Scotland and Ireland (and southwest England); and an 'Inland Zone' heading down the Rhine. Overlying this is a 'pentagon', based on London, Paris, Milan, Munich and Hamburg. We should not fixate on schemes like these, but they undoubtedly feed into EU regional policy discourse. The full list, as of 2006, of EU regional concepts and more concrete projects runs to 150 (Deas and Lord 2006: 1852–1854).

Within member states, the EU has insisted on the creation of regions in 'unitary' states which did not have them – for example in Ireland, which abolished its regions and then had to reinstate them. More importantly, it has encouraged regional authorities and even large cities to engage directly with the Commission, bypassing the member state governments. Many of the German Länder, for example, have permanent representation in Brussels. The Länder are however genuine regions, mini-states with real powers. The English regions, by contrast, never had much of a presence, and were stripped of what powers they had by the 2010–15 Conservative–Liberal coalition government.

As noted earlier, several of the successive enlargements of the EU were partly driven by concerns for democracy preservation, and this was also behind the dramatic expansion of cohesion policy in the run-up to the Eastern Enlargement of 2004 and its continuation in 2007 and 2013. At present, only small parts of formerly communist Europe are really plugged into the main economic circuits of the EU: notably car production in Slovakia and other forms of engineering in previously developed areas (Berend 1996; Berend and Bugaric 2015). Even in Germany, where post-communist transition came first, and with massive transfers from

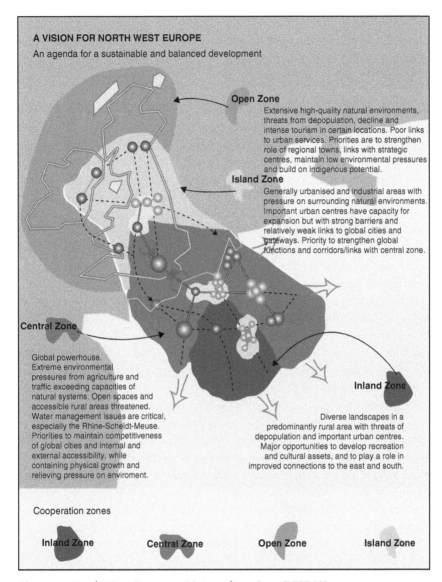

Figure 3.2 North West European Metropolitan Area (NWMA).
(Faludi 2004).

the West, financed by a special income tax levy for 'solidarity', the former German Democratic Republic lags behind on most measures except the quality of some of its infrastructure. Even if cohesion policy became a real priority for the EU, it is hard to see it moving beyond its present state of uneven development. This matters for Europe in a way it does not in the United States because of the linguistic and other obstacles to mobility in Europe and the political salience of the member states. A US state like

West Virginia can be left in relative poverty without the political fall-out that Europe has seen since it more or less deliberately impoverished Greece.

Migration within Europe is one of the great unknowns for anyone aiming to predict its future. Policy in the early years was confined to removing obstacles to free movement, and this was relatively modest: Italians (as well as Turks and Yugoslavs from outside the EEC) in Germany, Portuguese in France. With the fall of the Iron Curtain,[12] the situation was transformed: first, substantial movement in Germany from east to west and then from southeast Europe, Poland and the Baltic states (Eurofound 2015: 11–28). By 2010, 40 per cent of people from Albania and Bosnia and Herzegovina were living abroad, and over 10 per cent from the region as a whole. As well as Albania, many countries from the former Soviet Union and Yugoslavia have 15–25 per cent of their college graduates living abroad. Some of this migration may be internal to the former federations, but Poland and Romania also have 10–15 per cent of those with tertiary education living abroad (Heleniak and Canagarajah 2012). Western Europeans, especially xenophobic politicians in England, tend to focus on the impact of migration on the employment prospects of their less well-educated populations, and on overstretched health, education and welfare systems, but the effect of the 'brain drain' on the 'sending' countries is arguably more important in the longer term.

Migration is a good example of a broader issue: the recalcitrance of regional dynamics to policy interventions. Some governments, such as those in the UK, France and West Germany, attempted to organise and encourage migration, but these schemes were dwarfed by spontaneous movements, just as, despite attempts to revive declining areas, growth often took place in existing boom regions such as the 'M4 corridor' running west from London towards Bristol. As Steffen Mau (2010: 67) points out, 'More and more people are spending periods of time abroad without actually relocating, and the difference between mobility, temporary migration, and permanent migration is often blurred.'

A look at the United States may help to think about European migration. There, the decline of the 'rustbelt' and rise of the 'sunbelt' is driven partly by new forms of economic activity, for example those linked to low-cost assembly plants (*maquiladoras*) in Mexico, and partly by retirement migration – something which is also growing in Europe. UK pensioners go not only to the English-speaking former colonies (including Ireland) but also to Spain (where they and Germans make up much the greatest proportion), France, Italy and elsewhere in Europe (King *et al*. 2010: 88–89; Warnes 2009; Maddison, Murray and Chigbo 2013). The English, often portrayed as Europhobic, including, I'm afraid, in this book, are relatively willing to migrate for this purpose.

The EU has transformed the context for the regional nationalist movements which have been a permanent and increasingly significant accompaniment to the rise of the national state model and also to its partial eclipse in the past half-century. What has been called *internal colonialism* (Hechter 1975), the extension of state power from capital cities to the periphery, particularly strong in the eighteenth and nineteenth centuries as many states aimed to extend education and often to eradicate regional languages such as Gaelic or Breton, has produced a counter-movement of internal decolonialism, contesting rule from national capitals in forms which range from greater devolution of powers to full independence within the EU. The EU, as we have seen, has encouraged the formation of regions, while strongly discouraging anything like regional separatism – most recently in the Scottish referendum debate of 2014 and the ongoing controversy in Catalonia. But whatever stances the EU adopts, the most important fact is that its existence lowers the stakes for separatist movements, which can expect that if they successfully establish independent states they will immediately or eventually be admitted as new members of the Union. To put it crudely, however small your new state may be, it's unlikely to be smaller than Luxembourg, with just under half a million people. Costs of statehood are also reduced: with a common foreign and security policy, combined with NATO membership, there is no need to have diplomatic representation, armies, etc.

There are currently twenty-six countries with active separatist movements in Europe (including European Russia), and rather more movements aiming at independent statehood, rather than just devolution or greater autonomy, or unification with another state. Those with some prospect of success are in Belgium (Flanders and Wallonia), the Faroe Islands (currently part of Denmark), the Basque Country (spanning the border between France and Spain), Brittany, Corsica, Sardinia, Catalonia (also spanning the French–Spanish border), Galicia, the Canary Islands, Scotland, Wales and Turkey (Kurdistan).[13] In all these cases, except Turkey, the existing state has conceded various forms of partial autonomy. We may, however, see some new EU member states emerging from these movements, as we nearly did in the UK in 2014.

The EU has used its 'Europeanness' to reject membership applications from Morocco and to delay its response to those from Turkey, but it includes a number of (mostly French) territories outside Europe. Its population is also however incorporating a growing proportion of citizens and residents of non-European origin, though none of its member states has seriously internalised or adapted to the dynamics of this situation. The UK, for example, has always given the vote to the descendants of its former colonial subjects arriving from Ireland, Australasia, Africa, and South and East Asia, yet its restrictive immigration policies (including the notorious requirement of 'patriality')[14] and structural racism have created a political climate recently worsened by anxieties about internal immigration from other EU states in southeast Europe. Elsewhere in Europe, the predominant approach has been one of denial, manifested in the claim that (West) Germany was 'not a country of immigration'.[15] In France, for example, the ideology of a Republic of equal citizens, along with memories of the deportations of World War II, meant that statistical records of ethnicity were outlawed; only recently has this policy begun to be questioned as awareness has grown of the structural racism in French society (Simon 2008; Léonard 2015). In post-communist Europe, where immigration was largely unknown until 1989, the response has been extremely erratic and unpredictable – most recently in the 2015 asylum crisis.

As the EU's sense of itself as a territory has developed, there has been something of a revival of older (and, particularly in Germany, long-discredited) themes of 'geopolitics'. The 'heartland theory' of the English geographer Halford Mackinder (1861–1947) is not so much Eurocentric as Eurasia-centric, with Eurasia as the centre or 'pivot' of the 'World Island' made up of Europe, Asia and Africa.[16] In his much-quoted slogan, 'Who rules East Europe commands the Heartland; Who rules the Heartland commands the World Island; Who rules the World Island commands the World' (Mackinder 1919: 150). This may seem something of a historical curiosity, not least in its peripheralisation of the Americas, but it is striking that both Russia and the EU are much preoccupied with their surrounding territories or what in Russia is called the 'near abroad'. For the EU, this includes states with a prospect of eventual accession, such as Moldova and those in the Western Balkans, and those expected for the foreseeable future to be confined to various forms of agreement or 'partnership'. For the former, against the background of the Union's openness in principle to any democratic European state which meets certain economic and other requirements, there is what the German sociologist Georg Vobruba (2005) called the European 'dynamic', in which member states on the borders of the Union have an interest, other things being equal, in supporting their neighbours' accession (Germany for Poland and Czechoslovakia, Poland for Ukraine, and so on). This is partly for economic reasons, to reduce competition from lower-wage economies, but also issues of border security and political stability. The other side of the European expansionary dynamic is that, as Vachudová (2005: 71) puts it, 'the EU market from which a non-member is excluded will continue to expand'. Westernising politicians in post-communist prospective member states may also see political benefits in strengthening democracy in what is still a problematic region, even for EU members (Berend and Bugaric 2015). As we saw earlier, geopolitical considerations have played a part in all the enlargements except the first, though even there it can be argued that the accession of Ireland and the UK helped to improve the prospects of ending the civil war or 'troubles' in Northern Ireland, although this did not occur until 1998.

The other side of this process is of course the 'othering' of states and peoples portrayed as 'less European'. As William Wallace wrote:

> Each claimant to full European participation attempts to draw the boundaries of Europe around and behind it; to include all the countries of the Western tradition, of Catholicism and the Enlightenment, for Austria, Hungary and Poland; of the broader Christian tradition, for the southern republics of Yugoslavia, Romania, Bulgaria and Russia; of the secularising and modernising tradition, for Turkey.... Each group of claimants except Turkey and Russia, it should be noted, is as concerned to exclude those beyond it as to include themselves within the community of Europe: Hungarians, Czechs and Poles to shut out Russia; Serbs and Bulgarians to emphasize their distinctiveness from their Islamic neighbours; Israel to stress the divide between 'Judaeo-Christian civilization' and Islam.
>
> (Wallace, 1990: 18–19)

In many ways the EU resembles an empire, though a democratic one whose expansion is at the request of the states which join it. It is multinational, multilingual, with multilevel governance and a model of citizenship similar to that of the Roman Empire, where citizenship carries privileges denied to 'third-party' residents or visitors. Internal borders are open, and what counts is the external border or what the Romans called the *limes* (the origin of our word *limit*). In the past, this expansionary dynamic was uncontentious, except for a few Northern Irish protestants who associated the Rome Treaty with Roman Catholicism, but after 1989, when the expansion of the EU coincided with that of NATO, this conflicted with more traditional imperial conceptions in Russia, stripped in 1991 of its quasi-empire, the Soviet Union. Seen from Western Europe in the 1950s, the Soviet Union was a military threat which encouraged the process of European integration, but one which was far away, except for its presence in the 'satellites'. Russia now borders not just on Finland (and Norway and Turkey) but on former Soviet Estonia and Latvia, and has an 'exclave' around Kaliningrad, between Lithuania and Poland. These tensions came to a head in Ukraine in 2014, with the 'soft power' of the EU conflicting with the rather harder leverage of Russia and its energy resources, and in Crimea and the east of Ukraine, its finally unconcealed military force. It leaves a situation which is still unresolved.

If the EU is a territory, how is it administered, and how do its institutions interact with those of its member states? The next chapter examines these questions.

Summary points

What is now the EU began with very little in the way of regional or social policy, but with an underlying idea of territorial management which partly inspired the CAP, which for a long time amounted to around three quarters of the Community's budget and to some extent operated as a social and regional policy for agricultural districts. Partly intended to preserve small-scale farming which was only marginally profitable, it however delivers large subsidies to big producers.

The EU now has more substantial regional and 'cohesion' funds, though their redistributive impact, like that of the CAP, is very weak. Some regions have benefited considerably, including from improved transport links, but there is little political support for more serious redistribution of the kind seen between north and south in Italy and later between West and East Germany.

Further questions

What is meant by a 'Europe of regions' and is it a useful way of thinking about Europe?
How has the EU affected the place of regions in Europe?
'Location, location, location'. Does 'place' matter in contemporary Europe?
How useful is it to distinguish between 'civic' and 'ethnic' nationalism?

Further reading

Harvie, Christopher (1994) *The Rise of Regional Europe.* London: Routledge.
Jensen, Ole B. and Tim Richardson (2003) *Making European Space: Mobility, Power and Territorial Identity.* London: Routledge.
Jönsson, Christer, Sven Tögil and Gunnar Törnqvist (2000) *Organizing European Space.* London: SAGE.
Outhwaite, William (2016) *Europe Since 1989.* London: Routledge, 'Appendix on Territoriality', pp. 156–163.
Paasi, Anssi (2009) 'Regions and Regional Dynamics', in Chris Rumford (ed.), *The SAGE Handbook of European Studies.* London: SAGE, pp. 464–484.
Therborn, Göran (2006) 'Why and How Place Matters', in Robert E. Goodin and Charles Tilly (eds), *The Oxford Handbook of Contextual Political Analysis.* Oxford: Oxford University Press, pp. 509–533.

Notes

1 Between 1958 and 1965, it also accounted for 90 per cent of Community legislation (Knudsen 2009: 3).

2 Knudsen (2009). For France, see Mendras (1970); more generally Mendras and Cole (1991); Mendras (1997).
3 See http://ec.europa.eu/regional_policy/sources/information/pdf/brochures/interreg_25years_en.pdf
4 Even in the UK, where agriculture had become capitalist at a much earlier stage, financial support was higher in the early 1950s than in any of the EEC's founding member states (Knudsen 2009: 53).
5 Or in the words of the King James Bible (Matthew 13:12): 'For whosoever hath, to him shall be given, and he shall have more abundance'. This is also true of regional and 'cohesion' policies, if one looks not at the overall sums allocated to poorer regions but to amount *per person*; see Dunford and Perrons (2012).
6 See http://ec.europa.eu/eurostat/statistics-explained/index.php/File:Average_size_of_farms,_by_NUTS_2_regions,_2010_(1)_(hectares_of_utilised_agricultural_area_per_agricultural_holding)_RYB14.png
7 The concept of cohesion goes back to the sociologist Emile Durkheim's 1893 book on the division of labour, which he saw as contributing to social cohesion and 'solidarity' (Pahl 1991). The Council of Europe took it up the concept in 1999 (www.coe.int/t/dgal/dit/ilcd/archives/fonds/adm_social_cohesion_FR.asp), as did the EU. On cohesion, see Rumford (2000). On the Committee of the Regions, see Piattoni and Schönlau (2015).
8 See also http://eur-lex.europa.eu/legal-content/EN/TXT/?uri=URISERV:l60014
9 See, for example, Meijers and Romein (2003); Hall and Pain (2006).
10 For an example of a projected rail 'corridor' from Oslo to Berlin which would cut the travel time from over sixteen hours to seven, see Jensen and Richardson (2007) and news reports on www.coinco-berlin.de/ and www.north-south-initiative.eu/. It seems that this project, if it goes ahead, will be funded from private sources. It remains the case, as Chris Rumford (2000: 16) pointed out, that 'the patchwork of crossborder initiatives which comprise the flagship transport TENs are for the most part national projects which would have happened with or without the EU's help'. A more recent project is another rail tunnel, from Finland to Estonia.
11 It is unlikely that this inspired the highly contentious British rail project HS2, and I am not aware of any scheme to remove the other bottleneck with a causeway across the Channel. The inclusion of the whole of the UK in the final version is a bit of a mystery and may have a political explanation. For a more detailed analysis, see also Faludi (2004).
12 Even before 1989, there was considerable migration from Poland, which was easier to leave than anywhere else in the bloc. As a Polish colleague said to me in the late 1980s, the flights to America left full and came back empty.
13 This list discounts Russia and Ukraine, with their complex mixture of de facto breakaway states.
14 *Patriality* was a term used from 1971 to 1983, for Commonwealth citizens who had at least one grandparent born in the UK. The corresponding term now is the Ancestry Visa, with the same requirement. The idea seems to have been to afford a limited 'right of return' to the descendants of British emigrants to the (mostly white) Commonwealth.

15 This claim, made in 1982 in the coalition agreement between the conservative and liberal parties, which went on to draw the inference that 'all humanitarianly defensible measures should be taken to prevent the settlement of foreigners', was explicitly repudiated in 2000 by a government commission.

16 Mackinder (1904). See the image on https://en.wikipedia.org/wiki/Halford_Mackinder#/media/File:Heartland.png

References

Bausinger, Hermann (2000) *Typisch Deutsch: Wie Deutsch Sind die Deutschen?* Munich: Beck.

Berend, Iván (1996) *Central and Eastern Europe 1944–1993: Detour from the Periphery to the Periphery*. Cambridge: Cambridge University Press.

Berend, Ivan and Bojan Bugaric (2015) 'Unfinished Europe: Transition from Communism to Democracy in Central and Eastern Europe', *Journal of Contemporary History*, 50(4): 768–785.

Copsey, Nathaniel (2015) *Rethinking the European Union*. London: Palgrave Macmillan.

Deas, Iain and Alex Lord (2006) 'From a New Regionalism to an Unusual Regionalism? The Emergence of Non-standard Regional Spaces and Lessons for the Territorial Reorganisation of the State', *Urban Studies*, 43(10): 1847–1877.

Dunford, Michael and Diane Perrons (2012) 'Regional Inequality in the EU: How to Finance Greater Cohesion', *European Planning Studies*, 20(6): 895–922.

Elden, Stuart (2013) *The Birth of Territory*. Chicago: Chicago University Press.

Elden, Stuart and Jeremy W. Crampton (eds) (2007) *Space, Knowledge and Power: Foucault and Geography*. Aldershot: Ashgate.

Eurofound (2015) *Social Dimension of Intra-EU Mobility: Impact on Public Services*. Luxembourg: Publications Office of the European Union. www.eurofound.europa.eu/sites/default/files/ef_publication/field_ef_document/ef1546en_3.pdf.

Faludi, Andreas (2004) 'The European Spatial Development Perspective and North-west Europe: Application and the Future', *European Planning Studies*, 12(3): 391–408.

Foucault, Michel (1975) *Surveiller et Punir*. Paris: Gallimard. Tr. (1977) as *Discipline and Punish*, New York: Vintage Books.

Grant, Wyn (2009) 'Agricultural Policy and Protectionism', in Chris Rumford (ed.), *The SAGE Handbook of European Studies*. London: SAGE, pp. 260–276.

Hall, Peter and Kathy Pain (eds) (2006) *The Polycentric Metropolis*. London: Earthscan.

Hechter, Michael (1975) *Internal Colonialism: The Celtic Fringe in British National Development, 1536–1966*. London: Routledge and Kegan Paul.

Heleniak, Timothy and Sudharshan Canagarajah (2012) 'The ECA's Diaspora Populations Can Aid Growth and Development', Washington: World Bank Europe and Central Asia Knowledge Brief, 46, April. http://siteresources. worldbank.org/INTECALEA/Resources/1040211-1251905880790/KB46_ Diaspora_Final.pdf.

Jensen Ole B. and Tim Richardson (2004) *Making European Space: Mobility, Power and Territorial Identity*. London: Routledge.

Jensen, Anne and Tim Richardson (2007) 'New Region, New Story: Imagining Mobile Subjects in Transnational Space', *Space and Polity*, 11(2): 137–150.

King, Russell et al. (2010) *The Atlas of Human Migration*. London: Earthscan.

Knudsen, Ann-Christina (2009) *Farmers on Welfare: The Making of Europe's Common Agricultural Policy*. Ithaca: Cornell University Press.

Léonard, Marie des Neiges (2015) 'Who Counts in the Census? Racial and Ethnic Categories in France', in Rogelio Sáenz, David G. Embrick and Néstor P. Rodríguez (eds), *The International Handbook of the Demography of Race and Ethnicity*. Dordrecht: Springer Netherlands, pp. 537–552.

Mackinder, Halford J. (1904) 'The Geographical Pivot of History', *Geographical Journal*, 23: 421–37.

Mackinder, Halford J. (1919) *Democratic Ideals and Reality*. Washington, DC: National Defence University Press, pp. 175–193.

Maddison, David, Tom Murray and Onyebuchi Chigbo (2013) 'International Retirement Migration from Northern Europe to the Mediterranean: New Results on the Role of Climate with a Possible Application to Climate Change', in David Maddison, Tom Murray and Onyebuchi Chigbo (eds), *Regional Assessment of Climate Change in the Mediterranean*. Dordrecht: Springer Netherlands, Chapter 16, pp. 367–385.

Mau, Stephen (2010) *Social Transnationalism: Lifeworlds Beyond the Nation State*. London/New York: Routledge.

Meijers, Evert and Arie Romein (2003) 'Realizing Potential: Building Organizing Capacity in Polycentric Urban Regions', *European Urban and Regional Studies*, 10(2): 173–186.

Mendras, Henri (1970) *The Vanishing Peasant: Innovation and Change in French Agriculture*. Cambridge, MA: MIT Press.

Mendras, Henri and Alistair Cole (1991) *Social Change in Modern France*. Cambridge: Cambridge University Press.

Mendras, Henri (1997) *L'Europe des Européens*. Paris: Gallimard.

North West European Metropolitan Area (2000) *A Spatial Vision for North-West Europe: Building Cooperation*. The Hague: Ministry for Housing, Spatial Planning and the Environment.

Pahl, Ray (1991) 'The Search for Social Cohesion: From Durkheim to the European Commission', *European Journal of Sociology*, 32(2): 345–360.

Piattoni, Simona and Justus Schönlau (2015) *Shaping EU Policy from Below: EU Democracy and the Committee of the Regions*. Cheltenham: Edward Elgar.

Rumford, Chris (2000) *European Cohesion. Contradictions in EU Integration*. Basingstoke: Palgrave Macmillan.

Simon, Patrick (2008) 'The Choice of Ignorance: The Debate on Ethnic and Racial Statistics in France', *French Politics, Culture & Society*, 26(1): 7–31.

Vachudová, Milada Anna (2005) *Europe Undivided: Democracy, Leverage, and Integration After Communism*. Oxford: Oxford University Press.

Vobruba, Georg (2005) *Die Dynamik Europas*. Wiesbaden: VS Verlag für die Sozialwissenschaften.

Wallace, William (1990) *The Transformation of Western Europe*. London: RIIA/Pinter.

Warnes Tony (A.M.) (2009) 'International Retirement Migration', in Uhlenberg, Peter (ed.), *International Handbook of Population Aging*, Dordrecht: Springer, Chapter 15, pp. 341–363.

chapter 4

Institutional Europe

Having discussed Europe, including the EU, in broad terms, the book now turns to a more detailed introduction to the EU and other European institutions and the ways in which they relate to member states and regional sub-states. The 'original six' states which formed the ECSC in 1951 and, shortly afterwards, the EEC, included two where fascism had led to the recent war in which the other four were overrun and occupied and in which substantial parts of their populations were deported and murdered.[1] Reconciliation does not get much more dramatic than this.[2] On the other hand, they were all states with similar economic and social structures, and three, the Benelux states, had already collaborated closely in the immediate post-war years. The second, third and fourth enlargements brought in Greece, which had suffered a military dictatorship from 1967 to 1974; Spain and Portugal, whose fascist regimes had stayed out of the war; and finally Austria, which, like Germany, had been under four-power occupation after the war. The 2004 enlargement included six former communist dictatorships, and 2007 and 2013 continued this process. In retrospect it is perhaps surprising that what came after 2004 to be called 'enlargement fatigue' did not set in earlier. In some ways it did: as we saw, De Gaulle blocked the UK's accession twice in the 1960s, partly because of wider anxieties about expansion, and in 1977 the future president Mitterand said that Spain and Greece (and presumably Portugal) were not ready for accession. In the 1990s, the prospect of post-communist member states aroused more widespread anxiety, but the crisis which began in 2008 has turned the spotlight back to the South.

With all this diversity, it is perhaps surprising that the formal institutional structure of what is now the EU has remained so stable. Much of the weakness of EU democracy, as well as many of its other dysfunctional features, can probably be explained by the way in which a model developed for the six members of the ECSC at the beginning of the 1950s was gradually scaled up to the current EU and its nearly thirty member states. David Held and his co-authors have brilliantly described the way in which the world has become the victim of the *success* of post-war initiatives such as the UN, NATO and Bretton Woods. In this argument (Hale, Held and Young 2013: 224).

The ECSC was set up with a 'High Authority', a Council of national ministers, and a Court which seems to have been intended mainly to set limits to the activity of the High Authority (Rittberger 2012: 89). These were replicated in the EEC with the term *Commission*, taken institutions which are initially successful may become obstacles to further institutional innovation as in theories of 'path dependence' (see, for example, Outhwaite 2016, chapter 3). From the abortive European Defence Community, replacing the term *High Authority* but also made up of Commissioners nominated by the member states. There was also a Parliamentary Assembly, made up of national parliamentarians, but the legislative body for the EEC was termed the *Council of Ministers*, an umbrella for the various specialised ministers who attended the respective Council meetings. The Court had significantly greater powers than the ECSC Court, since it could also judge treaty breaches by member states.

The two anomalies in this structure were that there was no government and no parliamentary legislature. The Commission was a curious hybrid of a ministerial cabinet and a civil service, with powers to propose legislation and acting as the 'guardian of the treaties'. As Marc Abélès (1992: 11) wrote, 'In the absence of a real government, the parliamentarians cannot think in terms of government and opposition.'[3] The Parliament, although its powers included the 'nuclear option' of requiring the Commission to resign, had otherwise only a consultative role. In a critique that continues to be echoed, Alberto Spinelli complained that 'Europeans continue to be deprived of any institutional instrument that would permit them to be the European people and act as the European people'.[4] Instead, the Commission, like the Court, acted on behalf of the European people, while the Council and the Committee of Permanent Representatives (COREPER, from the French ***Comité des représentants permanents***) represented the member states.[5]

Over time each of these institutions has changed. The College of Commissioners has grown in size in order to preserve the principle that each member state be represented.[6] This should not be necessary, given that commissioners are officially independent of their states of origin, but one can understand how it happened. Despite an agreement that the number be capped at twenty-seven, with a rotation system applying thereafter, the EU currently has twenty-eight, after Croatia's accession in 2013.

The President of the College of Commissioners has acquired a more prominent role and, after the 2014 elections, the principle seems to be established that the 'lead candidates' (*Spitzenkandidaten*) of the parties will be elected by the party groupings in the Parliament and the presidency assigned to the candidate whose party has or can mobilise the largest majority. This means that most European voters are able in effect to vote for the Commission President by voting for their preferred party group. (In the 2014 elections this was possible in the UK for Labour, Liberal and Green voters, but not for supporters of the Conservatives, UKIP or the extreme right, whose party groupings did not put up candidates.) Despite criticism of the massive army of Eurocrats, the Commission staff number in fact just over 30,000, a little fewer than the UK's Department for Work and Pensions, which has less need for translation and interpretation. The Commission has in fact suffered from understaffing (Spence and Stevens 2006: 179).

The Council has now moved from requiring unanimity for its decisions to allowing, where necessary, for a vote on most matters by a qualified majority. This change was sparked by De Gaulle's refusal to attend in 1965, leaving an 'empty chair' and thus blocking Council business, and the 'Luxembourg Compromise' which ended the crisis, but in practice it was twenty years before majority voting became common. Importantly, however, there remains a national veto for accession applications and treaty changes. The Council made up of heads of state and government is now formally a separate institution, the European Council, and its membership includes the Council President and the President of the Commission. The High Representative of the Union for Foreign and Security Affairs, appointed by the Council, also participates in its meetings. He or she is also First Vice-President of the Commission.

The European Parliament (EP) has also grown in significance, as parliaments tend to do, with what one might call two-and-a-half main developments. First, the move to direct elections in 1979, which gave it greater legitimacy, though far from equal prominence with national legislatures in the minds of most Europeans. Second, from 1992, its legislative role, known as cooperation and co-decision, in conjunction with the Council and carefully structured in relation to different issue areas. *Co-decision*, now known as the *ordinary method*, applies for the bread-and-butter issues, with *consent* and *consultation* for others, such as the accession of new member states. The Parliament website currently includes the slightly defensive gloss that it can ask the Commission to present legislative proposals for laws to the Council. It plays a genuine role in creating new laws, since it examines the Commission's annual programme of work and says which laws it would like to see introduced.[7]

Since the Lisbon Treaty of 2009, it also has, in conjunction with the Council, the budgetary powers which we normally associate with parliaments and has exercised those in relation to new more intergovernmental institutions and practices (Pollak and Slominski 2015).

The half-measure, since 2014, is the Parliament's role in the appointment of the Commission President. This was previously a Council decision on which the Parliament had to be consulted, but it realised somewhat belatedly that this effectively gave it a veto power over the selection which it now decided to exercise, by inviting the parties to propose their candidates as part of the elections to the Parliament which take place every four years. This took the heads of state and government by surprise, and David Cameron attempted unsuccessfully to mobilise opinion against the nomination, but the principle now seems to be established.[8] It represents an extension of the Parliament's influence, as well as introducing a further element of Europeanisation to elections which remain otherwise fragmented on national lines (and where voting most often reflects national rather than European politics). The candidates took part in televised debates, in Maastricht, Florence and Brussels, very much like those in national elections. The turnout for elections, however, is low across Europe, and falling. The Parliament may have increased its institutional weight, but not its public profile. It also remains constrained by a ridiculous provision, agreed long ago with France, that it meet once a month not in Brussels, where its committees work, but in Strasbourg, over 200 miles away, on the French-German border. Franco-German reconciliation was welcome at the time, but 'la guerre est finie'.

The Court of Justice of the European Union, even more than the US Supreme Court, is central to the political system in which it sits, despite being located in Luxembourg, over 100 miles from Brussels. Starting from scratch, with only the Treaties as a base, and drawing as needed on legal principles in the law of the member states, it has gradually created something which walks, even if it does not talk, like an EU constitution. If the founding member states had known they were setting up a federal supreme court they would have probably thought again. Monnet, however, addressed the ECSC court in 1952 in the following terms: 'I greet you not only as the Court of the European Coal and Steel Community, but also as the prospective supreme federal European Court'.[9] The doctrines of 'direct effect' means that EU laws stand in direct relation to citizens independently of the national state legal systems, and the primacy of EU law means that the jurisdiction of the European Court of Justice (ECJ) is the final centre of European jurisprudence, something formally affirmed in the Lisbon Treaty. The Court does not have bailiffs, but it acts through the operation of national courts in member states.

The Court has often operated, sometimes decisively, as the pacemaker of the European integration process. Although one can find analyses by both insiders and outsiders stressing the voluntary of the pursuit of integration underlying this judicial activism (Maduro 1998), it is probably more accurate to regard it as a set of accommodations to specific situations (Everson and Eisner 2007). In the early years of this century, in particular, the European Court began to extend its traditional role in liberalising trade and mobility in a more starkly neo-liberal direction, with a string of judgements including *Volkswagen* and, most dramatically, *Viking* and *Laval* in 2007. In the absence of any coordinated European labour law or social policy, the Court took the alternative route of 'making the national welfare state regimes compatible with the internal market' (Habermas 1998: 146). It seems to be this, rather than any more ideological preference for neo-liberal strategies on the part of the Court, which explains the turn. The EU, in other words, failed to introduce a formal constitution, but it has developed a substantial body of law and a set of more informal understandings and institutional procedures of the kind which are familiar in the UK, which also lacks a written constitution.

How might we describe this structure, which Jacques Delors once called an 'unidentified political object'? The two models which can serve as reference points are an international organisation, like the UN or the Council of Europe, and a federal state like the United States or Germany. Just where it fits between these two extremes is hard to determine, since it is also an unidentified flying (or at least moving) object, whose final state, like its borders, is still undecided. Not only is the future unclear; specialists still disagree fundamentally about the past: the motivation behind the formation of the ECSC and EEC, with some stressing the heroic (or misguided) attempt to go beyond the national state model which had just produced two world wars and others seeing it as a means for national states to 'rescue' themselves in the post-war world (Milward 1992).

Between these two poles is perhaps the most fruitful model, developed recently by Chris Bickerton (2012). He suggests that we should see the EU as an association of 'member states', where these are no longer national states in the traditional form but states whose participation in the Union is an essential part of their nature. In other words, the concept of member state is not just a legal title which states acquire when they join, but 'a distinctive form of statehood' (Bickerton 2012: 15). Member states are 'entities whose self-understanding is inseparable from pan-European-level cooperation and policymaking' (Bickerton 2012: 49). In detailed studies of economic and foreign policy, he shows how member states have developed forms of concerted action where policy is made mostly in isolation from domestic electorates and the largely impotent European electorate. The EU, then, takes the process of international cooperation which can be seen in other late-twentieth-century innovations, such as the UN and the World Trade Organization, to a much higher and qualitatively different level. Even when member states such as the UK and Denmark opt out of common policies in the area of justice and home affairs, their 'governments are as keen as their peers to remain full players in the policymaking process and find multiple ways to circumvent the legal obstacles of the opt-out agreements' (Bickerton 2012: 40–41; see also Adler-Nissen 2011, 2014; Dyson and Sepos 2010; also the Special Issue of the *Journal of European Public Policy* [2015] on 'Differentiated integration in the European Union'). The EU should be seen not as an association of national states, nor as a new form of state in its own right, but as a project of *state transformation* (Bickerton 2012: 49).

An account of 'Institutional Europe' would be incomplete without some reference to the Council of Europe. Established in 1949, it is explicitly intergovernmental, focused on issues of democracy and the rule of law and cultural matters. Although it gave rise to the European Court of Human Rights it does not legislate directly, though it has a Parliamentary Assembly made up of parliamentarians from its forty-seven member states. It operates as a kind of outer circle of the EU, from which it is formally independent, though elements of its human rights law, based on the European Convention on Human Rights signed in 1950, intersect with EU law, notably the 'Social Chapter' of employment rights.[10]

The EU is clearly different from this intergovernmental model, but neither is it a federal state like the United States or Germany (or a confederation like Switzerland), with a fixed hierarchy of levels of governance having clearly delimited spheres of activity. Along with the primacy of EU law, there is a vaguer doctrine of 'subsidiarity', according to which decisions should be taken at the lowest appropriate level, from communes or parish councils through local and national government up to the EU level. Among the proposals for the future of the EU is the idea of a second chamber of the Parliament, representing national states or regions, as in the case of the US Senate or the German Bundesrat, and replacing the Council. This now seems if anything a little more remote than it did in 2000 when the German Foreign Minister, Joschka Fischer, proposed it (speaking in a private capacity).

Anthony Giddens (2014: 6), as noted earlier, has distinguished between what he calls EU1, the formal institutions of the Union, and EU2, the ad hoc groupings of heads of state or government in the leading member states 'where a lot of the real power lies, exercised on a selective and informal basis'.

A third alternative, federalism, he argues, 'is not an ideology but a pragmatic form of government, at its best flexible and adaptable'. I agree, though whether there is a political will to take this step remains to be seen.

Before addressing in the next chapter this and other proposals to democratise the EU, let us look more closely at the existing institutions. These have been a focus of important ethnographic and other research on the emergence and activities of a Europeanised administrative corps, working both in the institutions themselves and in the member states' representations. The research agenda, in other words, has moved from a main focus on policy to include one on process and the 'production of Europe' at the micro level.

Obeying the French sociologist Bruno Latour's injunction to 'follow the actors', we should ask first where they come from. A focus on EU professionals, in other words, calls attention to the biographical formation of those active in EU institutions, in very much the way pioneered by Cris Shore (2000) in his anthropological study of the Commission[11] and adopted by David Spence (2012) in his analysis of the European External Action Service (EEAS). European civil servants are recruited by competitive examination (the French *concours*) or, for a minority, delegated by member states. Jean Monnet (1978: 377, translation modified), the 'father' of the EU, wrote enthusiastically in his memoirs about the 'legend' of a 'new type of people' were being born in the institutions 'as in a laboratory', and 'the European spirit which is the fruit of working together', but the reality remains a little less dramatic.

Edward Page (1997: 87) wrote:

> The administration of the EU is a cosmopolitan bureaucracy. It has people at the top who have worked through the institutions, those who were parachuted long ago, and those who have just hit the ground. It has people on contracts, secondment as well as national civil servants passing through. ... Such diversity militates against the development of a common identity. In fact to deal with this diversity officials tend to make many assumptions about each other that emphasize such differences: officials from the 'north' behave differently from those from the 'south' . . .; political officials are simply reaping the rewards of earlier political loyalties; those on temporary contracts are working for a permanent job and seconded officials are working for their home state.

Recruitment is skewed by the attempt to appoint candidates proportionately from member states, though in the professional A-grade, Belgium is over-represented for obvious reasons (if you're in Brussels already you don't need to move house) and Germany and the UK under-represented.

(The UK's under-representation might be explained by poor competence in the required second language, but this hardly explains Germany's.)

While civil servants have become more professionalised over time, with specifically European experience, the commissioners have tended even more than in the past to come from careers in national politics. Didier Georgakakis (Georgakakis and Rowell 2013: 51) records 5 per cent prime ministers, 10 per cent foreign ministers, 14 per cent finance ministers, 4 per cent defence ministers and 30 per cent from other ministries, and another 10 per cent from other national political careers and 20 per cent diplomats or other national civil servants. Fewer than 3 per cent had been MEPs. He notes the way in which they often reshape their career biographies in documents and websites in a more 'European' way, in a context where they are in fact increasingly national career politicians with little prior EU involvement (Georgakakis and Rowell 2013: 48–49). Commissioners are supported by 'cabinets' of six advisors, and tend to appoint a mix of people who 'know the place' ('la maison') or other EU institutions and of outside recruits with specialised expertise, often from their own states, though since 2005 there is now a rule that at least three nationalities must be represented and that at least two cabinet members must be female.

A particular focus of the book by Cris Shore (2000) was the organisational culture of the Commission bureaucracy, described by one of the people he interviewed as 'a civil service *with attitude*' and by Jacques Delors in 1988 as the beginnings of a European government (Shore 2000: 143–144). He stressed, as his informants also did, the importance of *engrenage*, the interaction between the various cogs and wheels in the system, mediated by officials who share a common administrative language, even if their native languages differ (Shore 2000: 147–153).

Whether or not they develop a cosmopolitan lifestyle, Eurocrats and more temporary member state participants are constrained by their work and by the ethos of technical competence and compromise to adopt a European perspective. In the words of Outhwaite and Spence,

> The culture of compromise attributes a crucial role to 'information and expertise' (Abélès and Bellier, 1996: 448), in itself a long-recognized part of the self-justification of Commission officials relying on the assumption that it is precisely their expertise, their comprehensive information, their view of the whole European setting as opposed to national officials' knowledge of individual (national) parts, which makes the Commission indispensable.
>
> (Outhwaite and Spence 2014: 435)

This flexibility applies in particular to the members of commissioners' cabinets, who acquire and deploy a much wider expertise than would be normal in a national administrative system. Working for commissioners who are part of a collective body, they are required to provide the necessary information for meetings of the College. Cutting across this generalising and Europeanising tendency, which eurosceptics often call 'going native', is the question of institutional location within the EU: between those working in the Commission or Parliament and those more intergovernmentally oriented in the Council.

These 'tensions' are in part structural, in the formal division between servants of the Community such as the European Commissioners, Commission officials and the judges of the European Court on the one hand, and the ministers and permanent representatives of the member states on the other, with members of the Parliament located somewhere in between.[12] Georgakakis argues against fixating on official identities such as, in this case, intergovernmental and supranational, and paying more attention to the positions of actors and their strategies in the 'field'. He gives the example of a temporary Commission official who might have been expected to take a 'French' line on the protection of the public interest in relation to the liberalisation of postal services but who was also heading towards a business career (Georgakakis and Rowell 2013: 233–234).[13] The context was one in which contrasting conceptions of public services in France and the UK gradually slid into one that endorsed Thatcherite privatisation and became the mantra of that part of the Commission wedded to free market idealism (Abélès and Bellier, 1996: 452–454; Bellier, 2000). Asked whether they agreed that the Commission should become a 'European government', officials were evenly divided (Kassim 2013).

Much depends on informal accommodations between incumbents of these various positions, as stressed, for example, by Keith Middlemas (1995) in his masterly study of the 'informal politics' of the EU. In Middlemas's (1995: xx) analysis:

> Informal politics are defined not so much by the players' status – any who wish and can establish credentials to the satisfaction of others can enter – as by the mode chosen to establish relationships. All players can choose between formal and informal modes and shades of grey between them. There is no dividing line – only a spectrum. Rules and conventions are policed on both sides, with many nuanced penalties for infringement. . . . To a minimum extent, all players, like member states themselves, must demonstrate an element of altruism (European-mindedness) as well as basic self-interest.

Member state representatives must, for instance, steer an intermediate path between the naked pursuit of what they perceive as their national interest and a wholly selfless devotion to the common European good. It is unacceptable for a minister to say in the Council that he or she is only concerned with the national interest, though Thatcher came close to this. Contrary to this minority viewpoint among leaders in EU countries, others concentrate on justification for European action, seemingly (though perhaps only seemingly) relegating 'national interest' to second order priority status. But it is equally unacceptable for politicians to return home to declare that, although the result of a meeting has been disastrous for their own member state, decisions taken were in the general interest of the Union and that is what really matters – a point of view also requiring elaborate justification through solemn appeals to the general benefits of EU membership and to the norms and procedures of the treaties.

Tension between national (member state) and Union interest is fundamental to the nature of the EU – indeed, a frequent theme of its self-justification (Bellier 2000: 60–62). Another technique is to reclassify a national interest as a European interest and thereby bolster political support. French farmers' interests are reclassified as the interest of European agriculture. Industrial capital's interest can be reclassified as a European, free-movement interest. The interests of finance capital are another interest from within the welter of divergent interests which the EU institutions might select as an interest that needs to be defended or promoted, and member states with diverse interests according to classes and categories within them have a prior decision to take over which interest is the interest they choose to advocate or defend at EU level. The rub for 'Europeanists' is that the reverse process is also true; a European interest can be reclassified as in no specific national interest.

The theme of compromise discussed above by Georgakakis has in fact long been at the centre of reflection on the EU and in particular on the Commission (Abélès and Bellier 1996: 445–448). As Pascal Lamy (1991: 76, cited in Abélès and Bellier, 1996: 442), who was Delors' *chef de cabinet*, put it:

> In the community system, priority is given to the building of consensus. There is no arbitration; there is simply a vote. And before the vote the ideal is to reach agreement.

What is lacking, perhaps, is a space for the delicate matter of the affirmation of *national* interest and the legitimate forms in which this can be articulated. This is, of course, an area fraught with internal contradictions, since while there is a political commitment to 'integration' at the highest level, the facts of everyday business are imbued with a discourse of protection of national interests, as opposed to praise for success in terms of supranational outcomes. A recent analysis of working groups of the Council is particularly relevant here. One of the UK negotiators interviewed, concerned with common agricultural policy reform, commented on the contrast between working groups dominated by national interests and a more consensual 'European' approach 'higher up the Council hierarchy where EU diplomatic cadres took over' (Clark and Jones 2011: 350).

This short account has aimed to convey a sense of the EU as a going concern, shaped partly by long-term visions but also by short-term accommodations and compromises. Similarly, its failure to produce a constitution of a kind familiar from the United States and other states[14] contrasts with the fact that it already has a very substantial body of constitutional law and practice, in which transnational processes and institutions take precedence over national ones. These interrelations are not well understood, and are at the limit sometimes indeterminate – as in the more or less hypothetical possibility of a member state defying a European Court ruling.

We are left then with the question whether the Union has the right institutions, in the right configuration, to operate effectively. Does an institutional model created for the six members of the ECSC still fit the needs of a political Union many times bigger? How can the formal institutions, and a 'community method' of decision-making be reconciled with the much more intergovernmental approach to other areas?

The EU had for a time a formal 'pillar structure' represented below. This is officially superseded by the Lisbon Treaty, which brought the three together, but in practice they remain distinct.[15]

The EU now has its own foreign ministry and diplomatic service, but we are not supposed to call it that. The External Action Service, established in 2011, is presided over by a High Representative for Foreign Affairs and Security Policy. It was accompanied with a (UK-inspired) caveat that this

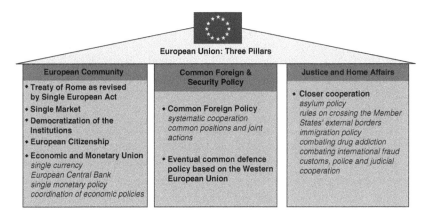

Figure 4.1 The Three Pillars.

Source: www.xanthi.ilsp.gr/kemeseu/ch1/images/3pillars.gif

Institutional Europe

will not affect the existing legal basis, responsibilities, and powers of each Member State in relation to the formulation and conduct of its foreign policy, its national diplomatic service, relations with third countries and participation in international organisations, including a Member State's membership of the Security Council of the United Nations.

(EU, Treaty of Lisbon 2007)

As well as ordinary diplomatic staff in 139 delegations and offices around the world, who complement and occasionally stand in for those of member states, it has currently nine 'Special Representatives' in problem regions: The Horn of Africa, Kosovo, Bosnia and Herzegovina, Afghanistan, South Caucasus, the Sahel, and Central Asia, and in the areas of Human Rights and the Middle East Peace Process. The EEAS is a laboratory-style experiment: not just in forming a new institution, but in creating a new group of professionals claiming for itself the attributes of an already existing profession. Some of the EU's new diplomats were diplomats before; some were not. They have competing interpretations of 'diplomacy', their roles within it and, indeed, the institutional homes of these differing interpretations (Spence 2012; Spence and Bátora 2015). Gaining status, being able to fulfil 'real' diplomatic roles without being attached to a state, may depend on the achievement of an autonomous space, now largely recognised in other areas of EU affairs such as agriculture or trade.[16]

In the area of Justice and Home Affairs, sometimes frivolously known as 'thugs and drugs', the EU has nine agencies located in different member states, of which the most prominent are the border agency FRONTEX (from the French *frontières extérieures*, the external borders of the EU) and the police Europol. In the latter, the UK once again dragged its feet over whether to participate, which it is entitled to do on an ad hoc basis, as one of its four, now three, 'opt-outs', along with those from Schengen and from monetary union.

The director of Europol, who had previously worked in the British police, described the situation in at lecture at University College London in 2012:

> Under the Lisbon Treaty, which came into force in December 2009, the UK's participation in EU JHA [Justice and Home Affairs] legislation is now governed by 2 protocols, which have more or less maintained the status quo: Protocol 19 concerning Schengen – the UK is deemed to be participating in the police and judicial cooperation measures of the Schengen acquis in which it already takes part, unless it decides to opt-out – and Protocol 21 concerning the JHA area – decisions in JHA will not apply to the UK unless it decides to opt-in.

He went on to describe how much of what the UK had conceived as its own prerogative had been eroded by subsequent legislation, traced the likely consequences of non-participation and concluded on a more personal note:

> Perhaps there are a few idealists among my former colleagues in the UK who pro-actively engage with Europol because they believe in the European integration project, but I haven't found many. They simply do it because they are pragmatic and Europol's support delivers tangible benefits in terms of disrupting more organised crime networks and putting more crooks behind bars. I guess they know as much as I do the value of the UK remaining closely involved in European police and justice cooperation instruments, in order to add value in fighting crime and terrorism. They are not in it to please the Commission or even the British Director of Europol – simply to help themselves in protecting British citizens.[17]

In a commentary by Statewatch, the civil liberties non-governmental organisation (NGO), appended to the summary of the lecture on the University College London website, Tony Bunyan agreed

> that the UK has been, and is, a major player on EU policing and internal security policies. However, there is little evidence that the UK's role has safeguarded civil liberties. . . . When it comes to internal security the UK is on the side of the hawks.

These and other opt-outs mean that the EU is increasingly not just an area of multilevel governance, but multiform in the sense that the membership of common policies is increasingly open. This can be viewed either as a welcome element of flexibility or as a dirty compromise which erodes the idea of community or union. Also relevant here is the 'Open Method of Coordination', in which the EU merely sets principles or 'benchmarks', and may 'name and shame' states which do not comply with them. Introduced formally in 2000, it has been used particularly in the area of social policy and social inclusion, where the EU has been almost entirely ineffective and where this may be better than nothing.[18]

A theme which has run through discussion of the EU since the 1990s, when the German Christian Democrat Union (CDU) politicians Wolfgang Schäuble and Kurt Lamers (1994) introduced it in a CDU discussion paper, is that of a flexible integration process which would formalise the distinction between a 'core' of closely integrated member states and a more loosely integrated periphery. This currently exists to some extent in the division between eurozone members and the rest, but only on a temporary basis, since all member states except Denmark (whose currency is anyway pegged to the euro and likely to remain so) and the UK are obliged to join the eurozone in due course. This, of course, made nonsense of the UK government's insistence, as one of its pre-referendum negotiating points, that eurozone members should not be allowed to commit to policies affecting the interests of the rest. As it happens, almost all the prospective euro states (apart from Sweden) have signed up to the new framework for euro governance; the other exceptions are the Czech Republic, which had an extreme eurosceptic president, and Hungary, which is courting suspension of its voting rights through a series of anti-democratic and illiberal measures. Only the UK has chosen not to sign up to any of these elements (Hix 2015: 188). An inner–outer division remains a possible future for the EU, but it is hard to see any advantage to it, except perhaps to keep the UK in. Until the accession process is complete, however, there will always be degrees of 'Europeanisation' as new members adapt to the Union, and some member states might prefer to remain in a position of qualified membership.

The very ambiguous term *Europeanisation* refers, among other things, to the interaction of national institutions with European ones (vertically) or with equivalent institutions in other national states in a European context.[19] This would include, for example, ministers in the Council, civil servants in the Commission and the other institutions, and judges and advocates-general (and their staff) in the Court. There are more ad hoc arrangements for the interaction of parliamentarians, though for a long time it was common in some countries for politicians to be members of the EP as well as their national parliaments (and sometimes mayors as well). There are, of course, formal arrangements for local scrutiny of legislation and other EU matters; a House of Lords Committee, for example, examined the JHA question mentioned above. Similarly, in the early years it was quite common for national courts to refer questions to the European Court of Justice (ECJ), but as its case law has developed and become better known this has become less common. Among reform proposals discussed in the next chapter are closer collaboration between the EP and national parliaments.

Summary points

The EEC began with a similar institutional structure to that of the earlier ECSC, and this has survived to the present, though now with a directly elected Parliament and a more powerful Court.

These two supranational institutions, like the European Commission, continue to be balanced and increasingly outweighed by the intergovernmental institutions of the Council, despite occasional suggestions that the Council could be transformed into a representative parliamentary body for the member states, along the lines of the US or French Senates or the German Bundesrat.

The first question we tend to ask about a state, even a regional state like Scotland, is who runs the government? This does not have a clear answer in the case of the EU.

Legal integration has gone further and faster than that in most other areas of the EU polity. European elites would probably not have agreed to set up what is effectively (in the areas for which it is responsible) a federal supreme court if the issue had been posed so directly.

The EU has something like a constitution, though attempts to formalise it have been notably unsuccessful, in the face of opposition where the electorates in some member states refused to support proposals in referendums.

Further questions

Why are the EU institutions so hard to understand?
Consider the phrasing: 'the so-called European Parliament' (Wolfang Streeck). Is this a bit unfair?
Consider the phrasing: 'the beginnings of a European government' (Jacques Delors). Is this a meaningful way of thinking about the European Commission?
Why has law played such an important part in European integration?

Further reading

Jones, Erik, Anand Menon and Stephen Weatherill (eds) (2012) *The Oxford Handbook of the European Union*. Oxford: Oxford University Press.

Shore, Cris (2000) *Building Europe: The Cultural Politics of European Integration*. London: Routledge.

Vauchez, Antoine (2016) *Democratizing Europe*. London: Palgrave.

Weiler, Joseph (1999) *The Constitution of Europe: 'Do the New Clothes Have an Emperor?' and Other Essays on European Integration*. Cambridge: Cambridge University Press.

Weiler, Joseph and Marlene Wind (eds) (2003) *European Constitutionalism beyond the State*. Cambridge: Cambridge University Press.

Notes

1 Italy moved in 1943 from the former category to the latter. After the war, France, along with the UK and US, joined in the occupation of Western Germany and the western sectors of Berlin and Vienna.

2 As Alan Milward (2002: 16) pointed out, in many historical accounts, 'the European construction remains a peace treaty based on the rejection of the politics of 1933–45'.
3 My translation.
4 Quoted by Gilbert (2012: 104).
5 Commissioners still have to take an oath 'neither to seek nor to take instructions from any Government or from any other institution, body, office or entity'. They serve Europe rather than the states which nominated them, and tend to refer to their states of origin euphemistically as 'the state I know best'. A British Commissioner (and father of the now more famous UK politician), Stanley Johnson (1987), published a semi-autobiographical novel. For more formal memoirs, see also the European University Institute's Oral History Project http://archives.eui.eu/en/oral_history
6 In the past the larger states actually had two.
7 www.europarl.europa.eu/aboutparliament/en/20150201PVL00004/Legislative-powers
8 We can at present only guess what would happen if a Commission President left office mid-term.
9 See Cohen (2013: 42).
10 There is some question whether the UK could repeal its Human Rights Act, which incorporated the Convention into English and Scottish law, without being bound by some of its provisions and the related case law, unless it also left the EU.
11 Shore, beginning his fieldwork in 1993, was surprised to learn that a research team had just produced a report for the Commission itself. This long-buried document was retrieved from https://hal.archives-ouvertes.fr/halshs-00374346/document (accessed 13.2.16). See also McDonald (1996).
12 On the Parliament, see, for example, Ringe (2009) and Pollak and Slominski (2015). As Georgakakis and Weisbein (2010: 96) note, however, 'Permanent representatives, who are supposed to be "national", are sometimes more international and permanent in the field than a Commissioner or a director of the Commission who are supposed to be real "Europeans"'.
13 Following the sociologist Pierre Bourdieu, he emphasises a social space shaped by a variety of resources and accumulated properties and also by socialising processes (*communalisation*). Institutional location, too, should be seen less as a precise determinant and more as generating a space within which actors have a margin of manoeuvre.
14 The Lisbon Treaty (Treaty on the Functioning of the European Union) runs to 150 pages.
15 See Lisbon Treaty.
16 Even here there was a lot of controversy, for example over the 'Open Skies' issue in the 1990s, when various member states negotiated independently with the US. The situation was finally resolved in 2007 with an agreement negotiated, as according to EU law and custom it always should have been, between the EU and the US.
17 See www.ucl.ac.uk/european-institute/highlights/europol

18 See www.cer.org.uk/publications/archive/bulletin-article/2000/open-method-co-ordination-innovation-or-talking-shop
19 Brian Hocking and David Spence (2005) have analysed the convergence of foreign and diplomatic services across Europe.

References

Abélès, Marc (1992) *La Vie Quotidienne du Parlement Européen*. Paris: Hachette.

Abélès, Marc, Irène Bellier and Maryon Mcdonald (1993) 'Approche Anthropologique de la Commission Européenne.' https://hal.archives-ouvertes.fr/halshs-00374346/document.

Abélès, Marc and Irène Bellier (1996) 'La Commission Européenne: Du Compromis Culturel à la Culture Politique du Compromis', *Revue Française de Science Politique*, 46(3): 431–456.

Adler-Nissen, Rebecca (2011) 'The Integration Doxa and the Practice Dimension of Sovereignty', *West European Politics*, 34(5): 1092–1113.

Adler-Nissen, Rebecca (2014) *Opting Out of the European Union: Diplomacy, Sovereignty and European Integration*. Cambridge: Cambridge University Press.

Bellier, Irène (2000) 'The European Union, Identity Politics and the Logic of Interest Representation', in Bellier and Wilson (eds), *An Anthropology of the European Union*. Oxford: Berg, pp. 53–73.

Bellier, Irène and Thomas M. Wilson (eds) (2000) *An Anthropology of the European Union*, Oxford: Berg.

Bickerton, Christopher (2012) *European Integration: From Nation States to Member States*. Oxford: Oxford University Press.

Clark, Julian and Alun Jones (2011) '"Telling Stories about Politics": Europeanization and the EU's Council Working Groups', *Journal of Common Market Studies*, 49(2): 341–366.

Dyson, Kenneth and Angelos Sepos (eds) (2010) *Which Europe? The Politics of Differentiated Integration*. Basingstoke: Palgrave Macmillan.

European Union (2007) Treaty of Lisbon Amending the Treaty on European Union and the Treaty Establishing the European Community. *Official Journal of the European Union*. C 306/255, 17 December 2007.

Everson, Michelle and Julia Eisner (2007) *The Making of a European Constitution*. London: Routledge.

Georgakakis, Didier and Jay Rowell (eds) (2013) *The Field of Eurocracy. Mapping EU Actors and Professionals*. Basingstoke: Palgrave, 2013.

Georgakakis, Didier and Julien Weisbein (2010) 'From Above and From Below: A Political Sociology of European Actors', *Comparative European Politics*, 8(1): 93–109.

Giddens, A. (2014) *Turbulent and Mighty Continent. What Future for Europe?* Cambridge: Polity.

Gilbert, Mark (2012) 'The Treaties of Rome', in Erik Jones, Anand Menon and Stephen Weatherill (eds), *The Oxford Handbook of the European Union*. Oxford: Oxford University Press, pp. 95–106.

Habermas, Jürgen (1998) *Die Postnationale Konstellation*. Frankfurt: Suhrkamp. Tr. (2001) as *The Postnational Constellation*, Cambridge: Polity.

Hale Thomas, David Held and Kevin Young (2013) 'Gridlock: From Self-reinforcing Interdependence to Second-order Cooperation Problems', *Global Policy*, 4(3): 223–235.

Hix, Simon (2015) 'Democratizing a Macroeconomic Union in Europe', in Olaf Cramme and Sara Hobolt (eds), *Democratic Politics in a European Union under Stress*. Oxford: Oxford University Press, pp. 180–198.

Hocking, Brian and David Spence (eds) (2005) *Foreign Ministries in the European Union. Integrating Diplomats*. Basingstoke: Palgrave.

Johnson, Stanley (1987) *The Commissioner*. London: Century.

Kassim, Hussein (2013) 'Europeanization and Member State Institutions', in Simon Bulmer and Christian Lequesne (eds), *The Member States of the European Union*. Oxford: Oxford University Press.

Lamy, Pascal (1991) 'Choses Vues . . . d'Europe', *Esprit*, October: 67–81.

McDonald, Maryon (1996) '"Unity in Diversity": Some Tensions in the Construction of Europe', in *Social Anthropology*, 4(1): 47–60.

Maduro, Miguel Poiares (1998) *We the Court*. Oxford: Hart.

Middlemas, Keith (1995) *Orchestrating Europe: The Informal Politics of the European Union*. London: Fontana.

Milward, Alan (1992) *The European Rescue of the Nation-State*. London: Routledge.

Milward, Alan (2002) 'Historical Teleologies', in Mary Farrell, Stefano Fella and Michael Newman (eds), *European Integration in the 21st Century*. London: SAGE, pp. 15–28.

Monnet, Jean (1978) *Memoirs*. New York: Doubleday.

Outhwaite, William and David Spence (2014) 'Luc Boltanski in Euroland', in Simon Susen and Bryan Turner (eds), *The Spirit of Luc Boltanski*. London: Anthem, pp. 425–444.

Page, Edward (1997) *People Who Run Europe*. Oxford: Clarendon Press.

Pollak, Johannes and Peter Slominski (2015) 'The European Parliament: Adversary or Accomplice of the New Intergovernmentalism?', in Christopher J. Bickerton, Dermot Hodson and Uwe Puetter (eds), *The New Intergovernmentalism: States and Supranational Actors in the Post-Maastricht Era*. Oxford: Oxford University Press, pp. 245–262.

Richardson, Jeremy and Berthold Rittberger (eds) (2015) Special Issue: 'Differentiated Integration in the European Union', *Journal of European Public Policy*, 22(6).

Ringe, Nils (2009) *Who Decides and How? Uncertainty and Policy Choice in the European Parliament*. Oxford: Oxford University Press.

Rittberger, Berthold (2012) 'The Treaties of Paris', in Erik Jones, Anand Menon and Stephen Weatherill (eds), *The Oxford Handbook of the European Union*. Oxford: Oxford University Press, pp. 79–94.

Schäuble, Wolfgang and Kurt Lamers (1994) 'Überlegungen zur Europäischen Politik', www.cducsu.de/upload/schaeublelamers94.pdf

Shore, Cris (2000) *Building Europe: The Cultural Politics of European Integration*. London: Routledge.

Spence, David (2012) 'The Early Days of the European External Action Service: A Practitioner's View', *Hague Journal of Diplomacy*, 7: 115–134.

Spence, David and Jozef Bátora (eds) (2015) *The European External Action Service. European Diplomacy Post-Westphalia*. London: Palgrave.

chapter 5

European democracy

How did Europe develop democratic politics? Other civilisations have decision-making processes which involve deliberation and the pursuit of agreement by majority voting or sometimes unanimity, but the combination of formal state machinery and a democratic decision-making process, with all sane adults having the right to have an input, is something of a European (and North American) speciality. We should remember, however, that this is quite a recent development. Despite its early adoption, in some of the ancient Greek city-states, for free *men*, and its theorisation over a millennium later in Rousseau's idea that all citizens should participate in legislation, and in Montesquieu's famous doctrine of the separation of powers (legislative, executive and judicial), the notion of 'one person one vote' was wildly subversive in most of Europe until well into the nineteenth century, with its extension to women on the same basis as men not until well into the twentieth (1928 in Britain, 1945 in France, 1971 in Switzerland).

I mentioned earlier the US historian Barrington Moore's *Social Origins of Dictatorship and Democracy: Landlord and Peasant in the Making of the Modern World* (1966). The full title conveys the essence of the argument that the way in which societies industrialise tends to shape their political structures. England's early move to capitalist agriculture, wage labour both here and in the cities, and a bourgeoisie independent of the state contrasts with the situation in Germany, where industrialisation came later and a class alliance between big landowners and the industrial bourgeoisie marginalised the middle classes and preserved an authoritarian state structure until 1918 (revived briefly from 1933 to 1945).

Political competition in Europe came to be structured, long before the establishment of full representative democracy, in the polarity between people often calling themselves *liberals* or *radicals*[1] and their opponents, who came to be called *conservatives*, often motivated by anxieties that the ideas of the French Revolution might spread.[2] This pattern was complicated in the early stages by the opposition between monarchists and their (sometimes republican) critics, and between established religion (Catholic in France, Anglican in England) and secularism (*laïcité*, meaning the separation of religion and state) or what in England was called 'non-conformist' Protestantism.[3] From the mid-nineteenth century there was a further element: the rise of socialism and labour movements, which produced, in varying combinations, parties like the Sozialdemokratische Partei Deutschlands (SPD) in Germany and Labour in Britain. By the early twentieth century, this had become a common pattern and the sociologist Werner Sombart (1906/1976) was asking why there is no socialism in the United States. With this as the main structuring opposition, liberals positioned themselves either in the middle, as in Britain, or on the right, as in most of the rest of Europe, while trading in both cases on their connection to liberalism in the broader sense of freedom and individual rights.

After World War II, social democratic parties often tried to broaden their appeal, turning from a shrinking working class to redefine themselves as 'catch-all' parties (Kirchheimer 1966) – successfully in West Germany in 1959 and unsuccessfully at the same time in Britain, where the transformation into 'New Labour' came only in the 1990s under Blair. Meanwhile, in the wake of the 1968 movements, there emerged new forms of politics, often informal and participatory and stressing 'new' issues such as the environment, gender equality and sexual liberation. This led to what has been called the GAL/TAN (Green-Alternative-Libertarian/Traditional-Authoritarian-Nationalist) polarisation of political opinion, which often cuts across the left/right divide (Hooghe, Marks and Wilson 2002). As discussed more fully in Chapter 7, this opposition is important for the politics of European integration, on which parties of the left and right tend to divide. The UK referendum of 2016 may be seen as a desperate and deplorably self-interested attempt by Cameron to keep his party together on this issue, or alternatively as a creative response to a serious division both in the party and in public opinion.

As late as the end of the 1970s, after the fall of the post-fascist Franco dictatorship, a Spanish researcher could find local politicians expressing scepticism about this new-fangled democracy business. In post-communist Europe, a generation later, it is not hard to find people expressing nostalgia for the old days. In 1945, however, it was clear that democracy was the default model for European politics. Many members of the fascist regimes in Italy, Vichy France and West Germany returned to power positions, but without a discernable influence on policy. Even the communist dictatorships established towards the end of the 1940s described themselves as 'people's democracies'. Member states of the EU were required to be democratic – a requirement formalised in the 'Copenhagen criteria' for accession.[4]

Given, then, that there was democracy of a kind in most of Europe, the question was whether and to what extent it also needed European-level democratic politics. In the early days of what has become the EU the answer was something like this: 'Yes of course, to an extent determined by progress of the integration process and cautiously implemented along with it'. This meant in practice a system of parliamentary assemblies recruited from national parliaments and, eventually, a directly elected parliament. It is worth recalling that Jean Monnet argued as early as 1953, in relation to the ECSC, that a parliament was indispensable, 'based on a desire to bring our institutions to life, a process in which, by necessity, this new European Parliament must play an essential part' (European Parliament 2010). Less

---

Amie Kreppel divides the history of the Parliament into four periods

The early years (1958–1969) include the initial creation and internal organization of the EP and a discussion of the formal role of the EP as established by the Treaties of Rome. The second period (1970–1978) covers the early period of EP development when it was granted partial budgetary control, adapted to the first enlargement, and prepared for direct elections. During the third period (1979–1986) the EP changed yet again, as its membership was doubled by the first direct elections and then later increased still further by the second round of enlargement. Most importantly, it was during this period that the Single European Act was passed, first granting the EP the opportunity to directly participate in the legislative process via the cooperation procedure. Finally, the fourth period of EP evolution (1987–1999) encompasses the expansion of the EP's power through the Maastricht and Amsterdam Treaties, including the addition and subsequent modification of the co-decision procedure as well as the third major enlargement.

(Kreppel 2002: 22)

Over the course of time . . . two crucial events occurred that dramatically changed the nature of the EP and the path of its institutional development: the creation of political party groups and the eventual acquisition of true, independent, legislative authority. The first occurred almost immediately; the second took thirty years. Together these two events have been the principal determinants of EP development and the transformation from consultative assembly to legislative body.

(Kreppel 2002: 53)

auspiciously, however, he described popular participation (with reference to France) very much in corporatist language of functional representation, referring to 'the trade unions, the industrialists, the administration ... associated with a plan of modernisation' (Monnet 1978: 278; see Magnette 2003).

We have already seen Spinelli's critique of the EEC's original Parliamentary Assembly. It was always envisaged, and included in the Rome Treaty, that the Parliament should be directly elected, but the Parliament's proposals were ignored by the Council until 1974, after which there was a further delay to accommodate the UK (Kreppel 2002: 60–69).

As I suggested earlier, much of the weakness of EU democracy, as well as many of its other dysfunctional features, can probably be explained by the way in which a model developed for the six members of the Coal and Steel Community at the beginning of the 1950s was gradually scaled up to the current EU and its nearly thirty member states. David Held and his co-authors have brilliantly described the way in which the world has become the victim of the *success* of post-war initiatives such as the UN, NATO and Bretton Woods. In this argument (Hale, Held and Young 2013: 224), 'the very success of global cooperation, by deepening interdependence, has led to the emergence of second-order cooperation problems'. Something like this certainly seems also to have happened at the European level, especially in relation to parliamentary democracy. Stefan Auer (2012: 77–78) has neatly brought out the paradoxes of this and other aspects of the EU's evolution:

> The attempt to build a European supra-democracy by undemocratic means has backfired. The attempt to turn the peoples of Europe into Europeans through a common currency, common citizenship and freedom of movement has resulted, paradoxically, in strengthening the forces of extreme nationalism. The attempt to weaken German influence in Europe ... by integrating it more firmly into a radically transformed EU has significantly increased economic and political imbalances, unwittingly empowering Germany vis-à-vis its European partners.

The elected parliament has surely got to be the main focus for questions about European democracy.[5] There *are* at least three other areas in which one might locate weaker forms of democracy: unanimity and/or majority voting in the Council; deliberative activity here, in the College of Commissioners and elsewhere and the relatively problematic referendums carried out in some member states on European issues; as well as the interaction of EU institutions with 'civil society'.[6] I'll discuss these later but begin with the Parliament.

All parliaments grow from small beginnings, as a former colleague who became a leading MEP reminded me when I teased him about his new job. The paradox of the EP is that the more powers it has managed to extract from the rest of the EU system, the less attention most Europeans pay to it. Turnout for the European elections has fallen from just under 62 per cent in 1979, when the first Parliament was directly elected, to around 43 per cent at the last two elections, with Czechs and Slovaks scoring in the teens. Turnout in national elections has also declined marginally in countries where voting is not compulsory (Luxembourg, Belgium, Greece and Italy), but from a much higher base. An EP spokesman put a brave face on the figures: 'The more pronounced descending turnout tendency of previous elections has well been contained (56.67 per cent in 1994, 49.51 per cent in 1999, 45.47 per cent in 2004, 43 per cent in 2009, 42.54 per cent in 2014)'.[7] Among close observers of European affairs, Wolfgang Streeck (2014), as noted earlier, refers dismissively to the 'so-called European Parliament'. Most recently, the Parliament now has around a third of eurosceptic MEPs, twice as many as the previous Parliament, with a substantial number who fundamentally reject it and call for the withdrawal from the EU of the states whose citizens they represent. Nathaniel Copsey (2015: 5) points out however that 'because of low turnout, support for radical anti-EU parties still amounted to only one in ten voters in both the UK and France'. For many European voters, EU elections come well after national ones in their perceived importance, and they are 'second-order' elections, offering a chance for a protest vote without consequences, which may be directed against the national government as much as or more than the EU.

We need however to ask what we might expect of the Parliament, in a context where what we have had in Europe is a set of rather halting attempts to remedy the perceived 'democratic deficit'[8] of the EU and a counter-argument which says, in essence, don't bother. One line of argument suggests that what the EU essentially is, and should be content to be, is a regulatory state, and that democracy need only exist at the realistic level at which it functions more or less well: that of the national state. We have already encountered Alan Milward's historical account of the way in which European integration 'rescued' and strengthened the member states and of its continuing centrality to EU politics. Andrew Moravcsik (1998, 2008) is the most prominent defender of this position. For him,

> the issues that matter most to voters remain overwhelmingly national, both in word and deed. Citizens continue to define their partisan allegiances on the basis of salient (thus largely national) issues, but have good reason to trust politicians and parties to represent their interests in Brussels.
>
> (Moravcsik 2008: 340)

This position is harder to uphold now. The issues which voters *do* care about, according to Moravcsik (2008: 339), include, as well as defence and broadly welfare state issues, 'macroeconomic management . . . infrastructure spending . . . immigration . . . and the environment'.[9] In all these, the role of the EU has become vastly more important as the economic, environmental and immigration crises have become central. Voters may still focus their attention on national politicians and call on them to 'do something about this in Europe', but they will increasingly want to address the important figures directly, who may be national or European politicians. David Cameron happens to be my MP, but if I could have anyone's attention for half an hour it would be Merkel's. But I'm a UK and EU voter, so my only legitimate routes are at the national or European level.

Nor, I think, is it helpful to say that the EP is too imperfect to use. The German Constitutional Court argued in 2009 for the primacy of democratic national parliaments *unless and until there emerges a democratic European polity*. This line of argument replicates, not surprisingly, the line taken by opponents of cosmopolitan democracy, that it would only make sense if, in some unlikely future, there was a world state with a world government.

There is, in other words, a fundamental intellectual debate about the *place* of democracy in the EU which is now rare in relation to the *national* state. This compounds the problem to which, for example, Antje Wiener (2008: 204–205) has drawn attention, of the absence of shared cultural frameworks: 'as long as exclusively organisational practices such as voting are transferred to the transnational realm while cultural practices are not transnationalised in equal measure, the voting procedure will be perceived not only as distant, but also actually lacking . . . democratic legitimation'.

It seems too easy to assume that a union of democratic states is *eo ipso* democratic, but a poor cook can make a dog's breakfast out of the best ingredients. The EU cannot, I think, claim to be fully democratic while its legislature takes the form it currently does. European democracy, we might say, has only two sets of problems: structural and functional. Structurally, the Parliament lacks the most fundamental legislative competences. At least the UK's House of Commons can *in extremis* trump the Lords and presumably talk the monarch out of exercising her theoretical veto power: the EP, by contrast, can dismiss the Commission but not circumvent the Council. The more serious problems are, however, functional: as John Palmer (2006: 106) neatly put it,

> European elections are simply *not about enough* at present to capture the imagination and enthusiasm of the electorate. A vote in the European Parliament election has no executive outcome.

The 2014 election provides a partial answer to this charge. As we saw earlier, one outcome was that the predominance of Christian democrats over social democrats after the election meant that the only candidate for Commission President whose selection could command a majority in the Parliament was Jean-Claude Juncker, who was appointed despite the reservations of several heads of state and government, and particularly David Cameron. More generally, it can be argued that

> despite the fact that there is no real *process* of political representation at this level, in that there are no European parties competing for the votes of a European electorate, the aggregation of the *outcomes* of national processes still leads to a reasonable congruence between the European electorate and the European Parliament.
>
> (Mair and Thomassen 2010: 30)

If we ask what sort of polity the EU is, there are further arguments for a more optimistic view of the Parliament. As analysts such as Joe Weiler and Hauke Brunkhorst have argued, in their different ways, the EU *does* have a kind of democratic constitution, but not one which anyone much recognises as such, and it is easy to see why.[10] Even the most sophisticated account of the EU's 'mixed constitution' (Telò 2011) fails to convince in the light of the current crisis in which, as Sonia Lucarelli (2011: 204) points out, the EU institutions 'have deprived the member states of sovereign powers without providing adequate guarantees that the overall multilevel system is based on a principle of governance for, by and with the people'.

As we saw earlier, attention has in any case shifted, with good reason, from the EU institutions, most recently the Court, to the intergovernmental level. If the 1980s were the decade of talk about the democratic deficit, the 2010s look like being the decade of 'post-democratic executive federalism'. The term *executive federalism* entered the discussion in a relatively optimistic analysis of the EU by the legal theorist Philipp Dann. Dann (2002: 3) defined the EU as a 'semi-parliamentary democracy': 'a system based on a negative parliamentary power to determine the executive and a consensual method of decision making'. Executive federalism more broadly is, he suggested, a feature of many federal systems in which 'making laws is the domain of the federal (in the EU: supranational) level but implementing that same law is the domain of the state (or here: national or even subnational level)' (Dann 2002: 5). In the case of the EU, the three components of executive federalism are 'an interwoven structure of competencies' (p. 7) complemented by a single institution or 'institutional core' (p. 12), in this case the Council of Ministers (pp. 6–9), and mediated by substantially consensus-based decision-making (pp. 9–12). Dann (p. 9) cites the model of consensus democracy advanced simultaneously but independently by

Arend Lijphart and Gerhard Lehmbruch, in which 'culturally, religiously, linguistically or otherwise divided societies developed an original mode of decision-making which enables them to find a peaceful way of dealing with cleavages and conflicts'. In a federal system of the kind often found in such societies, the 'weaving together of legislation and implementation . . . demands the prominence of executive actors in the law-making procedure of the federal level since only the bureaucracy of the sub-level has the knowledge, resources and power to render the common legislation workable' (p.13).

> *Federalism* is a system of rule in which one or more layers of regional government have constitutionally guaranteed powers. In Germany or the United States, for example, the states have their own parliaments (and, in the United States, supreme courts) and are responsible for some legal and policy areas (for example education in Germany). The UK now has substantial regional devolution, with a Scottish Parliament and parliamentary assemblies in Wales and Northern Ireland, but is not a federal system. The UK parliament could unilaterally change the status of the other parliaments and governments or executives. Asymmetric federalism is a system where some regions have greater constitutional powers than others (Von Beyme 2005).
>
> The EU has some elements of federalism, such as the primacy of EU law in certain areas and a common currency which almost all member states are obliged eventually to adopt, but is not a federation, since member states have veto powers in some domains, such as the accession of new member states, and now also have the constitutional right to leave the EU, as Greenland, an autonomous territory of Denmark, did in 1985. EU citizenship derives only from citizenship of a member state and the EU's foreign policy, so far as it has one, is on an intergovernmental basis.
>
> Source: Von Beyme, Klaus (2005) 'Asymmetric Federalism Between Globalization and Regionalization', *Journal of European Public Policy,* 12(3): 432–447.

What role has the EP in this system? Quite a substantial one: 'the EU will not be a parliamentary system but the EP already is a strong parliament' (p. 23). Dann distinguishes between two types of parliament: the debating parliament found in Europe (including of course the UK) and the 'working parliament' exemplified by the US Congress, where the action is focused not in the debating chamber but in committees and where the Congress works within a system of separated powers. The Bundestag, he suggests, is a cross between the two types; the French Assemblée Nationale largely fails *either* to influence legislation *or* to control the executive. The EP, he suggests, is a variant of the working parliament which he terms a 'controlling parliament', notably in its negative power to dismiss the Commission. A certain 'political deficit' is the 'drop of oil' which helps the complex system to function (Dann 2009: 370).

Thus the EP 'makes the best of an overall problematic institutional setting'. (Here Dann points to the analogy with the German Bundestag.) Dann takes the demands of democracy more seriously than the partisans of the regulative state. His argument from Germany has however the disadvantage that, whereas it would be hard to find a German citizen who saw the activities of his or her Landtag or local Senate as more important than those of the Bundestag, it is equally hard to find a European who would see the activities of the EP as more important than those of their *national* parliament. Nor is the German polity dominated by unelected politicians and senior officials (with the partial exception perhaps of the judges of the Federal Constitutional Court) in the way the EU polity is. There may well be good reasons for this, but it does not reinforce democratic legitimacy.

Since Dann moved on to other topics, his term *executive federalism* has taken on a more polemical edge, marked by Habermas' addition of the adjective *post-democratic* and the assertion 'Europe must choose between transnational democracy and post-democratic executive federalism' (Habermas 2012: 12).[11] 'Executive federalism', already 'implicit in the Lisbon Treaty', threatened to 'expand . . . into a form of intergovernmental rule by the European Council, moreover, one which is at odds with the spirit of the treaty' (Habermas 2012: 52). These tendencies have of course been present in the ECSC/European Community/EU from the beginning, notably in the Franco-German alliances with which they began and which have continued to the present. Habermas's principle (Habermas 2012: 28–29 *et seq.*) that we have a kind of double mandate as citizens of national states and of Europe (and also, one might add, of cities, regions, etc.) seems the right starting point for working out alternatives.

All this reinforces the theme I have stressed throughout this book: that we need to look both at the EU and at the member states themselves. Vivien Schmidt (2006) provided one of the best analyses of the interface between the European and national levels. Briefly, Schmidt shows how essentially unitary states like the UK[12] and France interact differently with the EU from more decentralised ones like Germany:

> Europeanization . . . has been more disruptive to simple polities with unified structures like France and Britain, where the traditionally powerful executive has given up significant autonomy and control, as

> a result of the diffusion of decision-making upward to the EU, downward to more autonomous regional authorities, and sideways to more independent judicial authorities.
>
> (Schmidt 2006: 54–55)[13]

Schmidt's conclusion at that time was relatively optimistic. As long as we recognise that the EU should be seen as a regional state and do not try to democratise it according to the model of national democracies, we can live with something like its present arrangements. 'Its "federal" checks and balances, its voting rules ensuring supermajorities, its elaborate interest intermediation process *with* the people, and its consensus politics go very far toward guaranteeing good governance *for* the people' (Schmidt 2006: 222–223). All that is needed is for the member states to recognise this and adapt their political discourse and practices accordingly. Since then, however, nearly a decade of economic crisis has put all this under considerable strain. In recent work, Schmidt (2015a, 2015b) has argued strongly for reestablishing the 'Community Method' in the governance of the eurozone and more broadly in the Union as a whole.

Chris Bickerton's (2012) analysis, mentioned in earlier chapters, suggests that the road is a good deal rockier. The transformation of national states into member states was also a way of shutting out European *societies* from the policy-making process. It was not just that the creators of the EU developed elitist and technocratic habits which have persisted into the present, creating complex and incomprehensible institutions, including an overcomplex architecture which marginalised the Parliament even when in 1979 it came to be directly elected. There was also a dynamic in the 1980s internal to member states, reinforced by their membership but independent of it, in which the broadly social democratic consensus sometimes described in the UK as 'Butskellism' (a conflation of the names of the Conservative Chancellor of the Exchequer Rab Butler and the Labour leader Hugh Gaitskell) was replaced by neoliberal economic policies formed without participation by, and in deliberate opposition to, trade unions or other social forces. The independence from government of central banks, built into the West German regional banks even before the creation in 1957 of the Bundesbank, and implemented in the UK by the Labour Chancellor Gordon Brown in 1998, was a central part of this strategy. Thatcher and her ministers had earlier deliberately minimised the economic role and responsibilities of the state, for example for employment, and curbed the trade unions. If the EU had not existed, European states would still have tended in this direction, though most continental states were less extreme, or more sluggish, than the UK. The EU's single market programme and monetary union were however a major element in this transformation in the case of member states. For Bickerton, this means that European politics has inevitably become polarised between technocracy on the one hand, both in the member states and in the European institutions, and populist protest and resistance. The next chapter examines the eurosceptic aspect of this in more detail.

As I noted at the beginning of this chapter, as well as focusing on the parliament we should also look at democratic elements in the other institutions and practices of the EU. The heads of state and government represented in the Council are democratically elected, as are most of the other ministers. Council voting is democratic, and if we include deliberation as an important qualitative aspect of democracy, this is also to be found there, as well as cruder forms of bargaining (Dann 2002: 10), and the same goes for the College of Commissioners (Egeberg 2006) and elsewhere (Joerges and Neyer 1997; Christiansen 2001).

Some member states are constrained by their constitutions to hold referendums on European issues (Hobolt 2006, 2009), and others, such as the UK, have twice chosen to do so. Across Europe there have been nearly fifty referendums on EU issues, notably membership and treaty ratification as well as single-issue referendums such as the Swedish and Danish ones which rejected the euro. Like the elections to the EP and despite the clear-cut alternatives presented, these have generally been determined by domestic concerns, sometimes irrelevant ones such as abortion in Ireland, which was not at issue but where the fear that the EU might enforce the liberalisation of Ireland's archaic abortion laws seems to have swayed many voters in the Nice Treaty referendum of 2001. There is also however some evidence that states which hold referendums record higher levels of support for the EU (Hug 2002: 78–82). As Hobolt (2009: 240) has shown, much depends on the quality of the information provided to the electorate, which was much better in the second than the first Irish Nice referendum. The EU itself has not held referendums, though Habermas (2001) and others have called for this from time to time in relation to constitutional change or more broadly. The closest approximation so far to a pan-European election was the 2014 EP election, where, as I noted earlier, many votes, though not those for the British Conservatives or some other parties in minority groupings, also counted towards the election of the Commission President.

A related issue is the interaction of EU institutions with 'civil society', which has been a substantial topic of discussion since the 1990s and was an important element in the White Paper on European Governance (European Commission 2001). The EU is certainly more open to input from civil society organisations than most member state governments outside the Nordic region. On the other hand, it shares with the Nordic countries a tendency to incorporate such organisations, encouraging them to become more professional and hence increasing the entry costs and the risks of exclusion for those which do not conform to established practice. Social movement organisations have tended to be marginalised by better funded and more 'respectable' lobbying organisations, not least the European Round Table of business executives. Beate Kohler-Koch (2010) suggests that the 'grass-roots' are often more like 'astroturf'.[14]

It is probably not surprising if post-democratic executive federalism has reinforced the already growing current of populist euroscepticism, embodied in Britain by UKIP. So far I have focused on executive federalism, but post-democracy at both national and European level deserves more serious attention. The debates on the EU's democratic deficit converged with diagnoses by Colin Crouch (2004, 2008) and others of trends in modern states in Europe and elsewhere towards post-democracy. As Crouch (2013) summarised his position in a recent interview,

> a post-democratic society . . . is one that continues to have and to use all the institutions of democracy, but in which they increasingly become a formal shell. The energy and innovative drive pass away from the democratic arena and into small circles of a politico-economic elite. I did not say that we were now living in a post-democratic society, but that we were moving towards such a condition.

EU politics certainly illustrates the post-democratic diagnosis of a combination of technocratic politics and media circus. It tends to be trivialised in the image of national leaders battling in Brussels and blaming it for policies which they have often endorsed (Hobolt and Tilley 2014). How far does the EU protect European democracy? A regime like Berlusconi's would presumably have been much the same whether or not Italy had been a member of the EU, though its membership may have made his eventual removal easier. Claus Offe and others have warned that extending EU-level democracy might further undermine democratic practices in the member states, and the eurosceptics discussed in Chapter 7 believe that it already has.[15]

We are left, then, with the dilemma to which, in their different ways, Schmidt, Offe and Streeck (as well as many others) have pointed: whether to strengthen what is left of national democracies by cutting back the powers of the Union, as Streeck recommends, or to attempt to democratise it. In focusing on the interplay between the interests, more or less well understood, of the Union and the member states and the institutions representing them, we may have paid too little attention to two other tensions. First, the underlying tension between the overall institutional matrix of the Union and what Giddens (2014) calls EU2 and in practice has often meant the Franco-German couple, with Germany very much in the driving seat. Second, that between the largely centrist (social or Christian democratic) integration project and the market liberalisation whose underlying dynamic was better understood by marxist and neomarxist analysts than by those who focused on its surface appearance in the removal of *geographical* barriers to trade.

The growing financial, economic and social catastrophe of the last few years has surely undermined the plausibility of a 'regulatory-state' approach and the neoliberal drift in legal and political integration diagnosed by Richard Münch (2010) and more recently by Streeck. Even the administration of the monetary union, let alone European public policy as a whole, is too fraught and contentious to be bagatellised by intergovernmental manoeuvring. The apparent truism that you need a demos, a people, to have a democracy may be more of a half-truth. Habermas counters it by standing it on its head, with the argument that the growth of a world society and public opinion calls for strategies to go beyond political fragmentation (Habermas 2012: 44).[16] As Habermas (2014: 87) has noted, arguments for continuing the unification of Europe now take a defensive form. Sadly this is also true of democracy, and it is no accident that the critique of technocracy with which he began his career is again a major theme of his polemics.

In a similar vein, Ivan Krastev (2012: 7) moves however from a pessimistic paradox to a more optimistic one:

> The EU is an elite project sustained by the European elites' respect for democracy. Today it is also an elite project endangered by the elites' fear of democracy. Unable to bring democracy to the European level owing to the lack of a European demos and frightened by the spectre of anti-European populism at the national level, many European politicians are ready pre-emptively to turn their backs on the Union.

But he goes on to note another paradox confronting these national elites:

> It is widespread disillusionment with democracy – the shared belief that national governments are powerless in the face of global markets – that may be the best hope for reconciling the growing tension between the goal of further European integration and the goal of deepening democracy in Europe.
>
> (Krastev 2012: 8)

One of the few bright spots in the otherwise dark picture of the EU's current state is that we Europeans still mostly 'trust' the EU more than our national governments and parliaments: 40 per cent compared to 31 per cent (European Commission 2015: 6). This is of course a backhanded compliment to the EU, which enjoyed, if that is the right word, a score of just under a third over the past few years, as compared with a similarly steady quarter or so for its national counterparts. The gap is now widening, which casts an interesting light on arguments that any attempt to democratise the EU risks further undermining democracy at the national and subnational levels at which it still more or less functions. We probably have to recognise that now is not the time to regale the increasingly desperate people of Europe with more constitutional or other innovations.[17] On the other hand, they are all too aware that (hopefully democratic) politics is needed in Europe to deal with global capitalism.[18] As Habermas (2012: 103) put it, 'Politics, not capitalism, is responsible for promoting the common good.' And as Vivien Schmidt points out,

> politicization, in any event, will be increasingly hard to avoid, given the awakening of the 'sleeping giant' of cross-cutting cleavages in member states, with the rise of splits between pro-Europeans and Eurosceptics in mainstream parties of the right and the left . . . and the likelihood of much more hotly contested, politicized EU elections than in the past, even if they remain second-order elections. . . . All of this could be a good thing for democracy.
>
> (Schmidt 2011: 33)

It may be that we need also to rethink the nature of democracy at both the national and the European level. In an important and neglected recent book, Jeffrey Green (2010) has argued for a spectatorial model of democracy focused on the regular exposure of political leaders to forms of interrogation which they do not control and manipulate. Modern publics have neither the time nor the inclination to engage substantially with political issues, but as more or less informed spectators they can exercise an important supervisory function. Theories of representative democracy put too much stress on the electoral process, and those of direct and deliberative democracy raise unrealistic expectations, while a modified version of plebiscitary democracy can enforce what he calls 'candour' on political leaders. In an argument which resonates with Crouch's discussion of post-democracy, Green in a sense sets a spectatorial thief to catch the post-democratic media-manipulative thief (Berlusconi, Erdogan and others), recognising, as Habermas and other democratic theorists have done, the implications of the fact that we now have an essentially mediated relationship to political debate.

How might this approach illuminate European politics? Green urges us to turn our attention to political *leaders* rather than legislative *outputs* – an approach which seems at best inappropriate to the EU and at worst to reinforce the current emphasis on EU2 and intergovernmentalism. On the other hand, theories of the EU as a regulatory and audit-based state do capture an important aspect of its operations, and of the more effective areas of activity of the EP. In national politics, too, for example in the UK, there has been a notable shift of emphasis in the recent past from the show in the Chamber to the investigatory role of parliamentary committees.

The EU's current political leaders might not stand up well to spectatorial democracy, but the politics of the Union, though for geographical reasons inevitably remote from most of its citizens, is a good deal more open to scrutiny than those of most member states, and its representatives relatively open to public attention – where they can attract it. This is clearly open to the charge of paternalism, but there is perhaps the possibility of a virtuous spiral in which upgraded EU presidents, high representatives and commissioners begin to look and act like representatives of a serious political entity. As Antoine Vauchez (2016) has argued, the deliberations of the 'independent' institutions of the Union, in particular the Court, the European Central Bank and the Commission, could usefully be opened up much further. An EU which addressed these internal issues, as well as questions of social policy and the overarching global crisis of capitalism, might do much to revive democracy at the national and the European level.

In this chapter I have focused on democracy in the member states of the EU, but we should not forget Europe's remaining undemocratic regimes, in Russia and Belarus, and the shaky state of democracy in Ukraine, Armenia, Azerbaijan, Georgia, Turkey and parts of the Western Balkans. The 2015 Freedom House report had the pessimistic headline 'Discarding Democracy: Return to the Iron Fist'. Within the Union there is at least the sanction of Article 7 of the Lisbon Treaty, according to which serious human rights breaches by a member state can result in a suspension or loss of voting rights in the Council. So far the Union has not used this provision, though it is coming close to doing so in relation to Hungary. When the extreme-right Austrian Freedom Party entered a ruling coalition in 2000, the EU imposed ineffective diplomatic sanctions until the withdrawal of the party's leader Jörg Haider. This seems to confirm the impression that, while the EU has considerable leverage over states in the run-up to accession, this does not continue afterwards. While some Europeans, for example in the Romanian presidential election in 2014, seem to have viewed their association with the EU as a protection against post-communist corruption and authoritarian politics, some of the eurosceptics discussed in Chapter 7 are democrats hoping that withdrawal from the EU, or scaling down its integrationist ambitions, might revive national democracy.

Summary points

After the Second World War, the Western European democracies were mostly restored, though with post-fascist regimes surviving in Portugal and Spain and a military dictatorship in Greece from 1967 to 1974.

Democracy came to much of communist Europe in 1989 and the following years, making those states eligible in due course to apply for EU membership.

Despite the EU's important role in strengthening democracy in post-communist Europe and to some extent in the rest of the world, its own structures are only democratic in a rather weak and indirect sense. There has been some disagreement over whether this 'democratic deficit' is a matter of concern, but it is now clear that the 'permissive consensus' is over.

Further questions

Why is contemporary Europe largely democratic? Is it likely to remain so?
Is the EU democratic (enough)?
How does the internal structure of member states affect their position in the EU?
How does the EU affect the internal structure of member states?

Further reading

Blokker, Paul (2014) *New Democracies in Crisis? A comparative constitutional study of the Czech Republic, Hungary, Poland, Romania and Slovakia*. London and New York: Routledge.

Caramani, Daniele (2015) *The Europeanization of Politics. The Formation of a European Electorate and Party System in Historical Perspective*. Cambridge: Cambridge University Press.

Cramme, Olaf and Sara Hobolt (eds) (2015) *Democratic Politics in a European Union under Stress*. Oxford: Oxford University Press.

Ferrin, Mónica and Hanspeter Kriesi (2014) 'Europeans' Understandings and Evaluations of Democracy', Topline Results from Round 6 of the European Social Survey. http://www.europeansocialsurvey.org/permalink/800ea36f-3a8d-11e4-95d4-005056b8065f.pdf

Friedrich, David (2011) *Democratic Participation and Civil Society in the European Union*. Manchester: Manchester University Press.

Schmidt, Vivien (2006) *Democracy in Europe. The EU and National Polities*. Oxford: Oxford University Press.

Vauchez, Antoine (2016) *Democratizing Europe*. London: Palgrave.

Notes

1 This broad sense of the two terms can still be found in some political cultures. In the US, for example, the term *liberal* is used, often pejoratively, to refer to any vaguely progressive orientation. *Radical* survived as a label for two parties in

France: the centre-right Parti Radical and the centre-left Radicaux de Gauche, who split off in 1972. The radicalism of the Parti Radical was partly in its support for secularism (*laïcité*), as well as a broader leftism which it shed after a few years in the early twentieth century.
2. The sociologist Karl Mannheim (1927) brilliantly analysed this reaction in a book which is still worth reading. For the more specific case of England, see Thompson (1963).
3. In some countries there were also substantial agrarian parties, some of which still survive, for example in the Nordic countries and Poland.
4. For a judiciously pessimistic discussion of some of Europe's new democracies, see Blokker (2014).
5. As Habermas (2015: 94) argues, 'A generalization of interests *that cuts across national borders* is only possible in a European Parliament organized into party groupings.'
6. On these see Outhwaite (2010; 2012); Outhwaite and Spence (2014). For a comprehensive and sceptical overview of some of these areas of deliberation, see Schmidt (2012); also Crespy (2013).
7. www.euractiv.com/sections/eu-elections-2014/its-official-last-eu-election-had-lowest-ever-turnout-307773
8. The term *democratic deficit* was introduced by David Marquand (1978) and was a major focus of discussion in the 1980s. As Mark Warren (2009: 18) points out, 'The claim that the EU was in democratic deficit reflected not a democratic past that was eroding, but rather the growing democratic expectations that came with political integration, combined with institutions – the European Parliament in particular – that can and should be measured according to democratic norms.' See also Spence (2011).
9. As Jürgen Habermas (2015: 56) writes: 'Even when all members of an international organization are flawless democracies, the legitimation of the individual member states is increasingly insufficient to justify decisions of the organization as a whole as cooperation becomes closer and the interventions agreed upon become more invasive.'
10. As the then External Trade Commissioner Pascal Lamy (2004: 40) wrote, 'The European space today is a space without democratic magic. The machine is there, but it's not alive.' See also Lamy (2004: 55): 'Europe is a political project, without having invented the language it needs.'
11. In *Ach, Europa* (Habermas 2008) the inside cover blurb declares the end of his 'optimism about European politics', and this is given added emphasis in the subtitle of the English translation, 'the faltering project' (Habermas 2009).
12. The UK, like Spain, has of course now substantial devolution to Scotland and to a lesser extent to Wales, and the Blair government reversed Thatcher's abolition of metropolitan institutions in London and elsewhere. Its political style however remains essentially unitary, reinforced by a strongly majoritarian voting system in which coalitions have historically been rare.
13. Without going into the details, I suggest that Schmidt (2009: 402) is right to insist on the greater flexibility of a federal state. More broadly, this is clearly one of the reasons why Germany, accustomed to federalism and all the messiness

of 'joint decision traps', is more comfortable with the architecture of the EU than is the UK, which has not yet learned to handle the implications of its relatively recent devolution.
14 See also Friedrich (2011); Liebert and Trenz (2011) and the EU's civil society website: http://ec.europa.eu/transparency/civil_society/.
15 A minority of eurosceptics are of course also anti-democrats.
16 Mark Warren (2009: 19) makes a related point: 'The electoral machinery of democracies is an increasingly poor fit with the complex, pluralistic, multilevel business that governing has become.' See also Schmitter and Trechsel (2004); Schmitter (2015). The increasing differentiation of the EU, with the various opt-outs noted earlier, also poses serious problems for European democracy (Fossum 2015).
17 For some otherwise attractive suggestions, see Simon Hix (2008), Mark Warren (2009), Ferenc Miszlivetz (2009), Steven Hill (2012) and Vivien Schmidt (2012; 2015a; 2015b). See also the special issue of the *German Law Journal* (2013: 441–712) on 'Regeneration Europe' and a discussion paper by the Spinelli Group (2013).
18 Colin Crouch (2012) has argued powerfully that we might look to the capacities of social movements rather than politicians (national and, by implication, also European) to curb the power of transnational corporations. On the impact of globalization on European politics, see the interesting analysis by Kriesi *et al.* (2012).

References

Auer, Stefan (2012) *Whose Liberty Is It Anyway? Europe at the Crossroads*. London, New York and Calcutta: Seagull Press.

Bickerton, Christopher (2012) *European Integration: From Nation States to Member States*. Oxford: Oxford University Press.

Blokker, Paul (2014) *New Democracies in Crisis? A Comparative Constitutional Study of the Czech Republic, Hungary, Poland, Romania and Slovakia*. London and New York: Routledge.

Christiansen, Thomas (2001) Intra-institutional Politics and Inter-institutional Relations in the EU: Towards Coherent Governance? *Journal of European Public Policy*, 8(5): 747–769.

Copsey, Nathaniel (2015) *Rethinking the European Union*. London: Palgrave Macmillan.

Crespy, Amandine (2013) 'Deliberative Democracy and the Legitimacy of the European Union: A Reappraisal of Conflict', *Political Studies*, 62(S1): 81–98.

Crouch, Colin (2004) *Postdemocracy*. Cambridge: Polity.

Crouch, Colin (2008) 'British Professor: We Are Living in a "Postdemocracy"'. *Deutsche Welle* 13.09.08. www.dw.de/dw/article/5/0,,3617727,00.html

Crouch, Colin (2012) 'As Much Market as Possible, as Much State as Necessary', in Henning Meyer and Jonathan Rutherford (eds), *The Future of Social Democracy*. Basingstoke: Palgrave Macmillan, pp.74–89.

Crouch, Colin (2013) http://blogs.lse.ac.uk/politicsandpolicy/five-minutes-with-colin-crouch/

Dann, Philipp (2002) Looking Through the Federal Lens: the Semi-Parliamentary Democracy of the EU. Jean Monnet Working Paper 5/02. New York: NYU School of Law.

Dann, Philipp (2009) 'Die Europäischen Organe'. In Armin von Bogdandy and Jürgen Bast (eds), *Europäisches Verfassungsrecht*. Berlin and Heidelberg: Springer, pp.335–388.

Egeberg, M. (2006) 'Executive Politics as Usual: Role Behaviour and Conflict Dimensions in the College of European Commissioners'. *Journal of European Public Policy*, 13(1): 1–15.

European Commission (2001) 'European Governance. A White Paper'. http://europa.eu/rapid/press-release_DOC-01-10_en.htm

European Commission (2015) Standard Eurobarometer 83 First Results – Autumn 2015. Luxembourg.

European Parliament (2010) From the Schuman Declaration to the birth of the ECSC: The Role of Jean Monnet. CARDOC No. 6 - Annex IX. http://www.europarl.europa.eu/pdf/cardoc/24663-5531_EN-CARDOC_JOURNALS_No6-complet_low_res.pdf

Fossum, John Erik (2015) 'Democracy and Differentiation in Europe', *Journal of European Public Policy*, 22(6): 799–815.

Friedrich, Dawid (2011) *Democratic Participation and Civil Society in the European Union*. Manchester: Manchester University Press.

Giddens, Anthony (2014) *Turbulent and Mighty Continent. What Future for Europe?* Cambridge: Polity.

Green, Jeffrey (2010) *The Eyes of the People. Democracy in an Age of Spectatorship*. New York: Oxford University Press.

Habermas, Jürgen (2001) 'Why Europe Needs a Constitution', *New Left Review*, 11, September-October: 5–26. http://newleftreview.org/II/11/jurgen-habermas-why-europe-needs-a-constitution

Habermas, Jürgen (2008) *Ach, Europa*. Frankfurt: Suhrkamp.

Habermas, Jürgen (2009) *The Faltering Project*. Cambridge: Polity.

Habermas, Jürgen (2012) *The Crisis of the European Union: A Response*. Cambridge: Polity.

Habermas, Jürgen (2014) 'Für ein starkes Europa' – aber was heißt das? *Blätter für deutsche und internationale Politik* 3, March: 85–94.

Habermas, Jürgen (2015) *The Lure of Technocracy*. Cambridge: Polity.

Hale, Thomas, David Held and Kevin Young (2013) 'Gridlock: From Self-reinforcing Interdependence to Second-order Cooperation Problems', *Global Policy* 4(3), September: 223–235.

Hill, Steven (2012) 'A Blueprint for Redesigning European-level Parliamentary Democracy', *Social Europe Journal*, April.

Hix, Simon (2008) *What's Wrong With the European Union and How to Fix It*. Cambridge: Polity.

Hobolt, Sara B. (2006) 'Direct Democracy and European Integration', *Journal of European Public Policy*, 13(1): 153–166.

Hobolt, Sara B. (2009) *Europe in Question. Referendums on European Integration*. Oxford: Oxford University Press.

Hobolt, Sara B. and James Tilley (2014) *Blaming Europe? Responsibility Without Accountability in the European Union*. Oxford: Oxford University Press.

Hooghe, Liesbet, Gary Marks and Carole J. Wilson (2002) 'Does Left/Right Structure Party Positions on European Integration?' *Comparative Political Studies*, 5.8 (November): 965–989.

Hug, Simon (2002) *Voices of Europe: Citizens, Referendums, and European Integration*. Lanham, MD and Oxford: Rowman & Littlefield.

Joerges, Christian and Jurgen Neyer (1997) 'Transforming Strategic Interaction into Deliberative Problem-solving: European Comitology in the Foodstuff Sector', *Journal of European Public Policy*, 4(4): 609–625.

Kirchheimer, Otto (1966) 'The Transformation of Western European Party Systems', in J. Kohler-Koch, Beate (2010) 'Civil society and EU democracy: "Astroturf" representation?', *Journal of European Public Policy* 17, 1, pp. 100–116.

Krastev, Ivan (2012) 'The Political Logic of Disintegration: Seven Lessons from the Soviet Collapse', CEPS Essay, www.ceps.eu

Kreppel, Amie (2002) *The European Parliament and Supranational Party System. A Study in Institutional Development*. Cambridge: Cambridge University Press.

Kriesi, Hanspeter, Edgar Grande, Martin Dolezal, *et al.* (2012) *Political Conflict in Western Europe*. Cambridge: Cambridge University Press.

Lamy, Pascal (2004) *La Démocratie Monde: Pour Une Autre Gouvernance Globale*, Paris: Seuil.

Liebert, Ulrike and Hans-Jörg Trenz (2011) The New Politics of European Civil Society. Abingdon: Routledge.

Lucarelli, Sonia (2011) 'Debating Identity and Legitimacy in the EU. Concluding Remarks', in Sonia Lucarelli, Furio Cerutti and Vivien A. Schmidt (eds), *Debating Political Identity and Legitimacy in the European Union*. Abingdon: Routledge, pp. 193–206.

Magnette, Paul (2003) 'European Governance and Civic Participation: Beyond Elitist Citizenship? *Political Studies*, 51(1): 144–160.

Mair, Peter and Jacques Thomassen (2010) 'Political Representation and Government in the European Union', *Journal of European Public Policy* 17(1): 20–25.

Mannheim, Karl (1927) *Das konservative Denken*. Tübingen: Mohr. Tr. (1986 and 2007) as *Conservatism*, London: Routledge.

Marquand, David (1978) 'Towards a Europe of the Parties'. *The Political Quarterly*, 49(4): 425–445.

Miszlivetz, Ferenc (2009) '"Lost in Transformation": The Crisis of Democracy and Civil Society', in Mary Kaldor, Henrietta L. Moore and Sabine Selchow (eds), *Global Civil Society*. Basingstoke, UK: Palgrave.

Moore, Barrington (1966) *The Social Origins of Dictatorship and Democracy. Landlord and Peasant in the Making of the Modern World*. Harmondsworth: Penguin.

Monnet, Jean (1978) *Memoirs*. New York: Doubleday.

Moravcsik, Andrew (1998) *The Choice for Europe: Social Purpose and State Power from Messina to Maastricht*. Ithaca, NY: Cornell University Press; London: Routledge/UCL Press.

Moravcsik, Andrew (2008) 'The Myth of Europe's "Democratic Deficit"', *Intereconomics*, November-December, pp. 331–340. https://www.princeton.edu/~amoravcs/library/myth_european.pdf

Münch, Richard (2010) *European Governmentality: The Liberal Drift of Multilevel Governance*. London: Routledge.

Outhwaite, William (2010) 'Legality and Legitimacy in the European Union', in Samantha Ashenden and Chris Thornhill (eds), *Legality and Legitimacy: Normative and Sociological Approaches*. Baden-Baden: Nomos pp. 279–290.

Outhwaite, William (2012) *Critical Theory and Contemporary Europe*. New York: Continuum.

Outhwaite, William and David Spence (2014) 'Luc Boltanski in Euroland', in Simon Susen and Bryan Turner (eds) *The Spirit of Luc Boltanski*. London: Anthem Press, pp. 425–444.

Palmer, John (2006) 'The Future of European Political Parties', *European View* 3, Spring. http://www.1888932-2946.ws/ComTool6.0_CES/CES/E-DocumentManager/gallery/European_View/_copy_3.pdf

Schmidt, Vivien (2006) *Democracy in Europe. The EU and National Polities*. Oxford: Oxford University Press.

Schmidt, Vivien (2009) 'Re-Envisioning the European Union: Identity, Democracy, Economy,' *Journal of Common Market Studies*, 47, Annual Review: 17–42.

Schmidt, Vivien (2011) 'The Problems of Identity and Legitimacy in the European Union: Is more Politics the Answer?', in Furio Cerutti, Sonia Lucarelli and Vivien A. Schmidt (eds) *Debating Political Identity and Legitimacy in the European Union*. London: Routledge, 2011, pp. 16–37.

Schmidt, Vivien (2012) 'Democracy and Legitimacy in the European Union Revisited: Input, Output *and* Throughput', *Political Studies*, 61: 2–22.

Schmidt, Vivien (2015a) 'Forgotten Democratic Legitimacy: "Governing by the Rules" and "Ruling by the Numbers"', in Matthias Matthijs and Mark Blyth (eds), *The Future of the Euro*. New York: Oxford University Press.

Schmidt, Vivien (2015b) 'Changing the policies, politics, and processes of the Eurozone in crisis: will this time be different?', in David Natali and Bart Vanhercke (eds), *Social Policy in the European Union: State of Play 2015*. Brussels: etui, pp. 33–64. http://www.etui.org/Publications2/Books/Social-policy-in-the-European-Union-state-of-play-2015

Schmitter, Philippe (2015) 'The crisis of the Euro, the crisis of the European Union and the crisis of democracy in Europe', in Jody Jensen and Ferenc Miszlivetz (eds), *Reframing Europe's Future: Challenges and Failures of the European Construction*. Abingdon: Routledge, pp. 181–188.

Schmitter, Philippe and Alexander Trechsel (2004) *The Future of Democracy in Europe. Trends, Analyses and Reforms*. Strasbourg: Council of Europe. http://www.nonformality.org/wp-content/uploads/2006/07/2-Greenpaper.pdf

Sombart, Werner (1976) [1906] *Why Is There No Socialism in the United States?* London: Macmillan.

Spence, David (2011) 'Deconstructing EU Governance: How the European Commission Constructed EU Governance Policy and How it Attempts to Export It', in J. Wunnerlich and D. Bailey (eds), *The EU and Global Governance* Abingdon: Routledge, pp. 59–78.

Spinelli Group (2013) A Fundamental Law of the European Union. www.spinelligroup.eu/article/fundamental-law-european-union

Streeck, Wolfgang (2014) *Buying Time: The Delayed Crisis of Democratic Capitalism*. London: Verso.

Telò, Mario (2011) 'Three European Constitutionalisms and Their Respective Legitimacy Requirements: Explaining the *Longue Durée* Stability of the European Polity', in Sonia Lucarelli, Furio Cerutti and Vivien A. Schmidt (eds), *Debating Political Identity and Legitimacy in the European Union*. Abingdon: Routledge, pp. 93–114.

Thompson, Edward P. (1963) *The Making of the English Working-Class*. London: Gollancz. Reprinted by Penguin.

Vauchez, Antoine (2016) *Democratizing Europe*. London: Palgrave.

Warren, Mark (2009) 'Citizen Participation and Democratic Deficits: Considerations from the Perspective of Democratic Theory' in Joan DeBardeleben and Jon Pammett (eds), *Activating the Citizen. Dilemmas of Participation in Europe and Canada*. Basingstoke: Palgrave MacMillan, pp. 17–40.

Watt, Andrew (2013) 'Cyprus: Risking the European Ship for Ten Euros of Tar', *Social Europe Journal* 18.3.13.

Wiener, Antje (2008) *The Invisible Constitution of Politics: Contested Norms and International Encounters*. Cambridge: Cambridge University Press.

chapter 6

People's Europe

The slogan of a 'Europe of peoples', where it is not just used to mean one of nation states, directs attention to the theme of this chapter: the everyday reality of Europe for European citizens and residents. As in previous chapters, we need first to ask what has been happening in Europe as a whole before looking more closely at the dynamics introduced, or reacted to, by the EU.

Mobility of various kinds is at the centre of the chapter. The massive flow of refugees and 'displaced persons' from east to west, particularly into West Germany, in the years just after World War II was followed, as the economic recovery of Western Europe gathered pace, by labour migration both within Europe and from outside. By the time of the economic downturn in 1973, there had been major movements from Ireland to the UK; from Portugal, Spain and North Africa to France; and from Italy to Switzerland and West Germany, which also attracted considerable numbers of migrants from Yugoslavia, Greece and Turkey. By 2010, all of the 'Western' European countries except Finland had over 5 per cent of migrants in their population. 'Skilled' migrants from India (those with tertiary education) moved in large numbers to the United States, Canada and also the UK.[1]

European populations became more diverse, richer and also more secular (especially in countries like Scotland, Ireland, Italy and Poland). Discrimination (often with a religious basis) against women, ethnic minorities and people with minority sexual preferences has been officially outlawed, and although it continues on a subterranean basis the changes in the legal framework are quite remarkable. In the UK, for example, Thatcher's Conservative government in 1988 banned local authorities, and hence schools, from 'promoting' homosexuality. Only a quarter of a century later, Cameron's otherwise equally extreme Conservative-led government presided over the legalisation of gay marriage. Some of this diversification and liberalisation can be attributed to the EU or the Council of Europe's Human Rights jurisdiction, while other elements are largely independent of them. The point is however that, as with the post-war labour migration into and across Western Europe or the extension of air travel, it often made little difference in practice whether this was intra-EU or from outside. It was opposition in Poland and elsewhere in the bloc and Gorbachev's role in the USSR, rather than the EU, which ended communism in Europe. And it was this, along with budget air travel, which made a weekend trip from Western Europe to Poland or Lithuania, or a weekly commute to work in the other direction, a realistic prospect for many Europeans.

It was however the EU which provided the legal underpinning for mobility of this kind. The Schengen Agreement of 1985 on borderless travel formalised a practice which had already become fairly common in Western Europe, where controls had become mostly perfunctory. But a Belgian friend teaching at a French university in the late 1970s had to become French in order to progress her career. She received a document stating that she was 'well assimilated and spoke French fluently'. When she pointed out that it was her native language she was told that that was just the standard formula. A few years later this nationality requirement was abolished, in accordance with EU law.[2] The integration of European labour markets has an important social protection dimension. Waltraud Scheikle (2015: 142) points out that this means that Europeans can move freely if employment opportunities dry up at home, retaining their pension rights and other welfare entitlements: 'This is a risk-sharing mechanism of the Single Market that has been triggered by the eurozone crisis.' And as Adrian Favell (2009: 177) points out in relation to freedom of movement, 'the European Union is a unique space . . . there is nothing like this kind of politically constructed post-national space anywhere else on the planet'. In some ways the EU is more closely integrated than the United States, which we think of rightly as a unified state. Kathleen McNamara (2015: 128) notes that European hairdressers can practice across the Union, while in the United States they have to pass separate tests in order to move their workplace from one state to another.

How much use do Europeans make of these rights? As of 2014, 19.9 million, or just under 4 per cent, were resident in another member state.[3] Over half a million a year study in another member state, the largest number of them in the UK. More than half of 'young' Europeans (age 15–35) are willing to work in another European country for a shorter or longer period.[4] Rather curiously, the highest level of negative responses to this question came from Turkey, Italy, the Netherlands and Belgium; the UK was just below the average. Those most willing came from the north (Iceland, Sweden, Finland) or the southeast (Bulgaria, Romania). At the other end of the age range, there is substantial migration of retired people, mostly from the north (UK, Germany, Scandinavia, Netherlands, Belgium) to the south (Spain, Portugal, Italy and other Mediterranean states) (King *et al.* 2000), and also of mid-life migrants responding, for example, to redundancy in their native countries, such as Britons in France (Benson 2011). Juan Díez Medrano (2011: 38–39) notes the relatively high level of Anglo-Spanish marriages, reflecting the fact that the British, while largely abjuring a European identity, are prominent among those travelling to Spain for holidays or to live. Although intermarriage rates are low in Europe, between 1996 and 2007 'the odds that a Spaniard will marry another European have doubled or more in this period'.

For some of the more mobile, a number of 'Eurocities' offer attractive alternatives for work in a way which approximates to those available across their continent to North Americans. Adrian Favell and Ettore Recchi (2011: 59) conducted two major complementary studies. One was a quantitative study based on 5,000 telephone interviews with intra-EU migrants across western Europe (Britain, France, Germany, Italy, and Spain), who make up a proportion of the total population in low single figures: 2.7 per cent in the UK and France, 2.1 per cent in Germany, and just over 1 per cent in Spain and Italy. The only countries with substantially higher proportions are Belgium (6.4 per cent), Ireland (9.6 per cent), and nearly a quarter in Luxembourg. Recchi and Favell (2009) found that their respondents were substantially upper and upper middle class in origin.

> Upper and upper middle-class movers reach their highest number in Italy; around 45 per cent of British, French and Germans in Italy are drawn from classes I-II. Only Italians and Spanish in Germany (about 45 and 60 per cent respectively) from class V-VII are exceptions to this rule, fitting in larger numbers with the traditional immigrant profile as low-skilled or manual workers.
>
> (Favell and Recchi 2011: 63–64)

Favell (2008) also conducted a qualitative study based on sixty interviews and participant observation of mobile young and youngish professionals in London, Brussels and Amsterdam, pioneering 'Euro-stars' living in Eurocities. Although many had improved their material life-chances, especially women moving from Southern Europe, and they mostly welcomed the cosmopolitan experience, they often encountered administrative and cultural obstacles even in these ostensibly highly cosmopolitan and globalised cities. Favell and Recchi (2011: 74) summarise this as follows:

> Home countries of origin and foreign countries of residence alike have their way of re-asserting their norms, value systems and social hierarchies over the lives of these pioneers. They see their experiences and opportunities being *re*-nationalized by the weight of mainstream lives lived in national structures; they are often caught out on a limb in their life choice, out of time and place in terms of both the peers they left back home, and the natives living and working around them.

Even the very substantial numbers of migrants from post-communist EU states, who have benefited massively from freedom of movement in the early 2000s, have often stayed only for a few years, returning as the 2008 recessions hit Western and Eastern Europe. On the other hand, enough people have left some of the smaller states, such as the Baltic States, to create a serious demographic problem which is only now being realised. At the two extremes of post-communist Europe, parts of Eastern Germany are becoming seriously depopulated, while very large numbers of Russians say that they would rather live abroad, as many are now doing (Narizhnaya 2013). In many parts of Europe, of course, there has been substantial political controversy around immigration, though as a comparative study of Romanian migration to Spain and Italy demonstrates, this reflects local political contexts rather than anything about the migrant populations themselves. Simon McMahon (2015) notes that migrant populations of similar size were largely welcomed in Spain but were the object of a moral panic in Italy, where neofascists and the extreme-right Northern League had long been campaigning against immigration. Similar phenomena are found elsewhere in Europe, notably Fortuyn and Wilders in the Netherlands, the *Front National* in France and UKIP in the UK, where the dissident Conservative and later Ulster Unionist MP Enoch Powell had campaigned against immigration and Prime Minister Thatcher spoke in 1978 about people in Britain fearing that they might be 'rather swamped'.

On the related issue of support for free movement of workers within the EU, which of course was a fundamental principle from the beginnings of the European Community, it is alarming to note that, according to the European Values Survey of 1999–2000, only three states (Sweden, the Netherlands and Denmark) had a majority rejecting the suggestion that 'if jobs are scarce, employers should give priority to [nationals] over immigrants' (Halman 2001: 69). The average in the EU-15 was a third, and in the 2004–07 accession states, barely over 10 per cent. Interestingly, Ukraine and Russia had figures twice those of the EU post-communist states. Florian

Pichler (2009: 725) argues however that the apparent east/west difference is explained by structural factors, primarily GDP and 'sociopolitical culture'. Mau (2010: 105) records over three quarters of his German respondents agreeing with the statement, 'Every state should independently decide who's supposed to stay on the territory.'

What of those who do not migrate? First, there are *frontier workers*, defined as 'people employed or self-employed in one Member state, residing in another Member state to which they return, as a rule, daily or at least once a week'. Eurostat records just under 1.9 million in 2014, over 430,000 in France, 266,000 in Germany, 130,000 in Slovakia and around 100,000 in Belgium, Italy and Hungary. Much the largest number is into Switzerland, which is notoriously expensive to live in and whose three largest cities are in easy or, in the case of Zürich, quite easy reach of EU member states (MKW 2009: 24). Capital, too, is particularly mobile in border regions. Juan Díez Medrano (2011: 34–35) notes the existence in the financial sectors in Germany and Belgium of 'something akin to a "European" cluster of companies coordinating their investment strategies.... These findings do suggest that a European capitalist class is emerging in the densely populated and capital-rich areas at the intersection of Germany and the Low Countries. In fact, the finding is not surprising since it is precisely in this region that citizens identify most frequently as Europeans.' This is not just at the heartland of European integration since the 1950s, but the focus of work by Steffen Mau (2010), Jochen Roose (2010) and others on cross-border socialisation. Just as the globalisation of capitalist enterprise very often means, in the European region, its Europeanisation, so the globalisation of the social relations of individuals is better described as 'denationalisation', especially in the transnational environment of the EU (Mau 2010: 13).

Cross-border shopping is another possibility for many parts of Europe. The EU has ceased to examine this separately, rolling it in with e-commerce. Around half of internet shoppers have bought something from another member state, the highest proportion coming from Denmark, the United Kingdom and Sweden. In the area of virtual consumption, *Euronews*, broadcasting in thirteen languages and covering around the same number of households outside as inside Europe, substantially outperforms in Europe CNN and BBC World News put together. Most Europeans regularly use or will soon come to use the euro, or currencies pegged to it, like the Danish Krone. Whatever its current and perhaps endemic flaws, it is a fact of life[5] which, as we saw earlier, few Europeans would care to abandon. The currency and the EU symbol on car number plates are the two elements of the Union which are a daily reality across most of the territory. The symbol was borrowed from the Council of Europe, its twelve stars reflecting the membership only between 1986 and 1995, but the design of the currency is worth closer attention. The coins illustrate the dualism at the heart of the Union, with a shared face matched by a nationally differentiated one. The architectural features on the banknotes move through history, from classical to contemporary, as the value increases, but they are carefully designed not to favour the architecture of any specific member state, and the outline of Europe itself also varies between the various denominations.[6] This muted or wishy-washy character of the EU's self-representation is, as usual, either the result of a compromise or of a cautious anticipation of hostile reactions by one or more (or all) member states.

Another compromise product is the EU passport (see Figure 6.1). Like the euro coins, it includes on its cover page the names of the Union and of the respective member state. The order in which they appear, with 'European Union' at the top, was apparently argued over for at least a

Figure 6.1 UK Passport front cover.

© Shutterstock.

night, and no doubt much longer in preliminary discussions. The UK version, interestingly, has 'European Union' in a smaller font than the much longer 'United Kingdom of Great Britain and Northern Ireland', while the Belgian version, for example, has both in equal size, despite having to include the name of the state in its three official languages. Here anyway is another element of everyday Europe, no doubt taken for granted by most European citizens.

The European driving licence is another element, with the EU symbol in its corner including the initials representing the member state issuing it. (It is also in use in the European Economic Area and Switzerland, though the European Economic Area versions just have the initials.) All EU member states except Denmark and the UK issue national identity cards in a common format but without any EU symbolism. These can be used instead of passports for most internal travel, though UK border officials are sometimes suspicious of them. There is, however, no European identity card, and the one which was used for example in the Netherlands until 2001 was a local product.

Travel provides a good illustration of the way in which the reality of everyday Europe is shaped by geography, language and other structuring factors. Cross-border shopping in its physical as opposed to mediated form is pretty much confined in Britain (though not of course in Northern Ireland) to the 'booze cruise' to collect alcohol at prices less inflated by taxation, whereas for some other Europeans it may be just one supermarket alternative among others. Many countries automatically receive TV programmes from adjacent states – again something largely unknown in Britain.

The symbolism of the functional elements of everyday Europe has, as we have seen, been the result of quite laborious processes of construction. The same is true of more purely representational elements such as the flag, the anthem (Schiller's 'Ode to Joy' with Beethoven's music but without the words) and so on. The titles of EU officials, like the 'High Representative for Foreign and Security Policy' are also relatively muted in their symbolism. The EU's buildings, though sometimes architecturally impressive, do not form an ensemble like those in Washington or London. Although there has been since the 1970s a substantial effort to generate cultural symbols as well as more substantial cultural resources such as newspapers, TV, school textbooks and so forth, this has almost always involved an uphill struggle by the Commission against the resistance of member states. Tobias Thieler (2006: 6) stresses 'the continued determination of national elites to protect their near-monopoly over the tools of political identity creation from supranational interference' (see also Shore 2000; McNamara 2015).

States have always engaged in the construction of political symbols and historical and other myths. Manhole covers in Rome are still stamped with SPQR (*Senatus Populusque Romanus* – the Senate and the Roman People).

You may have been told in school that Louis XIV was very vain and liked to display himself as much as possible. However, he was also a highly innovative political operator; his court rituals were imitated across the rest of Europe. What Michael Billig (1995) brilliantly termed 'banal nationalism' is something we take for granted. The European effort to construct something like a 'banal supranationalism' was stymied from the start by the fact that the treaties explicitly excluded cultural matters, as Delors admitted in a speech to the Parliament in 1985, going on to say that 'we are going to try to tackle it [cultural policy] along economic lines' (Shore 2000: 45–46).

One resource was the 'Declaration on European Identity' of 1973, followed by the Tindemans Report of 1975 (Tindemans 1976) which called for the development of 'external signs of our solidarity', including a European Foundation which would support educational and cultural exchanges. The first direct elections to the Parliament in 1979 (and, as Shore [2000: 46] notes, the low turnout then and again in 1984) encouraged further efforts, such as the flag in 1985 and the Adonnino Report in the same year (Shore 2000: 46). Cultural policy was formally legitimated in the Maastricht Treaty in 1992.[7]

Much of everyday Europe is of course invisible. Europeans are often unaware of how much of their daily lives is structured by a framework of European rather than national law. Equal pay legislation in the UK, for example, was transformed by the EU. The UK's Equal Pay Act of 1970 was upstaged five years later by an EU directive which, based on the Rome Treaty, broadened the UK's restriction to equal pay for *the same* work to cover work of *equal value*, as included in the UK's later Equality Act. Trade agreements are negotiated by the EU, which also determines the rates of import duties, though the customs points are still attended by member state officials.

Education, too, has been shaped by the Bologna process as well as by Pisa and by exchange programmes at school and higher levels. For a significant minority of Europeans, higher education can include a period of study from three months to a year in another EU country (which may of course include overseas dependent territories such as Martinique or Réunion in the case of France). In 2012, around 5 per cent of graduates had this experience, and the total over the past thirty years since the programmes were established (following the usual disputes, which ended up in a Court case) is approaching three million.[8] There is no doubt that students who have had this experience have a much more 'European' orientation than those who have not, though it is of course possible that for some of them their mobility was a result of a pre-existing attitude rather than a cause. In a study of European identities of young people in ten European sites, Sue Grundy and Lynn Jamieson (2005) found a stark difference between those with an experience of trans-European mobility and those without. Only in Madrid were those with transnational experience no more likely to declare that being a citizen of the EU was important to them, and in Prague, Bilbao and Edinburgh the difference was particularly strong.

The theme of European identity has been much studied, possibly too much. There has been an assumption that, like Lewis Carroll's snark, it must be there somewhere, if only we could find the right way to capture it. For Ulrich Beck and Edgar Grande (2007), a flexible identity, including a European one, goes along with the political form of the EU. Claus Offe and Ulrich Preuss (2006: 195) argue similarly that

> the European Union is [the] first spatially extended union of a great number of highly distinctive peoples that is governed as a republican regime. It reconciles the main attribute of an empire – multinationality – with an essential quality of a republic, political freedom, the latter resulting from the voluntary character of the former.

This flexible model is linked, they suggest, to a cosmopolitan vision which transcends old-fashioned oppositions between inside and outside, us and them. A cosmopolitan Europe relativises conceptions of inside/outside, self/other, Europe *or* the nation-state: 'Europe is another word for variable geometry, variable national interests, variable concern, variable internal and external relations, variable statehood, variable identity' (Beck and Grande 2007: 6).

A very substantial amount of work has been done on the topic of European identity, which has been a regular question in the Eurobarometer polls and received remarkably consistent answers over time. Since 1992, and in fact much earlier, a roughly equal percentage of people (in the high 30s or 40s) say they feel European *and* British, German or whatever, or nationality *only*, with the latter, less 'non-Europeanist' alternative usually, though not always, in the lead. Those defining themselves as European only or European *and* nationality are a consistently tiny minority (2–7 per cent for the former and 5–10 per cent for the latter) (Eurobarometer 40 Years, no date but probably 2014). As we have seen, the 1973 Copenhagen summit produced a paper on 'European identity', defined as being based on a 'common heritage' and 'acting together in relation to the rest of the world'. The appeal to identity in some ways replaced appeals to the notion of integration as a self-evident good (Stråth 2002). There are major differences between countries, with Croats, Belgians and Slovaks scoring highest on Europeanness (66–70 per cent) and the UK and Ireland lowest (33–34 per cent), followed by Greece, Bulgaria, Romania and Portugal in the 40s.

Much of the earlier work on identity tended to focus on the topical issue of EU citizenship, which had been put on the policy agenda by the

Maastricht Treaty and subsequent actions in the 1990s (Eder and Giesen 2001; Liebert 2007). The citizenship theme has subsequently become more muted, perhaps because the EU's citizenship policy was itself so half-hearted, but the related theme of identity remains a major focus of work.

It is not possible, Bernhard Giesen emphasises, simply to Europeanise a national form of consciousness; 'For Europe is no longer as obvious as the nation has been' (Eder and Giesen 2001: 230). At a European level the only realistic option is a minimalist conception of identity which is constantly reshaped. Echoing Ernest Renan's famous remark in 1882 about *national* consciousness being a 'daily plebiscite', an agreement to reaffirm one's national identity, Eder (2001: 238–239) writes: 'the making of identity becomes daily political business.' As he puts it earlier in the book:

> In the transnational situation there is no longer a people on top of class, nation or ethnicity; there are rather a series of people (*demoi*) who identify at times with class, with nation or with ethnicity. The idea of a hierarchy of identifications is to be replaced by the idea of a network of cross-cutting identifications. These many *demoi* are held together by the reliability of an institutional framework they have accepted by voluntary agreement and which guarantees everybody the maximum fairness in real life.
>
> (Eder and Giesen 2001: 46)

There is then the further question whether a sense of European or EU identity conduces to support for further integration. The relation seems surprisingly weak. Taking it from the negative end, the fear that integration threatens national identity is quite widespread among Europeans: the average is 48 per cent for the EU-15, with a range from 38.1 per cent in Italy to 60 per cent in Britain, 65.5 per cent in Greece and 66.5 per cent in Northern Ireland (McLaren 2004: 898). This, however, does not strongly affect their support for the EU. As McLaren (2004: 897) points out, 'Even in Britain and Denmark – generally the most guarded of the Member States when it comes to national sovereignty – only between 30 and 35 per cent of those who fear a loss of national identity from the EU also think their country's membership of the EU has been a bad thing.'

A political identity cannot, according to Furio Cerutti, be fabricated. Cerutti deconstructs a Commission call for research on identity which 'could assess how official identity symbols (such as the EU flag, the anthem, the EU slogan, the passport, the Euro, the ".eu" internet domain name, city branding like Brussels Capital of Europe or European capital of culture, commemoration days, artistic festivals or scientific events), and personal experiences with the European Union are present in the citizen's everyday life' (European Commission 2009; Cerutti 2011: 3–4). To see the EU concocting a set of pseudo-national symbols as though it were a new state like South Sudan is not very convincing:

> It is only when the peoples and the elites in the EU and national institutions perceive that they are affected by the same choices, thus having a common road to follow, that they can take significant steps forward in identifying with each other and the institutions. In this sense, the creation of the euro was the most promising step forward in the past decades, both financially and symbolically.
>
> (Cerutti 2011: 5)

One indirect way of approaching issues of European identity deserves special mention: it is another inevitably imprecise but often-asked question about *trust* in other nationalities. Jan Delhey (2007) used this approach to address the question of social cohesion in the EU. The successive EU enlargements have by definition increased the geographical distance between member states and between citizens: Have they also increased social distance as measured by (mis)trust? Delhey (2007: 273) concludes from an analysis of Eurobarometer surveys that distance tends indeed to reduce trust, though common borders have no observable effect in the opposite direction:

> 'The integrative effect of enlargement depends on the extent to which acceding nations differ from the present club members in three main dimensions: level of modernization (mechanisms: prestige), cultural characteristics (mechanisms: similarity) and power in the international system (mechanisms: perceived threat)'.

Turkey is therefore particularly suspect for other Europeans, being poor, Muslim and large; Bulgaria and Romania were also relatively untrusted both by EU-15 citizens and by those in the 2004 accession round. On the positive side, there is a general increase in levels of trust, and this tends to increase with length of EU membership. There are however variations: 'For example, the Germans now trust the Poles less but trust the Czechs and Hungarians more than they did the Italians in the 1970s' (Delhey 2007: 267). As I stressed in the previous chapters, we should remember that Europeans trust EU institutions more than those in their states. Only in Sweden and Finland do respondents trust the European Commission no *more* than their national governments (and in tiny Estonia and Cyprus substantially less). The same is true of the EP, which is trusted more than national parliaments in all countries except Sweden, Denmark and Cyprus (Harrison and Bruter 2015: 170–171).

Discussions of European identity tend to merge into questions about the existence of a European public sphere. There are no substantial transnational European media, with the partial exception of *Euronews*, so most discussion centres on the ways in which *national* media treat European topics individually and collectively, in syndication and other joint activities.[9] As Thomas Risse (2015: 3) writes:

> European public spheres do not emerge above and beyond local-, national- or issue-specific public spheres in some abstract supranational space but rather through the Europeanization of these various spheres.

Europeanization in this context is standardly measured by the prominence of European issues, the openness to non-national European actors, and sometimes, more contentiously, a sympathetic or supportive attitude to the EU (Risse 2015: 46). A study by Ruud Koopmans and Paul Statham's (2010), covering seven West European states, illuminates not just the public sphere but many other areas of EU politics and civil society. In his own chapter in the volume, Paul Statham (2010: 292) concludes soberly that 'the substance of the European Union's public sphere "deficit" consists in the over-domination by elite actors of Europeanized debates'. Rather than trying to arouse a largely dormant European civil society, or to increase the powers of an EP which is inevitably remote from most voters, Statham suggests that 'the supranational European institutions holding power would be better off strengthening their communicative links to citizens and seeking legitimacy through national parliaments and media, rather than engaging in another round of top-down efforts to engage a remote and inattentive citizenry'.[10]

This would align EU politics more closely with a well-established finding of studies of European media. Michał Krzyżanowski, Anna Triandafyllidou and Ruth Wodak (2009), in a volume concerned with a series of 'crisis moments' in late twentieth and early twenty-first century Europe, also stress the pervasive 'national filter' through which issues affecting Europe are presented. The approach Statham suggests would probably work better in continental Europe than in the more detached countries of Scandinavia and, even more so, the UK.[11]

The elitism of much writing about the EU reflects the more serious problem of the perception, which can hardly be questioned, of European integration as an elite project. Popular attitudes are also shaped by occupational class and income. Not only is there a smooth downward slope in support for the EU (and, closely related, the idea that one's own country has benefited from membership) as one moves 'down' the class structure from professionals to manual workers, but for any given occupation (*except for manual workers*) the perception that one's country has benefited rises with income (Leonard 1998: 26–27). This is a gift to the populist parties discussed in the next chapter, and a source of anxiety for social democrats like Leonard. Neil Fligstein (2008) focuses on the class slope of Europeanisation. There *is* a European society: 'Europe-wide social fields are being built where people and organizations from different countries come routinely to interact' (p. 9). And there *are* Europeans, but these form a small minority: 'There exists a European society for the group of educated, mobile people who are middle or upper-middle class' (p. 206). The 'Euroclash' (pp. 217–218) from which the book takes its title is that between two intersecting trends: one towards closer integration and the other towards a defensive focus on the nation-state, mobilising those who have lost out in the processes of globalisation and Europeanisation.[12] Once again, the globalisation of recruitment to elite positions in business, universities or sport tends, in the European region, to mean its Europeanisation. Recchi and Favell (2009) found that their respondents were substantially upper and upper middle class in origin.[13]

Fligstein may overstate his case; Copsey (2015) provides a more measured analysis, though especially for relatively immobile Europeans and those far from their national borders the integration process is likely to seem remote and irrelevant. As the Romanian-British political scientist Ghiță Ionescu (1974: 19–20) foresaw,

> there are endless reasons ... why European integration may not be carried to a successful end. But if there is one single reason why European integration might falter, through the EEC's own doing, it will be the failure to communicate directly with European society.[14]

The conclusion I think has to be that for most Europeans in the EU, except for a minority who countenance withdrawal, the Union is a fact of life. Just what they understand by it is however less certain, which in a way is not surprising when its ultimate extent, both geographically and in terms of degree of integration, remains in dispute. The EU's self-justificatory discourse also weaves between historical, cultural, economic, geopolitical and other narratives, as does public opinion. Eurobarometer has attempted to capture these different dimensions by asking, in slightly loaded terms, question such as those seen in Figure 6.2 about 'positive results'.[15]

Migration, as we have seen, has transformed notions of European identity and is having a substantial impact on labour markets and class structures across Europe – including many regions which had not previously been main destination countries. At the same time, hostility to (im)migration has fuelled the largely populist critiques of European integration which are the subject of the next chapter. The combination of geopolitical crises, especially in the Middle East, issues of voluntary and forced migration (refugees), and the tensions in the eurozone put the EU, and Europe

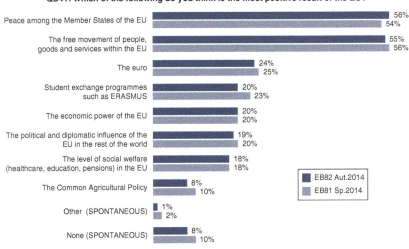

Figure 6.2 Which of the following do you think is the most positive result of the EU? © Eurostat.

as a whole, in a much tenser environment than around the turn of the century.

Summary points

Following the mass movements of populations after World War II and the labour migration into Europe and from south to north in the 1950s and 1960s, Europeans have again become more mobile, though not to anything like the same extent as in the United States.

Although the principle of free movement of labour was a central part of the Rome Treaty, transnational migrants within the EU still face legal and other obstacles.

There are elements of a European identity, but for most Europeans it is very much secondary to national or regional identities.

Many laws and policies originating at the EU level are administered and therefore experienced in a national framework.

Further questions

Is there a European social model?
What are some of the main ways in which the EU or other European institutions have affected you?

Has reading this book (so far) made you more or less inclined to

- move to/from Europe?
- live or work in another European state?
- work for a European institution?
- learn another European language?

Further reading

Checkel, Jeffrey T. and Peter J. Katzenstein (eds) (2009) *European Identity*. Cambridge: Cambridge University Press.

Enzensberger, Hans Magnus (1989) *Europe, Europe: Forays into a Continent*. New York: Pantheon.

Favell, Adrian (2008) *Eurostars and Eurocities: Free Movement and Mobility in an Integrating Europe*. Oxford: Blackwell.

Fligstein, Neil (2008) *Euro-Clash. The EU, European Identity, and the Future of Europe*. Oxford: Oxford University Press.

Klapisch, Cédric (2002) *L'Auberge Espagnole*. [Film].

Risse, Thomas (2010) *A Community of Europeans? Transnational Identities and Public Spheres*. Ithaca and London: Cornell University Press.

Notes

1. The UK is unusual in the extent of its 'ethnic monitoring', inviting people to declare their ethnicity even when, for example, joining a local library (www.ons.gov.uk/…/ethnic-group-statistics). This would be illegal in many other member states, notably France, where historical memories of Nazi deportations and an ideology of republican equal citizenship have maintained opposition until recently. Germany has included the categories of 'persons with a migration background' since 2005 and religious belief since 2011. A recent conference included a round table with the title 'Collecting Ethnic Data – no big deal or not an option?' https://idw-online.de/en/attachmentdata44883.pdf
2. Member states are allowed to make certain restrictions, for example in certain areas of public administration, subject to the requirement of 'proportionality'.
3. http://ec.europa.eu/eurostat/statistics-explained/index.php/Migration_and_migrant_population_statistics
4. Flash Eurobarometer 319b: Education and Training, Mobility, Employment and Entrepreneurship. http://ec.europa.eu/public_opinion/flash/fl_319b_sum_en.pdf
5. When I once showed some English banknotes to a French child, he said to his parents 'Hey, see what the English euros look like.'
6. See McNamara (2015): Chapter 6.

7   There had previously been some support for cultural activities from the Regional Fund and Social Fund. See www.europarl.europa.eu/facts_2004/4_17_0_en.htm
8   As Mau (2010: 73) points out, Germany is an interesting case because it imports as well as exports large numbers of students, whereas the UK is a big importer but small exporter, and Greece is the opposite.
9   Many papers produce regular supplements featuring articles from others. Project Syndicate, supported by a wide range of papers, makes material available in many Western European languages, as well as Arabic, Chinese, Hindi and Russian. For online media, see the very innovative study by Michailidou, Trenz and de Wilde (2014) (www.project-syndicate.org/about).
10 p. 306.
11 Statham's stress (p. 286) on the peculiarity of UK discourse on the EU is fully documented in the rest of the study, which covered five other member states (France, Germany, Italy, Netherlands and Spain) and one non-member (Switzerland).
12 See also Hix (2008) for a more detailed and nuanced account of EU political cleavages.
13 Class categories here are the Erikson, Goldthorpe, Portocarero scale, as used in the European Social Survey.
14 Cited by Catherine de Vries (2013: 434).
15 Eurobarometer 2014. Note that the number replying 'none' is not insignificant.

References

Beck, Ulrich and Edgar Grande (2007) *Cosmopolitan Europe*. Cambridge: Polity Press.

Benson, Michaela (2011) *The British in Rural France: Lifestyle Migration and the Ongoing Quest for a Better Way of Life*. Manchester: Manchester University Press.

Billig, Michael (1995) *Banal Nationalism*. London: SAGE.

Cerutti, Furio (2011) 'How Not to (Mis)understand Political Identity in the European Union', in Sonia Lucarelli, Furio Cerutti and Vivien A. Schmidt (eds), *Debating Political Identity and Legitimacy in the European Union*. London: Routledge, pp. 3–154.

Copsey, Nathaniel (2015) *Rethinking the European Union*. London: Palgrave Macmillan.

Delhey, Jan (2007) 'Do Enlargements Make the European Union Less Cohesive? An Analysis of Trust between EU Nationalities', *Journal of Common Market Studies*, 45: 253–279.

de Vries, Catherine (2013) 'Ambivalent Europeans? Public Support for European Integration in East and West', *Government and Opposition*, 48(3): 434–461.

Díez Medrano, Juan (2011) 'Social Class and Identity', in Adrian Favell and Virginie Guiraudon (eds), *Sociology of the European Union*. Basingstoke: Palgrave, pp. 28–49.

Eder, Klaus (2001) 'Integration through Culture? The Paradox of the Search for a European Identity', in Klaus Eder and Bernhard Giessen (eds), *European Citizenship between National Legacies and Postnational Projects*. Oxford: Oxford University Press, pp. 222–244.

Eder, Klaus and Bernhard Giesen (eds) (2001) *European Citizenship. Between National Legacies and Postnational Projects*. Oxford: Oxford University Press.

Eurobarometer (2014) Standard Eurobarometer 81: Public Opinion in the European Union: First Results. http://ec.europa.eu/citizenship/pdf/spring_eurobarometer_july_2014.pdf

Eurobarometer 40 Years (n.d.) http://ec.europa.eu/public_opinion/topics/forty_en.htm

European Commission (2009) FP7 Cooperation Work Programme: Socio-Economic Sciences and the Humanities. C5893 of 29 July 2009.

Favell, Adrian (2008) *Eurostars and Eurocities: Free Movement and Mobility in an Integrating Europe*. Oxford: Blackwell.

Favell, Adrian (2009) 'Immigration, Migration and Free Movement in the Making of Europe', in Jeffrey T. Checkel and Peter J. Katzenstein (eds), *European Identity*. Cambridge: Cambridge University Press, pp. 167–189.

Favell, Adrian and Ettore Recchi (2011) 'Social Mobility and Spatial Mobility', in Adrian Favell and Virginie Guiraudon (eds) *Sociology of the European Union*. Basingstoke: Palgrave Macmillan, pp. 50–75.

Fligstein, Neil (2008) *Euro-Clash: The EU, European Identity, and the Future of Europe*. Oxford: Oxford University Press.

Grundy, Sue and Lynn Jamieson (2005) 'Are We All Europeans Now? Local, National and Supranational Identities of Young Adults', *Sociological Research Online*, 10(3). http://www.socresonline.org.uk/10/3/grundy.html

Halman, Loek (2001) *The European Values Study: A Third Wave. Source Book of the 1999/2000 European Values Study Surveys*. Tilburg University: WORC.

Harrison, Sarah and Michael Bruter (2015) 'Media and Identity: The Paradox of Legitimacy and the Making of EU Citizens', in Thomas Risse (ed.), *European Public Spheres: Politics Is Back*. Cambridge: Cambridge University Press, pp. 170–171.

Hix, Simon (2008) *What's Wrong with the European Union and How to Fix It*. Cambridge: Polity.

Ionescu, Ghiţă (1974) 'Between Sovereignty and Integration: Introduction', *Government and Opposition*, 9(1): 3–20.

King, Russell et al. (eds.) (2000) *Eldorado or Fortress? Migration in Southern Europe*. London: Macmillan.

King, Russell et al. (2010) *The Atlas of Human Migration: Global Patterns of People on the Move*. London: Earthscan.

Koopmans, Ruud and Paul Statham (2010) *The Making of a European Public Sphere: Media Discourse and Political Contention*. Cambridge: Cambridge University Press.

Krzyżanowski, Michał, Anna Triandafyllidou and Ruth Wodak (2009) 'Conclusions: Europe, Media, Crisis and the European Public Sphere', in Anna Triandafyllidou, Ruth Wodak and Michał Krzyżanowski (eds), *The European Public Sphere and the Media: Europe in Crisis*. Basingstoke: Palgrave Macmillan.

Leonard, Mark (1998) *Rediscovering Europe*. London: Demos.

Liebert, Ulrike (2007) 'The European Citizenship Paradox: Renegotiating Equality and Diversity in the New Europe', *Critical Review of International Social and Political Philosophy*, 10(4): 417–441.

McLaren, Lauren (2004) 'Opposition to European Integration and Fear of Loss of National Identity: Debunking a Basic Assumption Regarding Hostility to the Integration Project', *European Journal of Political Research*, 43: 895–911.

McMahon, Simon (2015) *Immigration and Citizenship in an Enlarged European Union: The Political Dynamics of Intra-EU Mobility*. Basingstoke: Palgrave Macmillan.

McNamara, Kathleen (2015) *The Politics of Everyday Europe: Constructing Authority in the European Union*. Oxford: Oxford University Press.

Mau, Steffen (2010) *Social Transnationalism: Lifeworlds Beyond the Nation State*. London: Routledge.

Michailidou, Asimina, Hans-Jörg Trenz and Pieter de Wilde (2014) *The Internet and European Integration: Pro- and anti-EU Debates in Online News Media*. Opladen, Berlin and Toronto: Barbara Budrich.

MKW (2009) Scientific Report on the Mobility of Cross-Border Workers within the EU-27/EEA/EFTA Countries, MKW Wirtschaftsforschung GmbH, Munich.

Narizhnaya, Khristina (2013) 'Russians Go West', *World Policy Journal*, Spring. www.worldpolicy.org/journal/spring2013/russians-go-west

Offe, Claus and Ulrich Preuss (2006) 'The Problem of Legitimacy in the European Polity: Is Democratization the Answer?', in Colin Crouch and Wolfgang Streeck (eds), *The Diversity of Democracy: Corporatism, Social Order and Political Conflict*. Cheltenham: Edward Elgar, pp. 195–204.

Pichler, Florian (2009) '"Down-to-Earth" Cosmopolitanism: Subjective and Objective Measurements of Cosmopolitanism in Survey Research', *Current Sociology*, 57(5): 704–732.

Recchi, Ettore and Adrian Favell (2009) *Pioneers of European Integration: Citizenship and Mobility in the EU*. Cheltenham: Edward Elgar.

Risse, Thomas (ed.) (2015) *European Public Spheres: Politics Is Back*. Cambridge: Cambridge University Press.

Roose, Jochen (2010) *Vergesellschaftung an Europas Binnengrenzen: Eine Vergleichende Studie zu den Bedingungen Sozialer Integration*. Wiesbaden: VS Verlag.

Scheikle, Waltraud (2015) 'The Insurance Potential of a Non-Optimal Currency Area', in Olaf Cramme and Sara B. Hobolt (eds), *Democratic Politics in a European Union under Stress*. Oxford: Oxford University Press, pp. 137–154.

Shore, Cris (2000) *Building Europe: The Cultural Politics of European Integration*. London: Routledge.

Stråth, Bo (2002) 'A European Identity: To the Historical Limits of a Concept', *European Journal of Social Theory*, 5(4): 387–401.

Statham, Paul (2010) 'What Kind of Europeanized Public Politics?', in Ruud Koopmans and Paul Statham (eds), *The Making of a European Public Sphere: Media Discourse and Political Contention*. Cambridge: Cambridge University Press, pp. 277–306.

Thieler, Tobias (2006) *Political Symbolism and European Integration*. Manchester: Manchester University Press.

Tindemans, Leo (1976) 'European Union', *Bulletin of the European Communities*, Supplement 1/76. http://aei.pitt.edu/942/1/political_tindemans_report.pdf

chapter 7

Europeans against 'Europe'

Euroscepticism is an important feature of European politics, to a different extent across Europe and particularly strong in populist parties. The term is slightly misleading, since it refers not to the sort of critical and sceptical attitude which many internal or external observers of Europe display, the approach which Paul Statham (2010) and his co-authors call *eurocriticism*, but to a more fundamental opposition to the EU and its institutions. The rise of explicit euroscepticism, then, needs to be distinguished from the broader sentiment of unease or disillusionment which has been growing over time. A study of online discussion of the 2009 EP elections had over half of the comments displaying 'diffuse euroscepticism', mainly on cultural grounds, along with 15 per cent pro-European, 10 per cent supporting the status quo, 7 per cent anti-European, 5 per cent eurocritical, and 5 per cent 'altereuropean'.[1]

For most Europeans, decreasing enthusiasm for the EU coexists with the recognition of it as a permanent reality, but in some member states there are significant calls for withdrawal or for a radical scaling-down of the integration already achieved. As we saw in Chapter 5, the way in which EU politics is structured, both in the Union itself and in the member states, means that the only parties which really address European issues are the eurosceptic ones.[2] And the more eurosceptical parties there are in a given state, the greater the attention given to Europe (Risse 2015: 50). At the very least, attitudes to European integration add a further dimension to the polarisation of European politics between left and right, along with the GAL/TAN opposition.

Mark Leonard (2011: 3) has usefully presented eurosceptic parties in geographical terms. In the west, to begin with the simplest case, UKIP and many British Conservatives want to loosen or break the UK's ties with the EU, either through unilateral action or through the Union reshaping itself so that it becomes less intrusive on member states.³ The unilateral option of withdrawal is of course less simple than it seems, since an 'independent' UK would continue to be bound by all sorts of agreements with the EU and would probably ask for and be granted some closer form of association, such as that enjoyed by Norway in the European Economic Area or Switzerland, formally outside it but 'opting in' to a variety of common policies.

In the east, another fairly precise location, are a variety of parties in Poland, Hungary, the Czech Republic and Slovakia stressing their hostility to support for the wealthier southern states but in some cases also more fundamental opposition to the EU, sometimes seen as an intrusive successor to the Soviet Union which dominated their countries in the past.

The other two compass points are a little less precise. Leonard puts in the north the True Finns, the Danish People's Party, the Dutch Socialist Party and the Dutch and Austrian Freedom Parties, stressing, like those in the East though from a more affluent basis, their opposition to a 'transfer union'.

Leonard's 'south' includes the anti-austerity approach of the French Left Party and the extreme right National Front, the Lega Nord, which has shifted its emphasis from regional separatism from Italy to a broader extreme right and xenophobic programme, and the Communist Party of Greece.

Structurally, euroscepticism has tended to be understood in terms of the GAL/TAN polarisation of political opinion, briefly discussed at the beginning of Chapter 5, which often cuts across the left/right divide. It has also emerged from the conjunction of two trends: the drift towards populism in European politics in the early twenty-first century and the way in which European political leaders relied on a 'permissive consensus' over the development of the EU (Lindberg and Scheingold 1970), while tending to blame 'Brussels' for unpopular policies (Hooghe and Marks 2008).

As Vivien Schmidt (2006) and Justine Lacroix and Kalypso Nicolaïdis (2010) have shown, 'Europe' is framed differently in different national political cultures, and this has shaped the activities of eurosceptic parties and movements. Taken as a whole, however, eurosceptic politics is the only substantial political current explicitly focused on the EU; there is no corresponding integrationist party or group of parties. This makes euroscepticism analytically important, irrespective of the rise and fall of particular eurosceptic movements.

As I noted in Chapter 5, the politics of European integration cuts across the left/right division. Social democratic parties, such as Labour in Britain, were divided on the issue, and the first European referendum in the UK, just after the country had joined the Communities under the previous government, reflected this division. In the event, the political class lined up massively behind remaining in, with minority figures on the left and right, such as Tony Benn and Enoch Powell, respectively, calling for withdrawal. Tom Nairn (1973) explored the basis of Labour opposition to what was conceived, with some justification, as a business-oriented grouping of six countries whose growth and economic innovation were soaring ahead of the UK's. (A colleague joked that it might have been better to join Comecon: the quality of the UK's industrial output would far outshine even East Germany's, and the Channel would keep out the Warsaw Pact tanks.) By and large, however, it was parties on the far left and right which opposed European integration: the French Communists and Front National, for example. The communists in particular, suspected of being too pro-Soviet, had good reasons to play the national card, and in the last years of European communist rule they opposed the Single European Act of 1986.

Five years later, in France and elsewhere, there was substantial opposition to the 1992 Maastricht Treaty, which squeaked through a referendum in France but failed in Denmark, where a second referendum was held after the granting of some opt-outs. In the UK, John Major's Conservative government nearly fell, despite the UK's opt-out from the 'Social Chapter' on labour protection. Whereas the UK opposition to the treaty was backed by Thatcher and based in hostility to further integration, in France it was more focused on the neoliberal aspects of the treaty, under the slogan 'yes to Europe, no to Maastricht'.[4]

Thatcher's 'Bruges Speech' of 1988 is often cited as a major source of more recent euroscepticism, with her statement that 'we have not successfully rolled back the frontiers of the state in Britain, only to see them re-imposed at a European level with a European super-state exercising a new dominance from Brussels'.[5] Both forms of critique have continued since then, but the Thatcher version has become a good deal more strident, merging into what Alex Szczerbiak and Paul Taggart (2008a: 7–8) call 'hard' versus 'soft' euroscepticism. The former takes a strongly nationalist position and aims at withdrawal either in any circumstances (the UKIP position) or if the EU is not 'reformed' to suit the perceived 'national interest' (the modal Conservative position). 'Soft' eurosceptics, by contrast, tend to argue that reform is possible and would be in the interest of the EU as a whole, which should abandon further integrationist movement except in relation to the internal market. Other analysts have suggested a more complex differentiation between euroenthusiasts, eurorejects, eurosceptics and europragmatists, where the sceptics are pessimistic about the direction of European affairs and the pragmatists more optimistic (Kopecký and Mudde 2002). This seems a useful differentiation, especially in the

Central European case which was their main focus, since one can see something as inevitable, like the coming of winter, without welcoming it.

Such divisions are necessarily imprecise, since, for example, a successful anti-EU party such as UKIP will have to develop policies on other issues as well. Conversely, hard-right parties like the Front National will tend to vary their positions on the EU in response to particular developments such as the 2015 refugee crisis. As Szczerbiak and Taggart (2008a: 348–361) note, the place of European issues in a political system will tend to be determined by the degree of contestation within it. Systems of 'limited contestation', such as Germany, where most parties are in government at one time or another, will tend to have more of a consensus on the necessity of participation in the European project. Systems of more 'open contestation', where substantial parties are permanently excluded from government, are more likely to polarise around EU issues. The UK and France are possibly moving into this category, where UKIP and the Front National are able to mobilise significant numbers of voters.

Research on six Western European countries[6] over the past ten years by Edgar Grande, Hans Kriesi and others suggests a modification of the left/right and GAL/TAN model in relation to the EU, focused in particular on issues of immigration and European integration (Grande and Kriesi 2015: 204). They argue that the libertarian/authoritarian opposition has become less important, with a broader notion of cultural liberalism, along with European integration, now opposed to an anti-immigration emphasis. The resultant 'cleavage coalitions' cut across parties, and parties themselves may move between them:

1 a neoliberal-cosmopolitan coalition, combining economic and social liberalism;
2 an interventionist cosmopolitan coalition (Greens, social democrats – when not in power), trade unions and some social movements;
3 a moderate nationalist coalition (Christian democrats and conservatives, business associations – except in the UK);
4 an interventionist-nationalist coalition for economic protectionism (radical left and right in France and Netherlands, some social movements and trade unions);
5 a neoliberal-nationalist coalition (British business and Conservatives, extreme right in Austria and France).

Koopmans and Statham (2010: 272) suggest that 'what we are perhaps witnessing is the beginning of a process in which criticism of Europe becomes normalized within national party politics'. It is certainly the case that populist parties have substantially improved their position in this century by stressing economic interventionism and protectionism. The economic and euro crisis in the second decade seems not to have made much difference, though the immigration crisis of 2015 will undoubtedly have done so. In the European elections of 2009 and 2014, eurosceptics made up a substantial minority of MEPs, increasing to around a quarter in 2014, when UKIP came top in the UK, the Front National in France and the People's Party in Denmark. Syriza, which includes some eurosceptics, was in government. There are also several eurosceptic movements too small to form a parliamentary group among the so-called non-inscrits.

Overall, euroscepticism suffers from the paradox that its support is strongest in elections to the EP, where it tends to be marginalised by the majority pro-EU consensus of MEPs concerned with getting on with the job of legislation (Benedetto 2008). Those from UKIP and others are largely reduced to playing to the (national) gallery with disruptive protests. A parliament with a eurosceptic blocking majority would of course be a different matter. This raises the broader issue of the importance of euroscepticism. It is clearly a matter of serious concern if the most important and innovative European political project of the last half-century is losing the support of large numbers of citizens. In the United States people grumble about Washington but only a lunatic fringe wants to abolish the federal government or what some anti-semites call the 'Zionist Occupation Government'. Eurobarometer monitored for a time people's responses to the question of how they would feel if they were told tomorrow that the EU had been scrapped'.[7] Even with this rather stark question, the 2004 result had 43 per cent 'indifferent', against 39 per cent 'very sorry' and 13 per cent 'very relieved'. The major Western European countries were all close in their responses over time, except that Italians were much more prone to say 'sorry' and Britons much less (Rother and Langner 2004: 11).

Chris Bickerton points to an even more substantial problem, in which European politics in EU member states, and perhaps even those outside such as Norway and Switzerland, is increasingly polarised between technocracy and populism. The latter is mostly right-wing, though the Five Star Movement (M5S) in Italy is an exception, and UKIP has considerable appeal to former Labour supporters – as is also the case in France, where the Front National has long benefited from former Communists. As for technocracy, Bickerton (2012: 183) cites a Blair cabinet minister reported as saying that 'Depoliticizing of key decision-making is a vital element in bringing power closer to the people.'[8] Blair's Labour government was of course committed to a 'third way' between traditional social democracy and neoliberalism, and all political systems have a centripetal tendency in which parties move towards the political centre to capture voters, often including 'floating voters',[9] in the centre. Technocratic compromise at the European level reinforces a similar approach in domestic politics, with the further element that unpopular policies can be blamed on 'Brussels'.

Technocratically inclined politicians despise ordinary party members[10] and are at best suspicious of their voters, while populists favour uncritical admiration for the charismatic leader. Both are increasingly plebiscitary in their orientation. Bickerton (2012: 190) concluded that if we are to go 'beyond populist technocracy', that 'the first step would be to reclaim democracy from both populists and technocrats at the national level'. His more recent collaborative book (Bickerton, Hodson and Puetter 2015) is, if anything, even more pessimistic.

The examination of euroscepticism is actually a good way into looking at the different meanings of the EU in different states and social groups. To begin with the latter: farmers, as we saw earlier, are particularly closely engaged with the EU, though this is as likely to make them hostile to particular aspects of agricultural policy as supportive of the basic idea of the CAP. In the fullest survey available, published in 2000, only in Ireland and eurosceptic Denmark do two thirds of farmers think that the CAP is favourable to them. Overall in the then member states the proportion is reversed, with two thirds finding it unfavourable or very unfavourable. The UK and Germany were particularly hostile (Eurobarometer 2000: 8). On the other hand, two thirds approved of the upcoming changes in the CAP.[11] A 2005 study of France, Lithuania, Slovakia, Sweden and England (Gorton *et al.* 2008) paints a similar picture. Gorton *et al.* note a majority feeling that the EU imposed too many constraints on farmers' plans, and considerable scepticism about the ongoing reform measures. A French study in 2009 asked farmers how they would respond if the CAP were to be abolished in 2014. Two thirds said it would make no difference to whether they stayed in farming or left, though some said they would be less certain about their intentions and about 21 per cent said they would exit as a result (Latruffe, Dupuy and Desjeux 2013: 17, 21).

As with globalisation, Europeanisation is often evaluated in terms of its impact on 'winners' and 'losers'. Equality legislation can be assumed to benefit women, ethnic minorities and migrants, though there is a market liberal argument that, like minimum wages and other elements of labour protection, it worsens employment prospects. (This seems to have been the justification provided for the UK government under John Major demanding [and getting] an opt-out from the Social Chapter.) Whether measures which benefit the mobile harm the immobile is more controversial. To take a trivial example, the EU's recent action to ban excessive charges by mobile phone operators on calls made elsewhere in Europe was resisted on the grounds that they would protect their profits by raising their charges for domestic calls. More seriously, it has been argued that unrestricted intra-EU migration has worsened the employment prospects of native workers, especially those perceived as less well educated. The evidence is insubstantial, and employers who choose exclusively to employ migrants are usually aiming to breach minimum wage legislation or to exploit their vulnerable employees in other ways.[12] There is no doubt however that this fear has been a potent contributor to euroscepticism in the UK and elsewhere.

As for the national sources of euroscepticism, it is probably most useful to see it as just one expression of broader differences in the way the EU is perceived across its member states and prospective members. We can begin by taking Denmark and the UK as the countries which have resisted certain aspects of Europeanisation, expressed in their formal opt-outs, but even here the differences are very substantial. In the 2014 Eurobarometer, which reports roughly equal numbers of 'positive' and 'neutral' images of the EU, they are not among the three states with a majority of 'negative' images. These are Greece and Cyprus, which at present have particular reasons for disillusionment, but also Austria which, like the UK, stands out from the rest of Europe in its predominantly anti-EU press. The UK is more or less evenly split between the three alternatives, while Denmark has only 18 per cent negative, a little below the EU average. In Sweden the population has been quite eurosceptic, voting to join the EU in 1994 by only a tiny margin, but this is not reflected in the dominant parties, and opinion towards the EU actually became more favourable.

Both Denmark and the UK joined what is now the EU in 1973, amid anxieties about national autonomy which had led Norway to reject accession and underlay the UK's first referendum in 1975, where however the political class was massively in favour of remaining in, though with the main emphasis on the disadvantages of isolation ('We've got to stay in to get on').[13] In the UK, there was a residual attachment to the Commonwealth and to traditional trade links. Where the two countries diverged most was perhaps that Denmark was worried about levelling down its standards of consumer protection and social provision, whereas the UK, during the long period of Conservative rule from 1979 to 1997, was more resistant to levelling up to higher standards. Thatcher signed up to the Single European Act but soon wished, like at least one of her eurosceptic colleagues, that she had not. Although she was partly driven out of office for her anti-Europeanism, with her defeat cruelly exposed while she was in Paris, her party developed a eurosceptic orientation which sabotaged Major's successor regime and animated Ian Duncan Smith's period as party leader. Despite the strength of this euroscepticism, UKIP and a separate Referendum Party were formed in the early 1990s, with UKIP recording a major success in the 2014 European elections, drawing support from both Conservatives and Labour.

What is peculiar about the UK case is that the issue has always been posed much more starkly than anywhere else in terms of whether or not to remain a member of the EU.[14] The Danish People's Party, for example, declares roundly that it 'opposes the European Union' but is in the same EP grouping as the British Conservatives and is a good deal less strident on the issue than UKIP. Its predecessor, the Progress Party, like another extreme-right party, the Italian Lega Nord, was for a long time in favour of the EU. Even the Front National in France calls only for renegotiation of the treaties, though it wants to leave not only the euro and Schengen (which it wants abolished) but also the CAP, and to reverse the supremacy of European law. Like the Austrian Freedom Party, it would prefer to see a union of sovereign states in Europe, including Russia, which has lent it money, but not Turkey.

Whereas in many member states euroscepticism is often a by-product of opportunism by populist parties, in England and hence in the rest of the UK it seems to be hardwired. Chris Gifford (2014) ably traces the continuities between the UK's initial horror at the Schuman Declaration of 1950 which led to the ECSC, through to Cameron's promise of a referendum on membership, later sealed by his unexpected election victory in 2015. Whereas in the rest of Western Europe, the 'European rescue of the nation-state' (Milward 1992) was part of a strategy of economic reconstruction through European integration, the UK believed it had other ways of achieving the former and saw little need for the latter, in a world where economic links were being restored anyway on a broader basis. An on-off premarital relationship lasting over twenty years was followed by a marriage in which one of the partners constantly questioned whether it had been a good idea and increasingly asked if it was time to end it. Popular ignorance was so great that the referendum question could not be phrased as 'Should the United Kingdom be a member of the European Union?' in case it confused voters who did not know whether or not it was already a member (Gifford 2014: 166–167). Press coverage of the EU and other European institutions is peculiarly skimpy and unreliable for an otherwise mature democracy, and even among the political elite, it is not hard to find bizarre remarks such as the Labour Prime Minister Jim Callaghan's suggestion that withdrawal was not an option because it would upset the United States, or Gordon Brown suggesting that the European Commission was redundant (Gifford 2014: 76, 148).

As Kirsty Hughes (2015) pointed out before the outcome of the referendum was known, even a relatively strong majority for remaining in the EU would have perpetuated the UK's self-imposed marginalisation.[15] A split vote between an English 'no' and a 'yes' in the other parts of the UK would exacerbate existing tensions, while an English vote for Brexit, which at around 53 per cent would be enough to outvote the other nations, would achieve the break-up of the UK that it narrowly avoided, for better or worse, in 2014.

Having looked briefly at the comparison between the UK and Denmark, it is worth thinking about the comparison between the UK and France, a similar-sized post-imperial state. France was in at the beginning with Monnet and Schuman and the Franco-German 'motor' was a major dynamic force in European integration, even when successive enlargements diluted this influence (Schild 2010; Krotz and Schild 2013). The French public was rather uninterested in European affairs. Whereas the UK feared that European involvement would diminish what remained of its role as a world power, the French narrative was just the opposite: the EU was a way for France to continue to play a major role in the world, with Europe as an extension rather than a distraction. The institutional and administrative arrangements of the ECSC and EU were largely based on French models, and the Commission worked largely in French. De Gaulle was suspicious of enlargement and further integration, and blocked the Council's activities for a time in 1965, but on the whole he went along with the process. By the time of the 2009 European elections, the tensions between national and European narratives were beginning to open up, but the parties responded by skating over the issue, though several talked of 'changing Europe' and the Front National's slogan was 'Against the European Swindle'. Olivier Rozenberg (2011a) predicted 'the internalization of Eurosceptic claims by each political family', reflecting the ambiguity of French attitudes (Rozenberg 2011b). The successes of the Front National in the 2014 European elections and the 2015 regional elections have sharpened up these tensions. Even in the Front National[16] and parts of the extreme left, however, French euroscepticism is mostly soft rather than hard, and substantially motivated, as in the 'no' vote for the Constitution in 2003, by social concerns. On the other hand, the Front National has spoken of a referendum on EU *membership*, and a 'Frexit' would be much more destabilising for the Union than the loss of the UK/England.

The Federal Republic of Germany, founded in 1949 in the three western occupation zones, has had European integration built into its 'Basic Law' or constitution since 1992.[17] Except on the extreme right, the word *national* is highly suspect in Germany, and Germans have been among the most likely to describe themselves as Europeans. There have been occasional sceptical responses to EU integration from the Federal Constitutional Court,[18] and a growing opinion that Eastern enlargement and the introduction of the euro were premature, but otherwise euroscepticism was confined to the extreme right fringe, the National Democratic Party (NPD), German People's Union (DVU) and Republicans. The formation after unification of the Party of Democratic Socialism (PDS) added some soft eurosceptical notes, but German euroscepticism really began only with the formation of the Alternative für Deutschland (AfD) in 2013. AfD's history in some ways repeats UKIP's, beginning as a party heavy with academics and losing one of its founders and five of its seven MEPs as it lurched to the right. Here it was overtaken by the more sinister PEGIDA (Patriotic Europeans Against the Islamisation of the Occident), which however also does not call for withdrawal from the EU, though like the Front National and other extreme-right forces, it supports a Europe of strong sovereign states. AfD uses the same formula but has a more developed programme of reform for the EU; its residual MEPs sit with the British Conservatives in the European Conservatives and Reformists (ECR) group.

Italy, where regional loyalties are particularly strong and national politics has been particularly problematic, with the long period of rule by the deeply corrupt Christian Democrats followed by Berlusconi's bizarre antics, has been strongly pro-EU since the late 1960s. Recently, however, disillusionment with national politics has extended to the EU, against a background of economic stagnation and the refugee crisis (Lucarelli 2015). Even the protest parties however, the semi-fascist Lega Nord and the anti-establishment M5S, are so far soft eurosceptics.

Spain and Portugal, where EU membership came after the end of the long-lasting post-fascist dictatorships, were also traditionally supportive of the EU, but trust has crashed in both countries following the economic crisis, by 45 per cent in Spain and 31 per cent in Portugal between May 2007, just before the economic crisis broke, and November 2012.[19] Greece records an even higher loss of trust over the same period, from 63 per cent to 18 per cent. Even here, however, public support for EU and Eurozone membership remains solid, with outright anti-EU policies only in the communist party (KKE) and the neofascist Golden Dawn.

The Netherlands remains strongly in favour of EU membership, but with substantial criticism of its relatively high budget contribution and strong populist parties, notably the Freedom Party (PVV), whose 2012–13 electoral programme was focused on the opposition between 'their Brussels' and 'our Netherlands'.[20] In Belgium, the hard eurosceptic Flemish nationalist party Vlaams Belang has been outstripped by the softer New-Flemish Alliance (N-VA), which used to sit with the green group in the EP but is currently with the ECR group and is a member, like the Scottish, Welsh and Cornish nationalists in the UK, of the European Free Alliance (EFA), of progressive civic nationalist parties.[21] The French-language Rassemblement Wallon has no discernable European policy and generally argues for federalism in Belgium, with many supporters envisaging union with France if Flanders secedes from Belgium.

In post-communist Europe, the most striking feature is the low level of participation in EP elections, with Slovakia managing an impressive turnout in 2014 of 13 per cent, followed by the Czech Republic with 18 per cent. The next lowest, in the 20s, are also all post-communist states.[22]

Poland is the most favourably inclined to the EU, though the Law and Justice Party (PiS) is soft eurosceptic, sitting in the ECR group. In the Czech Republic the Civic Democratic Party (ODS) has been quite strongly eurosceptic, especially under the leadership of Václav Klaus, who was also president until 2013, though its voters were much less so. It also sits with the ECR group.

Hungary, as we saw in Chapter 5, is currently much more problematic, with Orbán defying the EU on a variety of issues. Hungarian euroscepticism, now stronger in its party representation than anywhere in the region after the 2014 elections, has a paranoid flavour: in a controversy over utility prices a Fidesz government spokesman said, 'The attacks . . . are coming from the international multinational companies and Hungary's left-wing opposition parties who in reality are working in cahoots to direct certain entities in Brussels to convince the European Commission to deliberately attack Hungary'.[23] At the December 2015 Fidesz congress, Orbán provided the following analysis of the EU:

> The European spirit and its people believe in superficial, secondary things, such as human rights, progress, openness, new kinds of families, and toleration. . . . These are nice and amiable things but really only secondary ones because they are only derivatives. . . . Europe doesn't believe in Christianity, in common sense, in military virtues, and doesn't believe in national pride . . .
>
> Today I . . . see a whole army of serious people with serious countenances who, convinced of their moral superiority, want to disparage the nation states of Europe and campaign for a United States of Europe. Trouble is waiting for us.[24]

Elsewhere, particularly in the Czech Republic and the Baltic States, euroscepticism is more often based on a neoliberal critique of regulation, though this can easily enough combine with more nationalist themes, as in the UK.

As Paul Taggart and Aleks Szczerbiak (2004: 80) noted, 'the key question is whether public opinion determines the shape of party competition, or whether party competition determines public opinion'. It is clear that the opportunity structure resulting from the distribution of parties and the nature of the electoral system has a major effect, but that public opinion will eventually find its expression, even in political structures and cultures like Germany's, inimical to euroscepticism. It seems likely to remain a strong element in EU politics for the foreseeable future; it may ultimately disappear, as in the United States, where 'states' rights' used to be a powerful theme, or alternatively lead to the abandonment of important aspects of the integration project.

Finally, we should note the more extreme version of anti-Europeanism represented by European citizens attracted by radical Islamism. In this highly transnational process, linking cities in Europe, Asia, Africa, North America and Australia, hostility to Europe from the outside, grounded in a broader rejection of 'Western' values, intersects with the resentments of Europeans from minority ethnic groups experiencing discrimination both at home and in the regions from which they or their parents or grandparents migrated. As in the time of the Spanish civil war (though the parallels should not be pushed too far), some people from countries in Europe and elsewhere are going to fight for or against a religiously underpinned form of fascism, reinforcing in turn more extreme politics back home. The next chapter explores the place of Europe in the contemporary world.

Summary points

The 'permissive consensus' in which European elites were mostly left to pursue integration as they saw fit has been succeeded by a much more politicised climate in which 'eurosceptic' parties have become influential, now holding around a third of the seats in the EP.

The extreme right is drawing support from its opposition to European integration, though there are also eurosceptic parties with a more centrist orientation, such as AfD and UKIP, and some also on the political left.

Only in the UK has the question of withdrawal from the EU become a key political question, though it could also become one in France if the Front National continues to gain support. A French withdrawal would be much more damaging to the EU than the loss of the UK.

Further questions

Is euroscepticism xenophobic?
'Yes to Europe, no to the EU.' Is this a coherent approach?
How do support for (and opposition to) the EU map on to other political divisions?

Further reading

Arzheimer, Kai (2015) 'The AfD: Finally a Successful Right-Wing Populist Eurosceptic Party for Germany?', *West European Politics*, 38: 535–556.

Arzheimer, Kai (n.d.) *The Eclectic, Erratic Bibliography on the Extreme Right in Western Europe*. www.kai-arzheimer.com/extreme-right-western-europe-bibliography

Merkl, Peter H. and Leonard Weinberg (2003) *Right-wing Extremism in the Twenty-first Century*. London: Frank Cass.

Notes

1 de Wilde, Michailidou and Trenz (2014: 185). The term *Altereuropean*, more common in France than in the English-speaking world, refers to a leftist orientation to EU reform of the kind often found in Green parties. See for example https://euroalter.com/.

2. The 2014 EP elections in the UK, which coincided in many areas with local government elections, were a particularly striking example. UKIP addressed the issue of the EU, which was almost entirely absent from the literature put out by the other parties.
3. I would be inclined to add to this list the Flemish nationalist Vlaams Belang, which describes itself as 'very reticent and critical' in relation to the intrusive aspects of EU policies.
4. See for example the critique by the political economist and Green MEP Alain Lipietz (1992).
5. www.margaretthatcher.org/document/107332. Cameron's Bloomberg speech in 2013, at which he promised a referendum, was described by the leader of the Conservative MEPs as 'pretty much a mirror image' of the Bruges speech. The difference is of course that Cameron, unlike Thatcher, countenanced the possibility that he would call for Brexit.
6. The first study included Austria, France, Germany, the Netherlands, Switzerland and the UK; the second replaced the Netherlands with Sweden.
7. The French and German versions are a little more muted, referring to 'disparition' and 'Scheitern'. For an interesting analysis of the gender gap in support for the EU, with women expressing lower levels of support than men in a wide variety of member states, see Liebert (1997); also Banducci and Netjes (2003).
8. This recalls a spoof advertisement for the British Social Democratic Party (a centrist group which broke from Labour in 1981 and later merged with the Liberals) which featured the slogan 'Keep politics out of politics'.
9. This term seems almost redundant in a time when 'dealignment', the weakening of party attachments, is so much a fact of contemporary political life.
10. The dissociation between many Labour MPs and other party members following Jeremy Corbyn's election as party leader is a particularly striking example, but Richard Crossman, normally seen as left-oriented, expressed a similar attitude in the 1960s in his introduction to Bagehot's *The English Constitution*: 'since it could not afford, like its opponents, to maintain a large army of paid party workers, the Labour Party required militants – politically conscious Socialists to do the work of organising the constituencies. But since these militants tended to be "extremists", a constitution was needed which maintained their enthusiasm by apparently creating a full party democracy while excluding them from effective power' (Crossman 1963: 41–42).
11. The 2003 Luxembourg Agreement replaced subsidies to production by a single farm payment per hectare of land maintained in good agricultural and/or environmental condition. A further agreement introduced in 2013 continues this policy. http://ec.europa.eu/agriculture/policy-perspectives/policy-briefs/05_en.pdf See also www.cap2020.ieep.eu/2015/6/10/keep-chewing-this-bone-a-trickle-of-ideas-on-a-future-cap
12. The UK government's demand that it be allowed to discriminate against other EU citizens by restricting their in-work benefits (something which a beginning student of EU law would know is illegal) reflects the overall situation in which low wage rates make larger numbers of workers eligible for these benefits.

13 A seminar in 1996 at King's College, London, brought together many of the protagonists: www.kcl.ac.uk/sspp/departments/icbh/witness/PDFfiles/European Referendum.pdf Also in *Contemporary British History*, 10(3): 82–105.
14 At least for those who know that it *is* a member. The UK displays one of the highest levels of ignorance about the EU. Asked three rather simple questions, only Latvians recorded a lower level of correct answers (http://blogs.lse.ac.uk/politicsandpolicy/brits-know-less-about-the-eu-than-anyone-else/). Austrians may, like the UK, have a largely eurosceptic press, but they are at least much better informed.
15 This applies to high-level political decisions and pronouncements rather than detailed negotiations by officials, where, as Simon Hix (2015) has shown, the UK has often participated fully and secured the outcomes it favoured.
16 The Front National website in December 2015 had a substantial paper recommending the dissolution of, or exit from the euro, but not from the EU (www.frontnational.com/pdf/fin-euro.pdf).
17 Article 23: www.bundestag.de/blob/284870/ce0d03414872b427e57fccb703634dcd/basic_law-data.pdf
18 Note the cautious wording of Article 23 of the revised Basic Law: 'With a view to establishing a united Europe, the Federal Republic of Germany shall participate in the development of the European Union that is committed to democratic, social and federal principles, to the rule of law, and to the principle of subsidiarity, and that guarantees a level of protection of basic rights essentially comparable to that afforded by this Basic Law. To this end the Federation may transfer sovereign powers by a law with the consent of the Bundesrat.'
19 www.ecfr.eu/page/-/Methodological_note_Euroscepticism.pdf
20 http://pvv.nl/images/stories/verkiezingen2012/VerkiezingsProgramma-PVV-2012-final-web.pdf. The programme (p. 15) shows projections of the 'non-Western' population spreading across the Netherlands like cancerous cells from 2010 to 2040.
21 www.e-f-a.org/about-us/
22 www.europarl.europa.eu/elections2014-results/en/turnout.html
23 *Budapest Beacon*, May 23, 2014: http://budapestbeacon.com/politics/many-faces-euroscepticism-hungary-central-europe/8251
24 http://hungarianspectrum.org/tag/viktor-orban/ My thanks to David Thompson for drawing my attention to this and the previous item.

References

Banducci, Susan and Catherine Netjes (2003) 'Gender, Supra-National Institutions and European Integration', ECPR Conference, Marburg, Germany.
Benedetto, Giacomo (2008) 'Explaining the Failure of Euroscepticism in the European Parliament', in Aleks Szczerbiak and Paul Taggart (eds), *Opposing Europe? The Politics of Euroscepticism in Europe*, Oxford: Oxford University Press, Vol. 2, Chapter 6.

Bickerton, Christopher J. (2012) *European Integration: From Nation States to Member States*. Oxford: Oxford University Press.

Bickerton, Christopher J., Dermot Hodson and Uwe Puetter (eds) (2015) *The New Intergovernmentalism: States and Supranational Actors in the Post-Maastricht Era*. Oxford: Oxford University Press.

Crossman, Richard (1963) *Introduction to Walter Bagehot, 'The English Constitution'*. London: Watts.

de Wilde, Pieter, Asimina Michailidou and Hans-Jörg Trenz (2014) 'Converging on Euroscepticism: Online Policy Contestation During European Parliament Elections', *European Journal of Political Research*, 53(4): 766–783.

Eurobarometer (2000) Standard Eurobarometer 53: Public Opinion in the European Union.

Eurobarometer (2014) Standard Eurobarometer 81: Public Opinion in the European Union: First Results. http://ec.europa.eu/citizenship/pdf/spring_eurobarometer_july_2014.pdf.

Gifford, Chris (2014) *The Making of Eurosceptic Britain* (2nd ed.). Farnham: Ashgate.

Gorton, Matthew, Elodie Douarin, Sophia Davidova and Laure Latruffe (2008) 'Attitudes to Agricultural Policy and Farming Futures in the Context of the 2003 CAP Reform: A Comparison of Farmers in Selected Established and New Member States', *Journal of Rural Studies*, 24: 322–336.

Grande, Edgar and Hanspeter Kriesi (2015) 'The Restructuring of Political Conflict in Europe and the Politicization of European Integration', in Thomas Risse (ed.), *European Public Spheres: Politics Is Back*. Cambridge: Cambridge University Press, pp. 190–223.

Hix, Simon (2015) 'UK Influence in Europe Series: Is the UK at the Top Table in EU Negotiations?', LSE EUROPP blog, 16 November. http://blogs.lse.ac.uk/europpblog/2015/11/16/uk-influence-in-europe-series-is-the-uk-at-the-top-table-in-eu-negotiations/

Hooghe, Liesbet and Gary Marks. 2008. 'A Postfunctionalist Theory of European Integration: From Permissive Consensus to Constraining Dissensus', *British Journal of Political Science*, 39(1): 1–23.

Hughes, Kirsty (2015) 'Can Europe make it? 3 Scenarios for the Outcome of the UK's EU Referendum', *opendemocracy*, 4 December. www.opendemocracy.net/can-europe-make-it/kirsty-hughes/3-scenarios-for-outcome-of-uk-s-eu-referendum

Koopmans, Ruud and Paul Statham (eds) (2010) *The Making of a European Public Sphere: Media Discourse and Political Contention*. New York: Cambridge University Press.

Kopecký, Petr and Cas Mudde (2002) 'The Two Sides of Euroscepticism: Party Positions on European Integration in East Central Europe', *European Union Politics*, 3(3): 297–326.

Krotz, Ulrich and Joachim Schild (2013) *Shaping Europe: France, Germany and Embedded Bilateralism from the Elysée Treaty to Twenty-First Century Politics*. Oxford: Oxford University Press.

Lacroix, Justine and Kalypso Nicolaïdis (eds) (2010) *European Stories: Intellectual Debates on Europe in National Contexts*. Oxford: Oxford University Press.

Latruffe, Laure, Aurélia Dupuy and Yann Desjeux (2013) 'What Would Farmers' Strategies Be in a no-CAP Situation? An Illustration from Two Regions in France', *Journal of Rural Studies*, 32: 10–25.

Leonard, Mark (2011) 'Four Scenarios for the Reinvention of Europe'. European Council on Foreign Relations. www.ecfr.eu/publications/C18/P8

Liebert, Ulrike (1997) 'The Gendering of Euro-skepticism: Public Discourses and Support to the EU in a Cross-national Comparison'. Bremen: Jean Monnet Centre for European Studies, CEuS Working Paper 1997/1. www.monnet-centre.uni-bremen.de/pdf/Euroscepticism.pdf

Lindberg, Leon and Stuart Scheingold (1970) *Europe's Would-be Polity: Patterns of Change in the European Community*. Englewood Cliffs: Prentice-Hall.

Lipietz, Alain (1992) 'Contre Maastricht, Parce que Pour l'Europe', *Silence* N. 157, September. http://lipietz.net/ALVP/VP_Maastricht.pdf

Lucarelli, Sonia (2015) 'Italy and the EU: From True Love to Disenchantment?', *Journal of Common Market Studies*, 53(1): 40–60.

Milward, Alan (1992) *The European Rescue of the Nation State*. London: Routledge.

Nairn, Tom (1973) *The Left Against Europe?* Harmondsworth: Penguin.

Risse, Thomas (ed.) (2015) *European Public Spheres: Politics is Back*. Cambridge: Cambridge University Press.

Rother, Nina and Tanja Langner (2004) 'Dimensions of Identification with Europe: Secondary Analysis of Comparative Surveys.' PIONEUR Working Paper no. 8, February. www.obets.ua.es/pioneur/documentos_public.php

Rozenberg, Olivier (2011a) 'Playing Softly with Euroscepticism: The 2009 European Elections in France', in Robert Harmsen and Joachim Schild (eds), *Debating Europe: The 2009 European Parliament Elections and Beyond*. Baden-Baden: Nomos.

Rozenberg, Olivier (2011b) 'Monnet for Nothing? France's Mixed Europeanisation', in Simon Bulmer and Christian Lequesne (eds), *The Member States of the European Union* (2nd ed.). Oxford: Oxford University Press.

Schild, Joachim (2010) 'Mission Impossible? The Potential for Franco-German Leadership in the Enlarged EU', *Journal of Common Market Studies*, 48(5): 1367–1390.

Schmidt, Vivien (2006) *Democracy in Europe: The EU and National Polities*. Oxford: Oxford University Press.

Statham, Paul (2010) 'What Kind of Europeanized Public Politics?', in Ruud Koopmans and Paul Statham (eds), *The Making of a European Public Sphere: Media Discourse and Political Contention*. New York: Cambridge University Press, pp. 277–306.

Szczerbiak, Aleks and Paul Taggart (eds) (2008a) *Opposing Europe? The Politics of Euroscepticism in Europe*, Vol. 1. Oxford: Oxford University Press.

Szczerbiak, Aleks and Paul Taggart (eds) (2008b) *Opposing Europe? The Politics of Euroscepticism in Europe*, Vol. 2. Oxford: Oxford University Press.

Taggart, Paul and Aleks Szczerbiak (2004) 'Supporting the Union: Euroscepticism and the Politics of European Integration', in Maria Green Cowles and Desmond Dinan (eds), *Developments in the European Union*, Vol. 2. Basingstoke: Palgrave Macmillan, pp. 65–84.

chapter 8

The future of Europe in the world

This chapter can be summed up in a sentence: in terms of population, share of world output and a number of other measures, Europe has become smaller in relation to the world. The combined EU and United States' share of world GDP has dropped from 60 per cent in 1990 to 45 per cent in 2012 (Copsey 2015: 157). An EU estimate has Europe and the United States in 2050 each making up a proportion of world GDP in the high teens, with China accounting for around a quarter and India a tenth.[1]

Jószef Böröcz (2015) has also explored some future scenarios, with the 'global economic weight' (share of world GDP) of the EU and United States more or less static from 1950 to 2010 and India and China on the rise, each a few points above or below 10 per cent (Böröcz 2015: Figure 2.1). Extrapolating these trends to 2060, we find China way ahead, with something like a two-thirds share, the United States with around a third, India catching up fast and the EU well below 10 per cent, even with its prospective enlargements taken into account (Böröcz 2015: Figure 2.2). His rather speculative alternative scenarios involve a fusion of the EU and the North American Free Trade Association (NAFTA) on the one hand, and with the former USSR on the other. Even these end up in 2060 somewhere between China and India: 'none of the three scenarios offer a viable solution to the task of maintaining the geopolitical privileges enjoyed by the states, capital and citizens that constitute key stakeholders in European integration' (Böröcz 2015: 32). For the moment, however, Western Europe, along with North America and Australia, is one of the three richest regions of the world.[2] As Chancellor Merkel pointed out in 2012, 'If Europe today accounts for just over seven per cent of the world's population, produces around twenty-five per cent of global GDP and has to finance fifty per cent of global social spending, then it's obvious that it will have to work very hard to maintain its prosperity and way of life' (Peel 2012).

We now think not so much about which countries are part of the world economy, but which ones still remain on the margins. The bulk of the world is now part of an integrated economic system, including most prominently the former communist countries, with China in the lead, and India, but also Brazil, Indonesia, South Africa and other parts of what used to be called the 'third world'.[3] Once again, this is something which would have happened in the absence of the process of European integration. The Western European empires (Belgian, British, Dutch, French, Portuguese) were on their way out as integration began, though it took some time for Europeans to realise this.[4]

The early years of the EEC were mainly focused inwards, but this changed after 1968. As Giuliano Garavini (2012: 242) writes:

> Western Europe, and the European Community in particular, had graduated from dragging its feet on international economic cooperation in the 1960s, to become its spearhead in the following decade: The 1971 approval of the Generalized System of Preferences; the ambition to play the role of 'most favored' partner of the developing world at the Paris European summit in 1972; the declaration on European identity and the launching of the Euro-Arab dialogue at the Copenhagen European summit in 1973; the joint signature of the Nine on the Final Act of the CSCE, the Lomé Convention, and the simultaneous launching of the G7 of industrialized countries and North-South dialogue in 1975.

The early stages of the EU were also however shaped by the Cold War and the Soviet threat, with all the founding members also in NATO, except for West Germany, which joined in 1955. Although France left the joint military command in 1966, the first enlargement in 1973, like the subsequent enlargements, brought in further members of the military alliance. Integration tended to move faster under two conditions: when the economic situation was good and the Soviet threat relatively great. As Copsey (2015: 155) writes, 'This dangerous, yet ultimately stable, period of domination by two non-European powers, the Soviet Union and the United States, helped Western Europe to undergo a relatively peaceful transition in its relationship with the rest of the world.'[5] Or as Jürgen Habermas (2006: chapter 3, last paragraph) put it, perhaps a little optimistically, 'With growing distance from imperial domination and colonial history, the European powers have also had the opportunity to *achieve a reflexive distance towards themselves.*'

Although the formal development of a common European security and foreign policy is a recent development, beginning around the turn of the century, the policies of EU member states very often converged, and their foreign services became less insular (Hocking and Spence 2005). Their cooperation in the Conference on Security and Cooperation in Europe, culminating in the final declaration at Helsinki in 1975, was not only crucial for legitimating the mobilisation of anti-communist activism in the citizens' initiatives or 'monitoring groups' following Helsinki, but also an impressive demonstration of European unity in a project the two superpowers treated as trivial. The United States saw it as simply ratifying the post-war status quo, while the Soviet Union treated the commitments to human rights as just another pious declaration without practical consequences.

If the EU is on a level with the United States in economic terms, and with a substantially larger population, it may seem natural that it should, or could, play a comparable role in world affairs, along with the United States, China, perhaps Russia and India, and regional groupings including one or more of these. Europe has a general interest in peace, prosperity and the democracy which it requires of its member states, and a regional interest on its southern and eastern borders, including in particular the states in the Western Balkans which are potential member states.[6] What remains undecided is whether it should aspire to pursue those interests in the same rather traditional and unscrupulous way as the other world powers[7] or project some alternative vision of 'soft power' or 'normative power Europe'. Whereas the EU's exclusive position as representing its member states in trade negotiations is firmly established, other aspects of its international role remain undefined.

The idea of Europe as a 'civilian power' was put forward first by the Anglo-French scholar François Duchène (1972), one of the pioneers of EU studies who worked for a long time with Monnet and whose biography he wrote (Duchène 1994). Ian Manners (2002, 2006) argued that, beyond the contrast between civilian and military power, we also need a concept of 'normative power': the power of ideas such as the norms of solidarity embodied in the EU treaties and other documents and practices, including notably the 'Copenhagen Criteria' of 1993 which laid down the conditions which future accession states had to satisfy and the 'Charter of Fundamental Rights' of 2000, given legal force in the Lisbon Treaty of 2009.[8] This idea is paralleled by Joseph Nye's conception of 'soft power' (Nye 2004) and the approach known as *constructivism* in International Relations, which stresses ideas and intersubjectivity in opposition to a 'realism' emphasising power politics. Soft power is in some ways similar to what Steven Lukes (1974, 2007) called 'three-dimensional power': the ideological shaping of ideas. A number of analysts of the EU have stressed the way in which member states commit themselves to principles and are then unable to escape the consequences.[9]

First, we should look more closely at the institutional framework of EU foreign policy as it has evolved into its present state. Europe nearly acquired a European Defence Community at a very early stage in the early 1950s, until French opposition killed it off. A generation later, the Maastricht Treaty of 1992 established a 'Common Foreign and Security Policy', continued in the treaties of Amsterdam and Nice and finally the Lisbon Treaty. This established the European External Action Service (EEAS), a European diplomatic service, and the post of High Representative for Foreign Affairs and Security Policy, the EU's foreign minister, who is developing a 'global strategy' to be completed in the summer of 2016. What does this amount to in practice?[10] It is not just defensiveness when the EEAS stresses its role in coordinating other aspects of EU policy, emanating from separate parts of the Commission. This aspect of its role is similar to that of a domestic foreign ministry. The need for this coordination is made clear by the EU's poor response to the situation in Ukraine in 2014, when a prospective trade agreement rapidly ramified into a major crisis. As for its independent action, it currently has 139 delegations or offices worldwide, complementing or sometimes standing in for the diplomatic representations of member states and engaging in independent activities ranging widely from normal diplomatic representation to peace-keeping missions such as that in Kosovo. The world is getting used to seeing the High Representative, who is also Vice-President of the Commission, signing international treaties and lining up alongside other world leaders. It is, however, significant that neither the current High Representative nor her predecessor is a top-flight politician such as a former prime minister. As usual in EU affairs, the Union's role is often restricted by member states concerned to preserve their traditional prerogatives in foreign policy. But as Copsey (2015: 191) stresses, 'The Eurozone crisis and the rise of new powers meant that Europe could no longer afford the luxury of so much squabbling between countries that hold generally similar views about the kind of world governance structures that European foreign policy is designed to promote and build.'

This is perhaps the area of EU policy where the approach which has been called the 'new intergovernmentalism' (Bickerton, Hodson and Puetter 2015) has the greatest purchase. Rather than focusing on the recent turf wars between the EEAS and the domestic governments and foreign ministries, it may make more sense to emphasise the longer history of cooperation in which, in Bickerton's words:

> National foreign policy strategies of European states are increasingly lifted out of both the Cold War context and the particular dynamics and concerns of domestic politics. Pursued by seconded national experts and by national diplomats, the development of EPC (European Political

Cooperation) reflected the uncoupling of state and society that was a key feature of this development of member statehood.

(Bickerton 2012: 169; see also Smith 2015)

In other words, rather than setting up a European interest in opposition to national interests, it may be helpful to see it as emerging from the coordination of various national perspectives, where the most important European interest is that Europe act *together*. As in Rousseau's political theory, the opposition between the general will and the 'will of all' is not perhaps as clear-cut as it is presented. What remains undoubtedly damaging, as noted earlier, is the lack of coordination between the EU's various representatives. As Bindi and Angelescu (2012: 331) write,

> These range from the high representative for foreign affairs and security policy, the council president, the commission president, the commissioner for enlargement and neighborhood policy, to the commissioner for external trade ... while non-Europeans were expecting a single voice in EU foreign policy after the Lisbon Treaty, the reality is that EU voices have multiplied, leaving partners more puzzled than ever.

It is still the case, as Henry Kissinger complained, that if you want to talk to the EU you don't know who to call.

Returning to the broader theme of the place of Europe in the contemporary world, it is clear that its image is increasingly bound up with that of the EU. Other states expect to deal with Europe as a whole, even if they also engage in bilateral arrangements with individual member states and play off one against the others. (These member states collude in this behaviour, as in the case of the UK's subservience to the United States and, more alarmingly, China and Saudi Arabia.) The colonial past of many of the leading member states is recalled by the survival of the Spanish enclaves in Africa, the British Overseas Territories (including the Falkland Islands/Malvinas), the French Territoires d'Outre Mer and the Dutch Caribbean territories (Adler-Nissen and Gad 2013). Despite all this, the EU can now present itself with some justification as the more acceptable face of 'the West' in a postcolonial world. Less aggressive than the United States, it is also more scrupulous than China in its dealings with, for example, Latin American and African regimes.

The years 2014–15 revealed the most critical issues for the EU's foreign relations: Russia on the one hand[11] and the Middle East and North Africa on the other. The Russian problem, as Mary Sarotte (2009: 214) notes, had been set up in 1989, when the withdrawal of the Soviet Union from east and central Europe left the former satellites mostly aiming for, sooner or later, membership of the EU and NATO. The alternative of a broader East–West European confederation rapidly fizzled out, as it had done earlier in the two German states. What Sarotte calls the 'prefab model' of the incorporation of much of post-communist Europe had the disadvantage that the west was 'creating a common European home of many rooms – just without one for Russia'. Because of its size, Russia might anyway have remained a large annex to the rest of Europe, but both NATO and the EU could undoubtedly have done much more to develop cooperation with Russia and the other members of the Commonwealth of Independent States which succeeded the Soviet Union.

President Putin is not alone in bemoaning, as he has done repeatedly since a speech in 2005, the break-up of the Soviet Union as a 'geopolitical catastrophe': in a recent survey (Levada-Center 2013), over half of respondents said they regretted it and that it could have been avoided, against just over a quarter saying they did not regret it. Whereas only 13 per cent favoured the 'restoration of the USSR in its previous form', two thirds supported closer union of the former republics or at least the continuation of the Commonwealth of Independent States in its present form, as opposed to complete independence, supported by only 11 per cent. An earlier survey in January 2011 had over three quarters 'definitely' or 'probably' in support of 'the opinion that Russia should restore its status of "Great Empire"'.

Running through late tsarism and the Soviet period to the present, the idea of the strong state (both internally and internationally) remains a constant. We should not perhaps be surprised to see this way of thinking among political and intellectual elites. What is more surprising is for it to be replicated in public opinion. In the Levada-Center (2013) survey cited earlier, nearly a quarter of respondents said they would like Russia to become 'a socialist state like the USSR', with a third each for the two alternatives offered: 'a state like Western states with a democratic government system and market economy' and 'a state with a special system and a unique course of development'. Surveys in 2002 and 2012 registered stable levels of support for the following statements:

> To ensure a successful development, Russia should become an open country, join the world community; otherwise we are doomed to fall behind other countries (58 per cent and 59 per cent, respectively).
> To ensure a successful development, Russia should not open to the world – otherwise openness will destroy our unique culture, whereas we should not be afraid of lagging behind others, as we have enough resources to be successful (42 per cent).

The same survey had a substantial minority wanting Russia to be

> A powerful military country, where the interests of the state and country's prestige and the position in the world is of paramount importance (30 per cent in 2002; 22 per cent in 2012).

> A comfortable and liveable country, where human well-being, interests and opportunities are the prime concern (70 per cent in 2002; 78 per cent in 2012).

In 2012, those who thought Russia needed democracy (nearly two thirds, as against a quarter who saw it as 'unsuitable') wanted this to be

> Like in developed countries of Europe and America (27 per cent)
> Like in the former Soviet Union (20 per cent)
> A special kind, which suits national traditions and the specific Russian character (38 per cent)

Of those who regretted the break-up of the USSR, equal numbers cited as the reason that 'People no longer feel they belong to a great power', and 'A single economic system is destroyed'. (Other reasons were more practical concerns about travel and so on.) Attitudes of this kind to Russia's position in the world, rather than Putin's personal charisma, such as it is, may explain the continuing popularity of Putin's rule. They are, of course, partly sustained by state propaganda in a country where the vast majority of citizens rely on state-controlled media, but they are also shaped by more substantial deep structures of a post-imperial consciousness.

Dmitry Trenin (2011: xiii) has written that 'it was in a fit of self-renewal, which also included an element of self-denial, that Russia in 1990–1991 simply shook off its empire – a move with few parallels in history'. He goes on: Russia . . . is a rare case of a former imperial polity having neither disappeared nor reinvented itself as a nation-state, but seeking to reconstitute itself as a great power, with a regional base and global interests. . . . While no longer a pretender to world hegemony and staying within its new, shrunken borders, Russia has been trying hard to establish itself in the top league of the world's major players and as the dominant power in its neighborhood. Even more strikingly, as it promoted its bid on the world stage, it has been striving, simultaneously, to keep itself in one piece. This is a dual adventure almost unparalleled in modern history.

For the moment, the empire functions mainly as an object of confused nostalgia for a gradually shrinking number of Russians and as a slogan legitimating a set of rather dangerous orientations in foreign policy. These are encapsulated in the other two themes: the *near abroad* and *Eurasia*. The *new abroad* is a relatively recent coinage from the early 1990s to refer to the former Soviet republics, with echoes of the Monroe Doctrine in the United States claiming US hegemony in its 'back yard'. *Eurasia*, by contrast, is a long-standing conception, going back at least to the late nineteenth century, which links a geographical region to an idea of Russia's special position, often as a bridge between Europe and Asia. Nurtured by Soviet émigrés, it returned as a trope of right-wing discourse and echoes through some of the survey responses cited earlier.

The current Russian regime, and perhaps any future one, will expect to play some sort of hegemonic role in the region, while suffering from a legacy of suspicion which undercuts its cultural resources of soft power and a variety of connections which have been sustained over the post-Soviet decades. The alternative of isolationism, which was an option for the United States, is probably not for a Russia with a host of unstable states around its borders, some of them cultivated by the United States.

In surveys such as those cited earlier, suspicion of the United States is particularly strong. The 2012–13 Levada survey recorded only 1 per cent of 'very positive' or 'likely positive' attitudes to President Obama, as against 16 per cent neutral and 76 per cent negative or likely negative. The United States was listed as the fourth country 'most unfriendly and hostile to Russia', sandwiched between Georgia, the Baltic States and Ukraine (with which Russia was already in a covert war). Six months later, 13 per cent of respondents felt 'good' about the United States, as against 81 per cent 'bad'. Attitudes to the EU, which had earlier been generally favourable, with 62 per cent positive as against 20 per cent negative in 2012, had by now caught up with the United States, with 20 per cent feeling 'good' and 71 per cent 'bad' – probably in the wake of the economic sanctions introduced following the annexation of Crimea and the incursions into Ukraine. Russians, like Belorussians and Ukrainians, had been feeling themselves 'less European' over the early years of this century (Korosteleva and White 2006), with rather little difference between 'European' Russia and the rest of the country. Maria Chepurina (2011) writes that, whereas a 1999 poll revealed that 79 per cent of Russians consider Russia to be a European country, while 21 per cent identify themselves with Asia, less than ten years later, in 2007, the Levada-Center, together with the EU-Russia Center, conducted a poll that revealed a completely opposite tendency. Only 20 per cent of the 1600 people polled considered themselves European, while 71 per cent did not. Moreover, 45 per cent considered the EU a potential threat to Russia, either financially, politically or culturally.

All this makes relations with Russia a particularly sensitive issue for the EU, widely perceived in Russia and also in much of Europe to be too subservient to the United States and NATO. This should not be exaggerated: even if the United States did not exist or embraced an isolationist foreign policy, there is a substantial body of opinion in the EU which is highly suspicious of Russia. The size of the country is, of course, a constant; imagine if North America were attached to Scotland, as it was a geological age ago, and Europe were heavily dependent on North America's mineral resources. Although Russia has been disinclined to deal with the EU as a whole, it has itself sponsored a variety of economic unions, most recently the Eurasian Economic Union, inaugurated in January 2015 and linking Russia with Armenia, Belarus, Kazakhstan and now Kyrgyzstan, which mirrors the EU in some of its formal structures (Commission, Council, Court, etc.).[12] A Clingendael Report (van der Togt *et al.* 2015) recommends a strategy of 'cautious engagement' with Russia and the Eurasian Union, rather than a more comprehensive partnership, currently seen as unfeasible in view of the state of Russian policy, or the other alternative of a more confrontational posture. In the longer term, it is possible that Putin's proposal in 2010 for an enlarged European free trade area 'from Lisbon to Vladivostok'[13] might be again a possibility.

The Russian problem intersects with the other main area of concern: the Middle East, with its terrorist threats and refugee crisis. As Peter van Ham (2015: 14) put it, after the Paris attack of November 2015, 'In an instant, Russia has turned from a quasi pariah state into a crucial coveted player and even potential partner to address the EU's new top security priority: to fight, and win, the "war" on jihadism, both in Syria and in Europe.' There is a further element for the EU: the long-delayed (and perhaps fading) prospect of Turkish accession would mean that the EU shared a boundary with Syria, Iraq and Iran, which also have substantial Kurdish minorities spanning the borders, as well as Georgia and Armenia.

The EU's main channel of real external influence, as opposed to just bustling around the world trying to be helpful, has been the accession process and its penumbrae of association agreements and so on. The various enlargements have undoubtedly had substantial effects, however incomplete.[14] As the enlargement process slows down,[15] however, and encounters more and more difficult terrain in the Western Balkans, the transformative promise seems less convincing. As Juncos and Whitman (2015: 209) write, 'If, after three decades of EU membership, Greece is still struggling to achieve economic growth and modernization and fighting corruption, how can the Western Balkan countries expect to overcome similar challenges?' The EU's 'Eastern Partnership' and 'Eastern Neighbourhood Policy' have also lost credibility, as well as seeming disturbingly colonialist in their orientation (Casier 2012; Grzymski n.d.).

Despite all these problems, the bottom line remains that it is only through the EU that European states can hope to have any serious influence in a world scene which has grown much more crowded and unpredictable. Copsey's stress on what he calls the 'common European interest in world politics' (Copsey 2015: 180–188) is important here. *Contra* Henry Kissinger, who argued long ago that the EU has only regional interests, it now has global interests without the will or the proper means to pursue them.

And yet, Europe has pioneered a new form of cosmopolitan political organisation which may prove attractive as a model for other parts of the world, as the national state model has done in the past. Jürgen Habermas (1994: 75) in a 1991 interview called this 'Europe's second chance', with a united Europe in what he later came to call a 'post-national constellation':

> We've watched the rise and fall of the great empires over the ages – the Romans and the Carolingians, the Portuguese and the Spaniards, the English and the French, the Russians and – it now virtually appears – the Americans. . . . Today, however, that force that Max Weber attributed to Western rationality could once again be gathering – and this time, I hope, free of all imperialistic ambitions and with so little narcissistic self-absorption that a Europe that has learned from its own history can help other countries emerge from *their* nineteenth centuries.

Habermas did not pursue here the theme of Europe as a democratic empire, but his later work is based around the argument that the national state is ill-equipped to deal with the challenges of globalisation. The term *post-national*, like many other '*posts*', is intended to convey the sense that the national is not simply replaced by another principle but continues in a different form: in this case a cosmopolitan union which he initially thought might take a federal form but increasingly presents, as we have seen, in rather more cautious terms (Habermas 1998; Grewal 2012). The idea of the EU as a new form of democratic empire was developed by Ulrich Beck and Edgar Grande (2004) and more fully by Jan Zielonka (2006). In Zielonka's image of a neo-medieval empire, different peoples, or *demoi*, coexist in a cosmopolitan and multilingual space, where, as in the Roman Empire, there is a common currency and the division between citizens of the empire and others becomes more important than internal borders between territories. (As we have seen, this division between EU citizens and 'third-party nationals' is a serious concern for current policy.)

The future of Europe in the world, then, is closely bound up with the future of transnational politics. The world has many more national states than a century ago, and for well over half a century the UN has provided a forum for them, while the permanent membership of the Security Council gave a special position to what were perceived in 1945 as the 'great powers': China, France, the Soviet Union, the UK and the United States.[16] Along with this and other intergovernmental organisations, such as the General Agreement on Tariffs and Trade, established in 1947 and which became the

World Trade Organization in 1995, and more recently the G6, G7 and G8 economic groupings, beginning in 1975, what we now know as the EU emerged as a radically different transnational body with a much more ambitious, if rather inexplicit, programme of 'ever-closer union'. This transformed its member states in ways which they often barely realised until after the event. As we saw earlier, the EP emerged as the world's first transnational directly elected parliament.

As world politics became more globalised, with agreements on topics ranging from economic issues to human rights binding most of the world's national states, the EU itself developed to fit this new world order, though without resolving the ambiguity between its intergovernmental and transnational identities. Within Europe itself, the EU, along with its penumbrae of non-members linked by special arrangements or partnerships, has become the overwhelmingly important political structure and reference point, rather as the Roman Empire was for southern and western Europe and, half a millennium later, the Holy Roman Empire was for central Europe. Its political role in the world, as opposed to that in its immediate sphere of influence (notably in relation to Russia), remains ill-defined.

It is important, though difficult, to estimate how Europe might have developed in the absence of what has become the EU. It is probably safe to assume that European wars were neither more nor less likely and that the end of European communism would have been neither accelerated nor delayed. Although the prospect of rejoining the rest of Europe was very important for opposition movements in communist Europe, the EU was only part of Europe's much wider appeal. By the time the first and largest wave of post-communist accessions took place in 2004 much of the economic 'transition shock' was already over, though preparations for EU membership may have made it harder, while aid from the EU in the PHARE and TACIS programmes may have mitigated some of the effects (Outhwaite 2016).

The prospect of accession was most important in relation to political transformation, first in Greece, Spain and Portugal and then in post-communist Europe, and undoubtedly made a substantial contribution to the strengthening of democracy in countries where it was particularly fragile. Whether the EU preserves European democracies from regressing into authoritarianism, as is currently threatened in Hungary and Poland and, with the rise of extreme right parties, in Western Europe as well, remains to be seen. Not all authoritarian parties and movements are hostile to the EU, and not all anti-EU movements are authoritarian, but there is a more than accidental affinity between these two strands of populist politics and, perhaps more importantly, those opposed to the EU will not be deterred by the threat that their membership might be suspended or terminated.

Economic estimates of the benefits of membership range from ten to twenty per cent for Europe as a whole, with one of probably the most reliable studies settling on a figure around twelve per cent. Campos, Coricelli and Moretti (2014: 25) found positive effects for all Western European member states except Greece.

> Focusing on the 1973, 1980, 1995 and 2004 enlargements, we find that per capita GDP and labor productivity increase with EU membership in Denmark, Ireland, United Kingdom, Portugal, Spain, Austria, Estonia, Hungary, Latvia, Slovenia and Lithuania. The effects tend to be smaller, albeit still mostly positive, for Finland, Sweden, Poland, Czech Republic and Slovakia.

Their tables compare the actual growth of real GDP per capita with a 'synthetic' estimate of what this would have been in the absence of membership. The benefits, they stress, tend to be cumulative, so the earlier accession countries tend to benefit more by 2014.[17] As has been shown however in the UK in the run-up to the 2016 referendum, disputable economic statistics can shape opinion, especially in a country with a heavily biased or politically manipulated press.

In the sphere of culture and everyday life, structures specifically related to the EU coexist with others which are largely independent of it. Budget air travel would exist in Europe without the EU, as it does in the United States; so would globalised consumption patterns, including that of service 'products' such as higher education. Eurovision is independent of the EU, though the marketing of the songs may be facilitated by European free trade. The globalisation, which in Europe often means Europeanisation, of sport is also an independent process, though the increasingly mobile players and coaches benefit from the EU's freedom of movement for employment. Wherever you look in these areas, you will find places where specifically EU-related elements contribute to a broader cosmopolitan pattern, and it is hard not to feel that a united Europe is an entity of the appropriate scale to mediate these relations.

As we approach the end of the second decade of the twenty-first century, and the EU approaches what for a human being would be retirement age, the future political shape of Europe remains uncertain. In my book on Europe since 1989, I offered two alternative prefaces to a hypothetical second edition, dated 2030. In the first, the EU gradually moves into a consensual form of federalism – a kind of multinational Germany. In the second, it falls apart as the former member states become increasingly authoritarian in their politics: thirty small versions of contemporary Russia. A film made in 2015 and transmitted and screened worldwide, *The Great European Disaster Movie*, traces the collapse of the EU from 2014 to a standpoint in the near future.[18] We should, of course, not overlook a third alternative, in which the project of European integration is abandoned but the member states survive in a more or less liberal and democratic form.

As we saw earlier, there is considerable support across Europe for maintaining something like the status quo, so we can begin by considering whether that is an option. The major question here is that of the euro. First, it is currently set to become the common currency of *all* member states except Denmark and the UK, which have a permanent opt-out arrangement (fairly meaningless in the Danish case as long as the Krone continues to be pegged to the euro). More seriously, the crises of the past years have shown fairly conclusively that the eurozone requires much closer coordination in order to function properly, even as a necessarily 'non-optimal' or 'sub-optimal' currency union. Thus the simple solution of removing the requirement that all member states adopt the euro would not help, though it might please Sweden and perhaps other member states, and would reduce the UK's isolation.[19]

Whereas in the past it often seemed as if the motor of the integration process was the legal integration pursued by the ECJ, the motor is now essentially the euro, demanding further monetary and fiscal integration which would not otherwise be on the agenda. What then about abandoning the euro and reverting to the now eighteen currencies which preceded it?[20] When Chancellor Merkel said in 2010 that 'if the euro falls, Europe falls', she was sticking her neck out to make a political point. The abandonment of the euro *might* start a domino process leading to collapse, or it might be managed at the cost only of a good deal of short-term dislocation and a substantial increase in transaction costs – perhaps less now than at the turn of the century because the technology has improved.[21] Wolfgang Streeck (2014, 2015; see also Streeck and Elsässer 2015), as we saw, has argued powerfully for the dissolution of the eurozone, though Streeck and Elsässer (2015: 19) think it is 'likely' that it will survive, despite its damaging consequences. The abolition of the euro, however, looks like a feasible alternative to the status quo, though it is striking that very few Europeans inside the eurozone want to leave it – even in Greece at the height of the crisis.

More ambitiously, we might think about the prospect of a much looser association of European states, without the law, currency or citizenship. As we saw, the extreme right tends to argue for something like this, and they also wish to control movement across their national borders, as UKIP does. It is true that much of European law and trade regulation could function on the simple basis that goods allowed in one country could be sold in any other. *Caveat emptor*! Consumers beware! External trade would be more problematic. UKIP wants to leave the EU and negotiate independent trade agreements with the rest of the world. A European association of states operating on this basis would, however, surely fall apart very quickly, as individual states undercut one another. Finally, we should remember that many EU member states have substantial regional separatist movements, and that the costs of secession are much higher in the absence of a larger transnational structure to which the new states could belong. This might discourage separatism, or alternatively the nationalism which dissolved the EU might go much further in the direction of the 'Balkanisation' of Europe.

It is hard, at least for me, to see this as in any way more attractive than the present EU. But Europe has experienced a wide variety of political forms, and it would be presumptuous to imagine that we have hit upon the ideal pattern, modified perhaps in a more or less federal direction, for the next thousand years. I continue to believe, however, that the project, formed in the midst of a hideously genocidal world war, of bringing together the states and peoples of Europe in an 'ever closer union' is something which most Europeans, and their neighbours elsewhere on our small planet, will continue to value.

Summary points

Economic growth and the emergence of independent states in the rest of the world have left Europe with a much reduced position, though its large population and economic output make it a major force in the world.

The EU has recently confronted direct external challenges in relation to Ukraine and the Middle East. What had earlier seemed like a quite distant prospect of an EU including Turkey and thus sharing a border with Syria, Iraq and Iran has now become dramatic, with vast refugee migrations from the region, throwing the EU into crisis both at home and in its foreign policy.

The EU has developed something like a foreign ministry and diplomatic service, but one which is still rivalled and undermined by those of (some) member states. It has not (yet) developed a coherent and coordinated international role, and may choose not to do so.

Further questions

What might Europe have looked like without the emergence of the EU?
Has Europe had it?
Consider the phrase: 'Economic giant and political dwarf'. Is this true of the EU?
Will there ever be a common European foreign policy? Should there be?

Further reading

Ziełonka, Jan (2014) *Is the EU Doomed?* Cambridge: Polity.
Bickerton, Chris (2016) *The European Union: A Citizen's Guide*. London: Pelican.

Notes

1 https://ec.europa.eu/research/social-sciences/pdf/policy_reviews/global-europe-2050-report_en.pdf; p. 53. There is also some explanation of the alternative scenarios on p. 3.
2 http://data.worldbank.org/indicator/NY.GDP.PCAP.CD/countries?display=map
3 The term was introduced in 1952 by Alfred Sauvy, with a conscious reference to the 'third estate' in pre-Revolution France. The 'West', including the EU, made up the first world, and the Soviet bloc and China the second.
4 The leading Belgian and EU politician Fernand Dehousse (1960: 524) declared in a speech that 'a French abandonment of Algeria would signify the retreat of Europe into itself'. See Garavini (2012: 45). Garavini (2012: 56) also cites the Dutch saying before it lost control of Indonesia in World War II that 'if the Indies are lost the Netherlands are fucked'. As we saw in the last chapter, British reticence about the EEC was substantially motivated by concerns about what remained of the UK's 'world role'.
5 The humiliation of France and the UK when they attacked Egypt in 1956 over the nationalisation of the Suez Canal is one of the main stages in this learning process.
6 Albania, Macedonia, Montenegro and Serbia are candidates for accession, along with Turkey, and Bosnia and Herzegovina, along with Kosovo, as potential candidates.
7 With perhaps the exception of India.
8 http://ec.europa.eu/justice/fundamental-rights/charter/index_en.htm
9 See for example Wiener (2008).
10 Browsing the EEAS site on 19.12.15, I found this slightly disappointing (and of course no longer applicable) message under 'Events': 'No event related to A Global Strategy on Foreign and Security Policy for the European Union found'. For a comprehensive discussion of the EEAS, see Spence and Bátora (2015).
11 For a fuller discussion of Russia, on which I have drawn here, see Outhwaite (2016).
12 See www.eaeunion.org/?lang=en#about
13 Cited by van der Togt et al. (2015: 71, no. 168). See also van Ham (2015) and Sherr (2015).
14 On the post-communist enlargements of 2004 and 2007, see Outhwaite and Ray (2005), Outhwaite (2016).
15 As Anna Szołucha (2010: 6) pointed out, the idea of 'accession fatigue' has a long history.
16 China was initially represented by the outgoing republican government, which took refuge in Taiwan in 1949, and from 1971 by the People's Republic of China. Russia took up the USSR's membership after its dissolution in 1991. The other ten members of the Security Council are elected for two years on a rotational basis.
17 See also the EP document 'Mapping the Cost of Non-Europe, 2014–19'. www.europarl.europa.eu/RegData/etudes/STUD/2015/536364/EPRS_STU(2015)536364_EN.pdf/. On the related issue of the benefits of EU spending, see Weiss (2013).

18 See the site of 'Wake Up Europe': www.wakeupeurope.eu/.
19 One of Cameron's more bizarre demands in the negotiations preceding the UK referendum was that the eurozone should not be able to take unilateral decisions affecting non-eurozone members. This might make sense in the short term, but not in a Union of thirty or so members with only one or at most two outside the eurozone.
20 Eighteen rather than nineteen, as the Belgian and Luxembourg francs were equivalent and could count as one currency.
21 The Union or the member states could force the banks to exchange currencies at less extortionate rates than at present. (In the days before the euro, an MEP travelled around the member states exchanging currency at each border and quickly reduced his starting amount of 100 ECU to zero.)

References

Adler-Nissen, Rebecca and Ulrik Pram Gad (eds) (2013) *European Integration and Postcolonial Sovereignty Games: The EU Overseas Countries and Territories*. Abingdon: Routledge.

Beck, Ulrich and Edgar Grande (2004) *Das kosmopolitische Europa*. Frankfurt: Suhrkamp. Tr. (2007) as *Cosmopolitan Europe*, Cambridge: Polity.

Bickerton, Christopher J. (2012) *European Integration: From Nation States to Member States*. Oxford: Oxford University Press.

Bickerton, Christopher J., Dermot Hodson and Uwe Puetter (eds) (2015) *The New Intergovernmentalism: States and Supranational Actors in the Post-Maastricht Era*. Oxford: Oxford University Press.

Bindi, Federiga and Irina Angelescu (2012) 'The Open Question of an EU Foreign Policy', in Federiga Bindi and Irina Angelescu (eds), *The Foreign Policy of the European Union: Assessing Europe's Role in the World* (2nd ed.). Washington, DC: Brookings, pp. 325–336.

Böröcz, Jószef (2015) 'Geopolitical Scenarios for European Integration: The Decades to Come', in Jody Jensen and Ferenc Miszlivetz (eds), *Reframing Europe's Future: Challenges and Failures of the European Construction*. Abingdon: Routledge, pp. 19–34.

Campos, Nauro, Fabrizio Coricelli and Luigi Moretti (2014) 'Economic Growth and Political Integration: Estimating the Benefits from Membership in the European Union Using the Synthetic Counterfactuals Method', IZA Discussion Paper No 8162, May. http://ftp.iza.org/dp8162.pdf

Casier, Tom (2012) 'European Neighborhood Policy: Living up to Regional Ambitions?', in Federiga Bindi and Irina Angelescu (eds), *The Foreign Policy of the European Union: Assessing Europe's Role in the World* (2nd ed.). Washington, DC: Brookings, pp. 99–117.

Chepurina, Maria (2011) 'Is Russian Identity European Identity?' In Focus: http://infocusrevue.com/2011/04/21/is-russian-identity-european-identity/#_edn13

Copsey, Nathaniel (2015) *Rethinking the European Union*. London: Palgrave Macmillan.

Dehousse, Fernand (1960) *L'Europe et le Monde. Receuil d'études, de Rapports et de Discours 1945–1960*. Paris: Librairie Générale de Droit et de Jurisprudence.

Duchêne, François (1972) 'Europe's Role in World Peace', in Richard Mayne (ed.), *Europe Tomorrow: Sixteen Europeans look ahead*. London: Fontana.

Duchêne, François (1994) *Jean Monnet: The First Statesman of Interdependence*. New York and London: Norton.

Garavini, Giuliano (2012) *After Empires. European Integration, Decolonization, and the Challenge from the Global South 1957–1986*. Oxford: Oxford University Press.

Grewal, Shivdeep (2012) *Habermas and European Integration: Social and Cultural Modernity Beyond the Nation State*. Manchester: Manchester University Press.

Grzymski, Jan (n.d.) 'Governing Neighbourhood: Governmentality of the EU's Borders'. Unpublished manuscript.

Habermas, Jürgen (1994) *The Past as Future*. Lincoln: University of Nebraska Press.

Habermas, Jürgen (1998) *Die postnationale Konstellation*, Frankfurt: Suhrkamp. Tr. (2001) as *The Postnational Constellation*, Cambridge: Polity.

Habermas, Jürgen (2006) [2004] *The Divided West*. Cambridge: Polity.

Hocking, Brian and David Spence (eds) (2005) *Foreign Ministries in the European Union. Integrating Diplomats*. Basingstoke: Palgrave Macmillan.

Juncos, Ana and Richard Whitman (2015) 'Europe as a Regional Actor: Neighbourhood Lost?', *Journal of Common Market Studies*, 53 (Annual Review): 200–215.

Korosteleva, Julia and Stephen White (2006) '"Feeling European": The View from Belarus, Russia and Ukraine'. *Contemporary Politics*, 12(2): 193–205.

Levada-Center and CSSP, Strathclyde (n.d.) *Russia Votes*. www.russiavotes.org

Levada-Center (2013) *Russian Public Opinion 2012–2013*. http://www.levada.ru/old/books/obshchestvennoe-mnenie-2012-eng (accessed 23.4.16) Place of publication: Moscow.

Lukes, Steven (1974) *Power: A Radical View*. London: Macmillan.

Lukes, Steven (2007) 'Power and the Battle for Hearts and Minds: On the Bluntness of Soft Power,' in Felix Berenskoetter and Michael J. Williams (eds), *Power in World Politics*. London: Routledge, pp. 83–97.

Manners, Ian (2002) 'Normative Power Europe: A Contradiction in Terms?', *Journal of Common Market Studies*, 40(2): 235–258.

Manners, Ian (2006) 'Normative Power Europe Reconsidered: Beyond the Crossroads', *Journal of European Public Policy*, 13(2): 182–119.

Nye, Joseph (2004) *Soft Power: The Means to Success in World Politics*. New York: Public Affairs.

Outhwaite, William and Larry Ray (2005) *Social Theory and Postcommunism*. Oxford: Blackwell.

Outhwaite, William (2016) *Europe Since 1989: Transitions and Transformations*. Abingdon: Routledge.

Peel, Quentin (2012) 'Merkel Warns on Cost of Welfare', *Financial Times*, 16.12.16. www.ft.com/cms/s/0/8ccof584-45fa-11e2-b7ba-00144feabdco.html#axzz3v4VCyoND

Sarotte, Mary (2009) *1989: The Struggle to Create Post-Cold War Europe*. Princeton: Princeton University Press, updated edition, 2014.

Sherr, James (2015) 'The New East-West Discord: Russian Objectives, Western Interests', Netherlands Institute of International Relations, Clingendael, December. www.clingendael.nl/publicatie/new-east-west-discord-russian-objectives-western-interests

Smith, Michael (2015) 'The New Intergovernmentalism and Experiential Learning in the Common Security and Defence Policy', in Christopher Bickerton, Dermot Hodson and Uwe Puetter (eds), *The New Intergovernmentalism: States and Supranational Actors in the Post-Maastricht Era*, Oxford: Oxford University Press, Chapter 5.

Spence, David and Jozef Bátora (eds) (2015) *The European External Action Service. European Diplomacy Post-Westphalia*. London: Palgrave Macmillan.

Streeck, Wolfgang (2014) *Buying Time: The Delayed Crisis of Democratic Capitalism*. London: Verso.

Streeck, Wolfgang (2015) 'Why the Euro divides Europe', *New Left Review*, 95 (September/October 2015): 5–26. http://newleftreview.org/II/95/wolfgang-streeck-why-the-euro-divides-europe

Streeck, Wolfgang and Lea Elsässer (2015) 'Monetary Disunion: The Domestic Politics of Euroland', *Journal of European Public Policy*, 23(1): 1–24.

Szołucha, Anna (2010) 'The EU and Enlargement Fatigue: Why Has the European Union Not Been Able to Counter Enlargement Fatigue?', *Journal of Contemporary European Research*, 6(1): 1–16.

Trenin, Dmitry (2011) *Post-Imperium: A Eurasian Story*. Washington, DC: Carnegie Endowment for International Peace. http://carnegieendowment.org/pdf/book/post-imperium.pdf

van der Togt, Tony, Francesco S. Montesano and Iaroslav Kozak (2015) 'Striking a Eurasian Balance in EU-Russia Relations', Netherlands Institute of International Relations, Clingendael, November. www.clingendael.nl/sites/default/files/Eurasian_Union_Report_FINAL.pdf

van Ham, Peter (2015) 'The EU, Russia and the Quest for a New European Security Bargain', Netherlands Institute of International Relations, Clingendael, December. www.clingendael.nl/pub/2015/eu_russia_rapport/

Weiss, Stefani (2013) *The European Added Value of EU Spending: Can the EU Help its Member States to Save Money?* Gütersloh: Bertelsmann Stiftung.

Wiener, Antje (2008) *The Invisible Constitution of Politics: Contested Norms and International Encounters.* Cambridge: Cambridge University Press.

Ziełonka, Jan (2006) *Europe as Empire: The Nature of the Enlarged European Union.* Oxford: Oxford University Press.

Postscript

I wrote this book in the run-up to the UK referendum on EU membership, and I was fortunately able at proof stage to update it here and there in the light of the result and also to add this postscript. If I were writing the book now, I would of course have omitted much of the discussion of the UK.

What we experienced in the UK was the conjunction of three phenomena: a world problem, a European or EU problem and a British (or, more properly, English and Welsh) problem. The world problem, well illustrated at the same time by the spectacular performance of two outsider candidates in the US presidential election campaign (one of them still in the running as I write), is a widespread disaffection with established political parties, political leaders and political systems as a whole and the rise of (mainly right-wing) populist politics. Ruth Wodak (2015: 181) writes that in 2000, when the Austrian far-right FPÖ entered a coalition government, 'probably very few scholars could have imagined that in 2014, such parties would be able to win the elections for European Parliament in France or the UK . . .'

The European problem is one of disaffection with the politics of the European Union and to some extent with the EU as a whole. This is most extreme in the UK but, as described in more detail in chapter 7, something which can be found to varying degrees across the Union. The same goes for the populist politics mobilised against it. Boris Johnson's comparison of the EU's integration strategy with those of Napoleon and Hitler was prefigured in 2014 by an Austrian MEP who called it a dictatorship, compared to which the 'Third Reich was probably informal and liberal' and that it was also a 'conglomerate of negroes'. (Wodak 2015: 63–4) He later apologised, unlike Johnson, who merely complained about the way the campaign had been dominated by sound-bites and twitter storms.

The British/English problem', a widespread unwillingness to see EU membership as a fact of life and a permanent ambivalence about the UK's membership, culminating in an even balance of opinion in the referendum campaign and a narrow majority for the leave option, can be seen in a broader context as the failure of the EU to attract three western European states and, so far at least, to reach a stable accommodation with others further east. Two of the westerners, Norway and Switzerland, remain outside the EU, but either a member of, or closely associated with, the European Economic Area. It remains to be seen whether this road will be taken by the UK, where anti-EU voters were misled to expect a fall in EU immigration. This could indeed be achieved, but not within the EEA, though the economic collapse which is likely to result from Brexit will reduce the appeal of England as a destination, and may make possible some compromise in which the UK remains in the EEA.

The UK referendum result does not, I think, change the 'don't know' assessment I made at the end of the last chapter of the book. What it does, however, is to sharpen up the issue of the Union's variable geometry or differentiated integration model. This is particularly important in relation to the euro, in terms of both widening (its prospective extension to all EU member states except Denmark, whose currency is however pegged to the euro and likely to remain so) and deepening (the closer integration of the Eurozone which all observers agree is required).

As discussed earlier, there was considerable debate in the long months preceding the UK referendum about a possible domino effect of Brexit, though less about a similar domino effect or, better, Pandora's box from Bremain. In either event, and we now know which is the reality, other member states might demand the same sort of special treatment afforded to the UK. The failure of these (admittedly trivial) 'concessions' to persuade the UK to remain has done little to change this. Nothing is easier than for member states to defer indefinitely their adoption of the euro, even if they are officially committed to it. Any plans for more intrusive surveillance and supervision within the Eurozone could be expected to reinforce this unwillingness to participate. The Schengen area is in some disarray, and another obvious area for opting out.

As far as the UK is concerned, the historian Brendan Simms (2016) has offered a striking projection which combines federalism within the Eurozone and a formal confederation with the UK and other states which wished to remain outside it, in something like the present European Economic Area. The confederation would supervise the Single Market and also, for example, the City of London, but would give Britain 'a much bigger role than Norway or Switzerland, and indeed than she has today . . .' (Simms 2016: 239) He notes, on the same page, that this was envisaged by Jacques Delors in 2012: 'If the British cannot support the trend towards more integration in Europe . . . I could imagine a form such as a European economic area or a free-trade agreement.'

Simms takes much more seriously than I would do the sense of Britain's special position as an established and, in the mid-twentieth century, undefeated democracy: 'Europe was designed to fix something that was never broken in Britain.' (Simms 2016: 237) Switzerland can perhaps more plausibly portray itself as a special case, since until 2002 it also declined to join the UN, despite providing its main European base in Geneva. The UK's sense of itself as distinct from the European continent is largely imaginary and grounded in a reading of history which stresses its maritime character and glosses over its permanent imbrication with the rest of Europe. (Ireland is two seas away from the mainland, not one, but has much less of a sense that this makes it somehow less European.) But as with the German *Sonderweg*, if you *think* you have a special path, you do.

How all this will pan out remains to be seen. It is hard to envisage much willingness in the rest of the EU to concoct a special position for a state which voted to leave it. What the UK has done is to place exit as an agenda item for the whole of the Union. As we saw, this can be found here and there in the rhetoric of some populist parties, but the UK's departure, however disastrous it turns out to be, does at least show that it is possible. This cuts more ice, as it were, than the departure of Greenland in 1985. Just as the Scottish independence referendum in 2014 has made it harder for Madrid to resist one in Catalonia, it is now hard to see how any member state could resist one if there were a significant demand for it.

In the UK itself, there will be a great deal of discussion comparing the two recent referendums, separated by less than two years. There was a morphological similarity, with the expectation that Scotland would vote no to independence followed by a last-minute panic that it would vote yes which brought together the three main UK parties. In Scotland, however, this may have helped to secure a no vote, though it further damaged the image of the Scottish Labour Party. In the UK referendum, it may even have had the opposite effect, with the consensus of most of the political class (though not the ruling Conservative Party) as well as virtually all independent expert organisations serving only to strengthen the sense that Brexit was a heroic, if risky, option. 'Very well then, alone', in the words of the famous cartoon as the rest of Europe capitulated to the Nazi invasion and the US stood aside. The UK's retreat has indeed been compared to that from Dunkirk in 1940, though with the difference that it is now the UK, rather than the rest of Europe, which has capitulated. By precipitating British exit through a gratuitous referendum, the British Conservatives gave the lead to movements across Europe that are almost all hostile to what are ostensibly its (and the EU's) foreign policy and human rights objectives.

The Scottish debate was however remarkably civilised compared to that later in the UK. Some 'no' supporters were accused of being unpatriotic, but there was little to compare with the temperature of the media debate in the UK less than twenty months later. The murder of a Labour MP and 'remain' supporter by a right-wing fanatic just over a week before the vote was the climax to months of mutual vilification by the two sides, and the referendum result has been followed by a massive increase in racist attacks and abuse.

Media bias was also extremely important. Unlike the situation in the Scottish referendum, the UK press massively supported Brexit.[2] As noted earlier (p. 123), the UK and Austria stand out for their eurosceptical press coverage, just as the UK and Latvia stood out in 2015 for their level of ignorance about the EU (p. 130 n. 14).) The BBC felt obliged to take a neutral position between the two camps. In what became a standard pattern, expert analyses were 'balanced' by a perfunctory rebuttal, often based on 'facts' which had long been shown to be false or misleading. One expert aptly compared the so-called debate to one between evolutionary biologists and creationists. When President Obama was criticised for predicting that a post-Brexit UK (or whatever remained of it) would be at the back of the queue for alternative trade deals with the US he rather plaintively suggested that, since there had been so much discussion of the issue, he had thought that people might be interested to have the opinion of the US President.

Separatist nationalism, to which the Brexit campaign can in some ways be assimilated, divides according to whether independence is valued whatever the cost or, alternatively, is seen as in any case the *least* costly option. Richer sub-states, like Slovenia in former Yugoslavia and Catalonia in Spain, have typically stressed the benefits of getting out from under an economically weaker union. This was contentious in the Scottish case, and the current lower oil price, as well as the depletion of the remaining fields, has made the issue more problematic. In the Brexit referendum, the EU was variously portrayed as a threatening super-state and as itself threatened by economic decline and political collapse. In a milder version of the second position, membership was seen as something possibly beneficial in the past but which the UK, its economic fortunes revived by Thatcherism, no longer needed or benefited from. This was typically conjoined with the rather better grounded argument that the character of what is now the EU had changed since the 1975 referendum, or at least since the Maastricht Treaty.

In the UK, however, the separatist vote seemed largely indifferent to the almost unanimous warnings of economic disaster, the beginnings of which followed immediately. However badly the result turns out for England and Wales[3], voters elsewhere in the EU may choose to follow suit. The UK, which had a great deal to contribute to the EU and Europe as a whole, and substantially reshaped the EU in the recent past, now has little to offer except disruption and dissension.

Notes

1. Like England, Wales was evenly split. Scotland was quite solidly for remain. In Northern Ireland, a late shift of opinion, as measured by a poll a week before the vote, raised leave from less than a quarter to nearly a third, with Catholics solidly for remain and Protestants shifting towards leave. (BBC 17 June: http://www.bbc.co.uk/news/uk-northern-ireland-36553552) In the final result, however, there was a substantial majority for the remain option.
2. http://www.theguardian.com/commentisfree/2016/jun/17/eu-referendum-battle-press-versus-democracy
3. Scotland is likely to choose independence within the EU. For Northern Ireland, the issue of reunification is back on the agenda, with the likelihood of a revival of the terrorism which had largely fizzled out by 2016. England, likely to be dominated by right-wing governments hostile to state aid, will presumably leave Wales (and Cornwall) to rot.

References

Simms, Brendan (2016) *Britain's Europe. A Thousand Years of Conflict and Cooperation.* Harmondsworth: Allen Lane.

Wodak, Ruth (2015) *The Politics of Fear. What Right-Wing Populist Discourse Means.* London: SAGE.

Appendix

Key legal cases in the history of the European Union

As noted at various places in this book, judgements by the European Court (ECJ/CJEU) have played a crucial part in the evolution of the Union.[1] This appendix lists some of the most important.

The two central principles, known as 'direct effect' and 'supremacy', were established in the 1960s. Direct effect means that courts in member states have to implement European law in relevant cases, thus removing the need to appeal to the European Court. *Supremacy*, as the term implies, means that European law takes priority over national law. There remains some controversy over this principle, with constitutional courts in some member states invoking their own local constitutional supremacy.

Van Gend en Loos v Nederlandse Administratie der Belastingen (1962–63)

A Dutch distribution company, Van Gend en Loos, brought this case against the Dutch customs authorities who had increased the customs duty charged on a chemical imported from West Germany. The court found that Article 12 of the Treaty of Rome, which prevented member states from increasing such charges, as part of the general programme of reducing internal tariff barriers, applied to this situation and that the company could recover the duty through the Dutch court.

The court justified its decision with the assertion that

> the Community constitutes a new legal order of international law for the benefit of which the states have limited their sovereign rights, albeit within limited fields and the subjects of which comprise not only member states but also their nationals. Independently of the legislation of member states, community law therefore not only imposes obligations on individuals but is also intended to confer upon them rights which become part of their legal heritage.

Direct effect was further developed in another case in 1976, *Defrenne v SABENA*. This extended the principle to cover the rights of private citizens and corporations, in this case the flight attendant against her employer.

The supremacy of European law was established in a test case, *Costa v ENEL* (1964), brought by an Italian shareholder in a private energy company which had been nationalised, and who refused, as a protest, to pay his electricity bill to the new state body ENEL. The Court held that he could not, as a private citizen, contest the Italian government's nationalisation decision on the grounds that it distorted the market (only the European Commission could do this). However, the principle was upheld that Mr Costa was entitled to raise the issue in his local court of the relation between national and Community law. As in *Van Gend en Loos*, the Court laid down the principle:

> As opposed to other international treaties, the Treaty instituting the E.E.C. has created its own order which was integrated with the national order of the member-states the moment the Treaty came into force; as such, it is binding upon them. In fact, by creating a Community of unlimited duration, having its own institutions, its own personality and its own capacity in law, apart from having international standing and more particularly, real powers resulting from a limitation of competence or a transfer of powers from the States to the Community, the member-states, albeit within limited spheres, have restricted their sovereign rights and created a body of law applicable both to their nationals and to themselves.

This principle of supremacy or *primacy* was restated in a 'Declaration' as part of the Lisbon Treaty of 2007, following cases such as *Marleasing* (1989–90) and *Simmenthal* (1978)[2].

Several member states maintain that their own constitutional courts or equivalents are entitled to decide on the local applicability of European law. The lead was taken by the very powerful German Constitutional Court, which concluded in 1986 that 'so long' as EU law followed the same principles of rights as that of the Federal Republic, it would not insist on reviewing legislation.[3]

In the UK, the *Factortame* case over fishing ran right through the 1990s. Although the principle of supremacy was conceded, the UK still seems to be kicking back, as it did recently in a Supreme Court ruling in 2014 on a case concerning the proposed high-speed rail line HS2, which included the following paragraph:

> 207. The United Kingdom has no written constitution, but we have a number of constitutional instruments. They include Magna Carta, the Petition of Right 1628, the Bill of Rights and (in Scotland) the Claim of Rights Act 1689, the Act of Settlement 1701 and the Act of Union 1707. The European Communities Act 1972, the Human Rights Act 1998 and the Constitutional Reform Act 2005 may now be added to this list. The common law itself also recognises certain principles as fundamental to the rule of law. It is, putting the point at its lowest, certainly arguable (and it is for United Kingdom law and courts to determine) that there may be fundamental principles, whether contained in other constitutional instruments or recognised at common law, of which Parliament when it enacted the European Communities Act 1972 did not either contemplate or authorise the abrogation.[4]

The Polish and Lithuanian constitutional courts also proclaimed in 2005 and 2006 respectively that EU did not take precedence over their constitutions. The Polish and Hungarian governments' current attempts to undermine the rule of law are likely to lead to further conflicts in this area.

Notes

1. See http://ec.europa.eu/competition/court/index.html
2. As well as the comprehensive EU sources, there is currently a more user-friendly site, last accessed on 17.2.16: http://www.caselawofeu.com/
3. *Re Wuensche Handelsgesellschaft*, BVerfG decision of 22 October 1986.
4. www.supremecourt.uk/decided-cases/docs/uksc_2013_0172_judgment.pdf

Index

1989 2, 8–9, 15, 42, 50–1, 53, 91, 138

Abélès, M. 58
accession 3, 9, 17, 21, 28, 36, 45, 50–1, 57, 59, 70, 78, 83, 90, 108, 128, 142, 144–5
accession fatigue 148
accession states, applicant states (see member states)
acquis communautaire 68
Adonnino Report 105
Africa 3, 15, 22, 33, 35, 49–50, 68, 98, 127, 135, 138
agriculture 22–4, 44–5, 47, 52–3, 66, 68, 76, 122, 129 (see also CAP)
Albania 4, 9, 44, 48, 148
Algeria 148
Altereuropean 117, 128
Alternative für Deutschland (AfD) 125
America 6, 13–14, 20, 27, 33–4, 44, 50, 53, 76, 100, 127, 134, 140, 142–3 (see also USA, Latin America)
Amsterdam 7–8, 78, 100, 137
Angelescu, I. 138
Armenia 9, 90, 142

Asia 3, 20, 22–3, 26–7, 33, 49–50, 68, 127, 141
Åslund, A. 29
Assemblée Nationale (France) 84
association agreements 142
Auer, S. 79
Australia, Australasia 49, 134
Austria 21, 25, 31, 41, 44–5, 51, 57, 90, 118, 120, 123–4, 129–30, 145
Azerbaijan 9, 90

Balkans, Balkan states 44, 50, 90, 136, 142, 147
Baltic (states) 9–10, 22, 25, 28, 42, 48, 101, 127, 141
'banal nationalism' 105
banana (blue/red) 10–11, 31, 36
Barcelona
Basque Country 9, 49
Bavaria 10
Beck, U. 36, 106, 119, 144, 147
Beethoven, L. van 7, 104
Belarus 9, 33, 35, 90, 142
Belgium 4, 6, 22–5, 42, 46, 49, 63, 80, 99–100, 102, 104, 106, 126, 135, 148–9
Benelux 4, 57

Benn, T. 119
Berlin 42, 53, 71
Berlusconi, S. 26, 87, 89, 126
Bickerton, C. 17, 21, 25, 36, 61–2, 85, 121–2, 137
Billig, M. 105
Bindi, F. 138
Blair, A. 77, 92, 121
Böröcz, J. 134
Bosnia–Herzegovina 11, 15, 31, 48, 68, 148
Bourdieu, P. 72
bourgeoisie 76
Braudel, F. 1
Brazil 135
Britain, British 3–4, 6, 12, 23, 25–6, 32, 45, 53, 68–9, 72, 76–7, 84, 86–7, 99–101, 104, 106–7, 118–21, 123, 125, 129, 135, 148 (see also UK)
British Overseas Territories 138
Brittany, Breton 12, 49
Brunet, R. 36
Brown, G. 85
Brunkhorst, H. 30, 82
Brussels 7–8, 14, 41, 46, 60, 63, 80, 87, 107, 118–9, 121, 126–7
Budapest 10
Bulgaria 4, 9, 25, 31, 37, 51, 100, 106, 108
Bundesverfassungsgericht (Federal Constitutional Court) 7, 81, 84, 125
Bundestag 83–4
Bunyan, T. 69
bureaucracy, bureaucratic 63–4, 83
'Butskellism' 85

Callaghan, J. 124
Cameron, D. 60, 77, 81–2, 99, 124, 129, 149
Canada 2, 21, 23, 25, 41, 98
Canary Islands 49
capital 15, 20, 23, 27, 29, 46, 66, 102, 143
capital cities 10, 44–5, 49,
capital of culture 107
capitalism 4, 21, 25–9, 35, 37, 40, 53, 56–8, 76, 89–90, 102
Catalonia 9, 49,
catholic(ism) 11, 34, 51, 77
Caucasus 9–10, 68
Central Europe 11, 119, 144
Central and Eastern Europe (CEE) 21, 138
Cerutti, F. 107–8
Channel Islands 3

charisma 122, 140
Chepurina, M. 141
China, Chinese 20, 33, 113, 134, 136, 138, 143, 148
Christian democracy 3, 44, 69, 82, 87, 120, 126
Christianity 51, 102, 127
Churchill, W. 5, 30
citizen(s) 2–3, 7, 14, 22, 29, 31–2, 34, 49–50, 53, 60, 69, 76, 80, 84, 90, 98, 102, 104, 106–9, 121, 127, 129, 134, 140, 143, 154
citizens' initiatives 136
citizenship 8, 14, 51, 67, 79, 83, 106–7, 112, 146
civil society 14, 79, 86, 93, 109, 23–4, 34–5, 40, 55, 69, 93, 106, 124–5
civil war 4, 51, 127
class 23, 76–7, 100, 102, 107, 109–10, 113, 119, 123
Clingendael Report (2015) 142
cohesion 24, 32–3, 35, 42, 45–7, 52–3, 108
Cold War 2, 19, 135
collective Bonapartism 30
colonialism 1, 6, 48–9, 135, 138, 142
 (see also empire, imperial)
 internal 49
Commission, European 4, 7, 14–15, 20–1, 30, 36, 46, 58–60, 63–72, 79, 81–2, 84–6, 88, 90, 92, 104, 107–8, 124–5, 128, 137–8, 142, 154
Committee of the Regions 45, 53
Common Agricultural Policy (CAP) 22–3, 44–5, 52, 67, 111, 122, 124, 129
common currency 23, 79, 83, 143, 146
 (see also Euro)
Commonwealth, British 2, 53, 123
Commonwealth/Community of Independent States (CIS) 27, 139
communism 1, 4–5, 8–10, 19–20, 23–4, 27–8, 35, 41–3, 46, 50, 57, 77–8, 91, 99, 121, 135–6, 144 (see also post–communism)
communist parties 118–9, 121, 126
community 51, 69, 139
Community, European Coal and Steel (ECSC) 4, 19, 22, 41, 58, 60, 67, 70, 79
Community, European Defence 5, 58, 136
Community/ies, European 4–5, 7, 14, 22, 41, 44–5, 52, 65, 70, 101, 119, 135, 154
'community method/system' 66–7, 85

Congress (US) 83
conservatism 54, 77, 97, 103, 116, 134–6, 144, 120
Conservative Party, British 46, 59, 85–6, 98–9, 101, 118–20, 123, 125, 129
constitution(alism) 61, 67, 83, 86, 125, 129, 153
  European 60–1, 67, 71, 82, 86, 89, 125
Constitutional Court (Federal/German) see Bundesverfassungsgericht
'constructivism' 136
consumption 102, 145
convergence 27, 73
Copenhagen, criteria 17, 77, 106, 135–6
Copsey, N. 44–5, 80, 110, 134–5, 137, 142–3
COREPER 58
corporatism 28, 79
corruption 90, 126, 142
Corsica 49
cosmopolitanism 8, 63–4, 81, 100–1, 106, 120, 143, 145
Council for Mutual Economic Assistance (CMEA/Comecon) 4, 42, 119
Council of Europe 9, 53, 62, 99, 102
Council of Ministers; European Council 7, 15, 21, 30, 58–60, 62, 65–6, 70, 79, 81–2, 84, 86, 90, 125, 138
Court of Justice of the European Union 7, 13, 21–2, 58, 60–1, 65, 67, 70, 82, 90, 105, 153–4
crime, criminality 2, 69, 20–1, 57, 91
Crimea 51, 141
crisis 6, 24–32, 36, 42, 57, 59, 82, 85, 90, 109, 120–1, 126, 137, 146–7
  of capitalism 3, 24, 26–32, 36,
  eurozone 6, 25, 28, 30, 32, 99, 121, 137, 146
  refugee/migrant 50, 120, 121, 126, 142
Croatia 9, 31, 37, 59
Crouch, C. 36, 87, 89, 93
culture, cultural 62, 64, 81, 83, 100, 104–5, 107–8, 113, 117, 120, 139, 141, 144
  political 91, 102, 118, 127
Cyprus 22, 37, 108, 123
Czech (Republic) 10, 25, 51, 70, 79, 108, 118, 126, 145
Czechoslovakia 4, 23, 50

DDR (see East Germany)
Dann, P. 30, 82–4, 86
debt 25, 27, 29, 32
De Gaulle, C. 5, 7, 41, 57, 59, 125
Dehousse, F. 148
Delanty, G. 16
Delhey, J. 108, 132,
Delors, J. 3, 20, 61, 64, 66, 71, 105
democracy 4–5, 7, 14, 23, 28, 30, 41, 44, 46, 50, 62, 67, 70, 122, 124, 129–30, 136, 139–40, 144–5
  deliberative 76, 79, 86, 89, 92,
  European Union 7–8, 31, 51, 58, 63, 76–93, 143 (see also Christian democracy, social democracy, post–democracy)
democratic deficit 80, 82, 84, 87, 91–2, 109
demography 33, 101
Denmark, Danish 21, 25, 29, 31–2, 41, 43, 45, 49, 69, 83, 86, 101–2, 104, 107–8, 119, 121–4, 145–6
deregulation 21
development 139
  regional 21, 45–7
development aid 36, 144
dictatorship 5, 23, 41, 44, 57, 76–7, 90
Díez Medrano, J. 100, 102
differentiation 93
'direct effect' (of EU law) 153
discrimination, anti–discrimination 7, 21–2, 98, 127, 129
Duchêne, F. 136
Duncan Smith, I. 123
Durkheim, E. 5, 53
Dutch (see Netherlands)

East Germany, DDR/GDR 4, 9, 23, 47, 52, 119
economies of scale 5, 23–4,
economists 5, 21, 29, 129
economy, economic system 4–5, 7, 19–40, 42–4, 46, 48, 50, 57, 61, 79, 81, 85, 87–8, 98, 105, 110–11, 119, 120–1, 124, 126, 134–6, 139–40, 142, 147
Eder, K. 107
Egypt 148
Elias, N. 22
elite 70, 87–8, 104, 107, 109–10, 124, 128, 139
emigration (see migration)
Empire, imperial (ism) 6, 11, 23, 51, 106, 124, 134–5, 140, 143

Russian, Soviet 23, 51, 139–40
EU as empire 34, 106, 143–4
England, English 1, 9–11, 17, 23, 31, 46, 48, 76–7, 92, 122, 124–5
English language 7, 13, 22, 25, 48
enlargement (*see* EU)
Erdogan, R.T. 89
Estonia 28, 35, 51, 53, 108, 145
ethnicity 50, 107, 112
Eurasia 1, 20, 50, 141–2
euro 25–32, 36, 44–5, 70, 86, 102–3, 107–8, 111, 121, 123, 125, 130, 146, 149 (*see also* common currency)
Eurobarometer 14, 106, 110, 121, 123, 140
Euronews 14, 102, 109
European Bank for Reconstruction and Development (EBRD) 9
European Central Bank 28–30, 36, 90
European Coal and Steel Community (ECSC) *see* Community, European Coal and Steel
European Council (*see* Council)
European Court of Human Rights (*see* human rights)
European Court of Justice (ECJ) (*see* Court of Justice of the European Union)
European Defence Community 58, 137
European Economic Area (EEA) 3, 104, 118
European External Action Service (EEAS) 63, 67–8, 137, 148
European Free Trade Area (EFTA) 41, 142
European integration/disintegration 4–5, 7–9, 15, 20, 22, 27–32, 34, 42–4, 51, 61–2, 66, 69, 71, 78, 80, 88, 90, 92, 99, 102, 106–7, 109–10, 117–20, 124–5, 127–8, 134–5, 145–6
European Parliament 7, 58–60, 62, 65, 70–2, 78–86, 88–90, 92, 105, 108–9, 117, 121, 126, 128–9, 148
European Regional Development Fund 45
European Round Table 20–1, 35, 87
European social model 22, 33, 111
European Union
  enlargement 4–5, 9, 24, 43–4, 46, 50, 57, 78, 108, 124–5, 134–5, 138, 142, 144, 148
Europeanisation 6, 34–5, 60, 70, 102, 110, 122–3, 145
Europol 68–9
euroscepticism 96, 116, 134–5, 146, 161

Falkland Islands/Malvinas 138
Faroe Islands 49
fascism, –ist 4–5, 41, 57, 77, 90, 101, 126, 128
Favell, A. 8, 14, 99–101, 110
federalism 15, 27, 30–2, 60–1, 63, 71, 82–5, 87, 92, 126, 130, 143, 145, 147
Fidesz 127
Financial Times 14
Finland 21, 44, 51, 53, 98, 100, 108, 118, 145
Fischer, J. 62
Flanders 49, 126
Fligstein, N. 110
Florence 60
Foucault, M. 42, 45
Fowler, N. 123
France 3–4, 6–7, 10, 12–13, 21, 23–6, 30–3, 41–6, 48–50, 53, 58, 60, 63, 65–8, 70–1, 76–9, 84, 87, 92, 98–102, 105, 112–13, 118–29, 134–9, 143, 148–9
freedom 2, 46, 77, 79, 92, 100–1, 106, 145
free movement 8, 15, 34, 46, 48, 66, 101, 111
Freedom House 90, 99
Freiheitspartei Österreichs (FPÖ) 90, 118, 124
FRONTEX 68
frontier workers (*frontaliers*) 102
Front National 101, 119–21, 124–5, 128

Gaelic 49
gal/tan parties 77, 117–8, 120
Garavani, G. 135, 148
gender 77
geopolitics 50, 110, 134, 139
Georgia 9, 15, 90, 141–2
GDR (*see* East Germany)
Georgakakis, D. 64–6, 72
Germany 10–12, 21–7, 30–4, 36, 42, 45–6, 48, 50, 52, 57, 60–4, 69, 71, 76–7, 79, 81–5, 87, 91–2, 98, 100–2, 106, 108, 112–13, 120, 122, 125, 127, 129–30, 135, 138, 145, 153, 155 (*see also* East Germany)
Giddens, A. 30–1, 87
Giesen, B. 107
Gifford, C. 124
globalisation 6, 19–35, 102, 110, 122, 143, 145
Gorbachev, M. 24, 99
Gorton, M. 122

governance 31, 33, 45, 51, 62, 69–70, 82, 85–6, 137, 41–2
governmentality 43, 45
Grande, E. 106, 120, 143,
Grant, W. 44
Greece, Greek 4–5, 7, 21, 24–8, 30–2, 36, 41–2, 44, 48, 57, 76, 80, 90, 98, 106–7, 113, 118, 123, 126, 142, 144–6
Green, J. 89
Grundy, S. 105–6
Guadaloupe 3
Guardian 21

Habermas, J. 8, 17, 30, 61, 84, 86, 88–9, 91–2, 135, 143
Haider, J. 90
Hamburg 47
health 14, 21, 48, 111
Held, D. 58
Helsinki 136
history, historical 5, 11, 22–3, 43, 72, 76, 80, 103–4, 110, 112, 135, 137, 140, 143, 148
Hix, S. 93, 113, 130
Hobolt, S. 32, 86–7
Hocking, B. 73
Holland (*see* Netherlands)
Hollande, F. 30,
Hughes, K. 124
human rights 2, 9, 62, 90, 127, 136, 144 (*see also* rights)
European Convention/Court/Declaration of 62
Human Rights Act (UK) 72, 155
Hungary, Hungarian 4, 6, 11, 28, 51, 70, 90, 102, 108, 118, 126–7, 144–5, 155

Iceland 3, 9, 26, 28, 99
identity 2, 104
European 14, 104–8, 110–11, 135, 146
ideology 50, 61, 63, 112, 136
immigration (*see* migration)
income 22, 31, 109
India 33, 98, 134–6, 148
Indonesia 135, 148
information technology 22
institution, institutional 3–7, 26–7, 29–30, 51–72, 78–9, 82, 84–7, 90, 92, 108–9, 111–12, 117, 124–5, 137, 154
intellectuals 139
interdependence 79

intergovernmentalism, 'new intergovernmentalism' 89, 136, 144
International Monetary Fund (IMF) 30, 36
internet 102, 107, 131
investment 33, 102
Ionescu, G. 110
Iraq 142, 147
Ireland, Irish 2, 7, 9–10, 13, 21–2, 24–6, 31, 34, 36, 41–3, 45–6, 48–9, 51, 83, 86–7, 98, 100, 104, 106–7, 122, 145, 146, 157–9, 161
Islam 11, 51 (*see also* muslim)
islamism 127
Israel 51
Italy, Italian 4, 7, 10, 21–2, 24–5, 30–2, 42, 45, 48, 52, 71, 77, 80, 87, 98, 100–2, 107–8, 113, 118, 121, 124, 126, 154

Jacoby, W. 27–8
Jamieson, L. 105–6
Japan 23, 25, 34–5
Jensen, A. 53
Jensen, O. 45
Johnson, S. 72
'joint decision trap' (Verflechtungsfalle) 92–3
Juncker, J.–C. 81
Juncos, A. 142
justice 61, 69
Justice and Home Affairs (JHA) 68–70

Kaliningrad 51
Katseli, L. 36
Kazakhstan 9, 141–2
Keynesianism, privatised 36
Kissinger, H. 138, 143
Klaus, V. 126
Kohler–Koch, B. 87
Koopmans, R. 109, 120
Kosovo 15, 36, 68, 137, 148
Kovács, M. 24
Krastev, I. 88
Kreppel, A. 78
Kriesi, H. 35, 93, 120
Kurds, Kurdistan 49, 142
Kyrgyz Republic, Kyrgyzstan 142

labour market 99, 110
laïcité 77
Lamy, P. 20, 66, 92,
'late capitalism' 29

language 7, 11–12, 34, 49, 63–4, 79, 92, 99, 102, 104, 113
Latin America 25, 138
Latour, B. 8, 62
Latvia 36, 51, 130, 145
Laval 61
law, legal 2, 7, 14, 22, 59–62, 70–2, 82–3, 86, 98–9, 105, 111, 124, 129–30, 146, 153–5
Lega Nord 126–7
legitimacy, legitimation 30–1, 59, 81, 84, 92, 109
Lehmbruch, G. 83
Leipzig 8
Leonard, M. 118
Levada Center 139–41
liberalism 20, 25, 46, 54, 59, 61, 70, 77, 91, 120, 129, 145 (*see also* neoliberalism)
liberalisation 61, 65, 86, 88, 99
Liechtenstein 3, 9, 43
life expectancy (*see* mortality)
Lijphart, A. 83
Lipietz, A. 129
Lisbon 7, 14, 30, 60–1, 68, 72, 84, 90, 136–8, 142, 154
Lithuania 36, 51, 99, 113, 122, 145, 155
lobbying 87
local government 128 (*see also* subsidiarity)
London 8, 17, 31, 46, 48, 92, 100, 104
Louis XIV 105
Lucarelli, S. 82
Lukes, S. 136
Luxembourg 4, 7, 13, 22, 31, 49, 59–60, 80, 100, 129, 149

Maastricht (and Maastricht Treaty) 7, 14, 30, 60, 78, 105, 107, 119, 136
Macedonia 31, 148
Mackinder, H. 50
Madrid 10, 106
Major, J. 119
managers 12, 33
Mann, M. 9
Mannheim, K. 92
Manners, I. 136
market 20–1, 29, 44, 65, 88, 122
  economy 25, 139
  single 3, 15, 20–1, 25, 29–30, 35, 61, 67, 85, 99, 119, 154
  social market economy 35, 50
  (*see also* labour market)

Marquand, D. 92
marriage 99–100, 124
Marshall Plan 4, 43
Martinique 3, 13, 37, 43, 105
Marxism 5, 88
'Matthew Effect' 45, 53
Mau, S. 48, 102, 113
McLaren, L. 107
McMahon, S. 101
McNamara, K. 8, 16, 99, 104, 112
Mediterranean 1, 11, 25, 100
member states (of EU etc.) 48–9, 51, 53, 57–72, 78–80, 82–92, 99, 102–13, 117–8, 121–4, 129, 136–8, 144–9, 153–4
Mendras, H. 22–3, 44, 53
Merkel, A. 26, 30, 81, 134, 146
Merton, Robert 45
Middle East 68, 110, 138, 142, 147
Middlemas, K. 65
migration 4, 10–11, 13, 28, 33–4, 42, 48–50, 53, 67, 81, 98–101, 110–12, 120–2, 147
Milan 46
military 4, 15, 19, 41, 51, 57, 90, 127, 135–6, 139
Milward, A. 6, 61, 72, 80, 104
minority 7, 98, 122, 127, 142
Mitterand, F. 57
modernization 44, 51, 79, 108, 142
Moldova 34, 50
Monnet, J. 5, 60, 63, 78–9, 124, 136
Monroe Doctrine 141
Montenegro 31, 36, 148
Montesquieu 76
Moravcsik, A. 80–1
Morocco 3, 49
Münch, R. 88
Munich 47
muslim 50–1, 95, 132

Nairn, T. 119
NAFTA 134
NATO 4, 41–2, 49, 51, 58, 135, 138–9, 141
NGO 69
nation (–al, –ality), nation–state 1–2, 6–9, 11–12, 14, 17, 20–2, 27, 29, 31–2, 35, 44–5, 49, 52, 53, 58–68, 70, 72, 78, 80–2, 84–5, 87–90, 98–9, 101–11, 118–27, 137–8, 140, 143, 146, 153 (*see also* supranational, transnational)

nationalism, –ist 5, 8, 77, 79, 105, 119–27, 129, 147
neoliberalism 28–9, 35, 61, 85, 88, 119–22, 127
Netherlands, Dutch 4, 12, 20–1, 25, 31, 46, 100–1, 104, 113, 118, 120, 126, 129–30, 135, 138, 148, 153–4
networks (transport, crime) 6, 46, 69
New York Times 14
Nice 7, 86, 137
Nordic counties 86, 92
Northern Ireland 9, 51, 83, 104, 107
Norway 3, 9, 31, 33, 41, 44, 51, 118, 121, 123
Nye, J. 136

Obama, B. 141
Oeter, S. 30
Offe, C. 87, 106
Open Method of Coordination (OMC) 69
Open Skies 72
optimal currency area 27,
Orbán, V. 126–7
Orwell, G. 20
Oslo 53
Ottoman Empire 11

Page, E. 63
Palmer, J. 81
Paris 7–8, 10, 46, 123, 135, 142
participation 78
party, parties 54, 59–60, 77–8, 80, 82, 86, 89, 91–2, 109, 117–29, 144 (*see also* individual parties)
Party of Democratic Socialism (PDS) (Germany) 125
passport 2, 6, 23, 103–4, 107,
'patriality' 50, 53
peasants 23, 44, 76
PEGIDA 125
PHARE 144
Pichler, F. 101–2
planning 46, 79
Podemos 28
Poland, Polish 4, 8, 10–11, 24, 31, 33, 48, 50–1, 53, 92, 98–9, 108, 118, 126, 144–5, 155
politics 1–9, 11, 15–16, 19–20, 23–6, 28, 25–31, 33–4, 42, 44, 48, 50, 52–3, 60–1, 63–72, 76–93, 99, 101–2, 104–7, 109, 111, 113, 117–30, 136, 139, 141, 143–8

populism 86–8, 109–10, 117–30, 144
Portugal 4, 69, 73, 102, 114, 119, 140, 159
post–communism 10, 17, 24, 27–8, 33–8, 44, 46, 50, 57, 77, 90–1, 101, 126, 135, 139, 144, 148
post–democracy 29, 82, 84, 87, 89, 103, 110
poverty 10, 15, 42, 48
Powell, E. 101, 119
power 15, 30, 33–4, 45–7, 49, 51, 58, 60, 62, 68, 70, 76–7, 79–93, 108–11, 121, 125, 129, 130, 135–7, 139–41, 143, 154–5
Prague 106
Preuss, U. 106
privatisation 24, 65
production 5, 20, 24, 42, 44, 46, 129
productivity 32, 145
Progress Party (UK) 127
propaganda 8, 140
property boom 26
public sphere 14, 109–9
Putin, V. 139–40, 142

racism 50
region 1, 6, 1–14, 20, 24, 27, 31, 33–4, 42–53, 57, 62, 68, 71, 83–6, 102, 110–11, 118, 125–7, 134, 136, 140–1, 143–4, 146–7
Europe as region 1, 33, 85, 102, 134, 136, 143
regulation, deregulation 21, 127, 146
religion 76–7, 112, 128 (*see also* Christianity, Islam, muslim)
Renan, E. 5
revolutions 23, 42, 77, 148 (*see also* 1989)
Rhine 10, 46–7
Richardson, T. 45–6, 53
rights 20, 53, 62, 76, 77, 83, 99, 127, 130, 136, 154–5 (*see also* human rights)
Risse, T. 109, 117
risk 6, 32, 86, 89, 99
Romania 4, 9, 25, 31, 37, 48, 51, 90, 100–1, 106, 108, 110
Rome (Empire, Treaty etc.) 9, 11, 45, 51, 67, 78–9, 104–5, 111, 143–4, 153
Roose, J. 102
Rousseau, J.-J. 76, 138
Rozenberg, O. 125
Rumford, C. 35, 53
Russia 3, 6, 9, 23–4, 27, 33, 36, 49–51, 53, 90, 101, 113, 124, 136, 138–45, 148

Index   167

Saint–Simon, H. de 5
San Marino 31
Sardinia 49
Sarkozy, N. 26, 30
Sarotte, M. 138–9
Saudi Arabia 138
Sauvy, A. 148
Scharpf, F. 27–8, 30, 32, 36
Schäuble–Lamers paper on EU 69
Schengen 2, 7, 34, 37, 68, 99, 124
Schiller, F. 7, 104
Schmidt, V. 31–2, 84–5, 87, 89, 92–3, 118
Scotland 46, 49, 71–2, 83, 92, 126, 142, 155
Second World War (see World War II)
security 2, 7, 14, 49–50, 59, 67–9, 104, 136–9, 6–7, 116, 141–3, 148
Security Council (see United Nations)
Serbia 31, 148
Shore, C. 63–4, 72, 104–5
Slovakia 10, 25, 36, 46, 80, 102, 106, 118, 122, 126
Slovenia 25, 27–8, 31, 36, 145
Smith, A. 21, 138
social democracy 110, 118, 120–1, 129
social movements 8–9, 14, 30, 49, 77, 87, 93, 118, 120–1, 126, 144, 147
social policy 22, 27, 44, 52, 61, 69, 90
structural funds 28, 36, 42–3, 45
solidarity 47, 53, 105, 136
Solidarity, Solidarność (Poland) 8
Sombart, W. 77
South Africa 134
sovereignty 29, 82, 107, 124–5
Soviet Union: see USSR
Spain, Spanish 1, 4–5, 7, 9–11, 21–2, 24–6, 28, 30–2, 36, 41–2, 44, 48–9, 57, 77, 90, 92, 98, 100–1, 113, 126–7, 138, 143–5
Spence, D. 63–4, 73, 92, 148
Spinelli, A. 58, 79, 93
Spitzenkandidaten 59
Stalin, J.V. 7
state(s) 3, 5–8, 12, 14–15, 19–20, 23, 27, 29, 45–6, 49, 51, 62, 71, 76–7, 80–92, 106, 119, 137–9, 143, 147, 154 (see also member states, nation-state)
'states' rights' (US) 128
Statewatch 69
Statham, P. 109, 113, 117, 120

Stockholm 10
Strasbourg 60
Streeck, W. 29, 36, 71, 80, 87–8, 146
subsidiarity 45, 62, 130
'supremacy' (of EU law) 153
surveillance 43
Sweden 10, 21, 25, 29, 31–2, 41, 44, 70, 86, 101–2, 108, 122–3, 129, 145–6
Switzerland 2, 9, 31, 33, 41, 44, 62, 76, 98, 102, 104, 113, 118, 121, 129
Syriza 28, 121
Szczerbiak, A. 119–20
Szelenyi, I. 17
Szołucha, A. 148

TACIS 144
Taggart, P. 119–20
tax, taxation 6, 26–7, 47, 104, 112, 140
terror, terrorism 2, 69, 142
Thatcher, M., Thatcherism 65–6, 85, 92, 98, 101, 119, 123, 129
Thieler, T. 104
Tindemans Report 105
Transatlantic Trade and Investment Partnership (TTIP) 21, 36
transition 24, 43, 47, 144
Trenin, D. 140
Triandafyllidou, A. 109
trust 80, 88, 108, 126
Turkey 3, 6, 9, 41–2, 44, 48–9, 51, 90, 98, 100, 108, 124, 142, 147–8
TV 14, 104

UK 2–5, 7–10, 20–2, 25–34, 41, 43, 45, 48–9, 51, 53, 57, 59, 61–72, 77, 79–81, 83–7, 90, 92–3, 98–106, 109, 112–13, 118–30, 145–6, 148–9, 155 (see also Britain, England)
UK Independence Party (UKIP) 59, 101, 118, 146, 120–30, 138
Ukraine 3, 15, 33, 50–1, 53, 90, 101, 137, 141, 147
unemployment 28, 42
United Nations, UN 9, 19, 37, 61–2, 68, 79, 143, 148
Urals 9–10, 17
US, USA 4, 14–15, 19, 21, 25–6, 32, 35, 48, 60, 71–2, 76, 83, 91, 102, 125 (see also America)
USSR, former USSR 1, 6, 19, 99, 134, 139–40, 148 (see also Russia)

168   Index

Vachudová, M.A. 50
values 14, 44, 101, 127
varieties of capitalism 25, 35
Vatican State 9
Vauchez, A. 90
Viking 61
Vlaams Belang 126, 129
Vobruba, G. 5–6, 50
Volkswagen 36, 61
Von Beyme, K. 83

Wales, Welsh 9, 12, 49, 83, 92
Wall Street Journal 14
Wallace, H. 20
Wallace, W. 51
Wallonia 49, 126
war, warfare 6–8, 42, 61, 141–2 (*see also* Cold War, World War I, World War II)
Warleigh, A. 35
Warren, M. 92–3
Warsaw Pact 4, 42, 119
Washington, D.C. 104, 121

Weber, Max 143
Weiler, J. 82
welfare, welfare state 14, 22, 33, 48, 61, 81, 99, 111, 125
Western Balkans (*see* Balkan states)
Whitman, R. 142
widening/deepening (of EU) 4
Wiener, A. 81
Wodak, R. 109
work, workers 2, 8, 12, 22, 24, 29, 44, 63–4, 79, 99–100, 102, 105, 109, 122, 129
working groups 66–7
World War I 6
World War II 2, 5, 8, 34, 50, 77, 90, 98, 111, 147–8
women 76, 98, 100, 122, 129

Yugoslavia 9, 11, 13, 31, 48, 51, 98

Ziełonka, J. 143
Zürich 102